In the Children's Aid

J.J. Kelso and Child Welfare in Ontario

In the Children's Aid
J.J. Kelso and
Child Welfare in Ontario

ANDREW JONES and LEONARD RUTMAN

UNIVERSITY OF TORONTO PRESS
Toronto   Buffalo   London

© University of Toronto Press 1981
Toronto Buffalo London
PRINTED IN CANADA

ISBN 0-8020-5491-9

Canadian Cataloguing in Publication Data

Jones, Andrew, 1950–
In the children's aid

Includes index.
ISBN 0-8020-5491-9

1. Kelso, John Joseph, 1864–   2. Social
reformers – Ontario – Biography.   3. Child welfare –
Ontario – History.   4. Children's Aid Society of
Toronto – History.   I. Rutman, Leonard,   II. Title.
HV745.05J66   362.7′092′4   C80-094414-3

Contents

Preface

The present-day system of child welfare in Canada dates from 1893, the year in which the Ontario legislature passed 'An Act for the Prevention of Cruelty to, and better Protection of Children.' Although there had been provisions for the indenture and institutionalization of neglected, dependent, and delinquent children on the statute books in Upper Canada during the previous hundred years, it was the 1893 act which first provided for the establishment of Children's Aid Societies with extensive legal powers to intervene in cases of child neglect and cruelty, and which gave official sanction to the foster care system of looking after mistreated children. These two radical departures from earlier policy were accompanied by the appointment of a government official to supervise child protection work. The person chosen to fill this position was John Joseph Kelso.

At the time of his selection as superintendent of neglected and dependent children, Kelso, although only twenty-nine years old, had already gained a reputation as one of Ontario's leading proponents of child welfare reform. He first came to public attention in 1887 when he stimulated the formation of the Toronto Humane Society, and as honorary secretary he guided the growth of that organization during its formative years. In 1888 he formed the Children's Fresh Air Fund and the Santa Claus Fund, out of which, in 1891, he founded the Toronto Children's Aid Society. This society became the model for the 1893 Children's Protection Act, which provided for the establishment of Children's Aid Societies throughout the province.

As superintendent of neglected and dependent children Kelso became responsible for the implementation of the Children's Protection Act. Between 1893 and 1934, the year in which he retired from the superintendency, he directed and promoted the establishment and development of Ontario's Children's Aid Societies. Largely through his efforts, societies were established in all areas of Ontario by 1914. He also played an important role in their spread throughout the other English-Canadian provinces. In 1921, with the expansion in scope of child welfare services, he was appointed administrator of Ontario's first Adoption Act and the Children of Unmarried Parents Act. Undisputedly, Kelso was the chief architect and builder of Ontario's child welfare system.

Kelso's reform activities extended beyond the services for neglected and dependent children for which he was directly responsible. He advocated a wide range of measures intended to protect children and contribute towards their well-being. He participated in the children's court movement, and was actively involved in closing reformatories, in organizing playgrounds in Toronto, and in advocating mothers' allowances. He also helped in various efforts to improve living conditions in the slums of Toronto, and played a major role in the settlement movement in Toronto.

Kelso occupies an important place in the history of Canadian social reform. This biography provides an account of the life and career of this social reformer and describes the various movements and issues in which he was involved. It should be of interest to the academic and professional as it traces the roots of social welfare services and the profession of social work. However, this biography is also intended for the general reader with an interest in Canadian history and social reform.

This account of Kelso's life and work has been based primarily on the materials in the Kelso Papers, which were presented to the Public Archives of Canada by Kelso's son, Martin, in 1974. J.J. Kelso was an inveterate collector of papers and documents relating to his career, and the Kelso Papers comprise twenty-nine volumes of correspondence, speeches, speech notes, diaries, journals, notes, drafts, notebooks, scrapbooks, circulars, newspaper clippings, and annual reports kept by him throughout his life. While this material provides an invaluable record of Kelso's activities, and of the issues and movements in which he was involved, this source has been supplemented by a number of theses and books which have examined various aspects of his work, and by other archival collections. All these materials are acknowledged in a detailed 'Note on Sources' at the end of the book, which is also intended as a guide for those who wish to consult further material on the man and his achievements. The use of notes in the main text has deliberately been kept to a minimum.

Acknowledgments

There are many people who have contributed to the publication of this book. James Albert and Phyllis Harrison can be credited for making arrangements with Martin Kelso to place his father's papers at the Public Archives of Canada. The research was greatly facilitated by the library and archival staff at Carleton University, the Archives of Ontario, and the Public Archives of Canada. The manuscript was typed at various stages by Doreen Hallam, Bev Gould, and Lynn Gunn. We appreciate their assistance.

Valuable comments and suggestions were made by Gene H. Homel, Joseph Laycock, Harriet Parsons, and Wayne Roberts. Dave McKendry provided considerable editorial assistance and we benefitted greatly from his advice. Martin and Helen Kelso were extremely helpful in talking to us, making private correspondence available, and commenting on early drafts. In acknowledging these contributions, we naturally assume full responsibility for the content of the book.

This book has been published with the help of grants from the Social Science Federation of Canada, using funds provided by the Social Sciences and Humanities Research Council of Canada, and the Publications Fund of the University of Toronto Press.

ANDREW JONES and LEONARD RUTMAN

Illustrations

Acknowledgment for permission to reproduce illustrations in this book
is hereby given to the
PUBLIC ARCHIVES OF CANADA
1 (C-4244), 2 (C-85881), 3 (PA-120548), 4 (PA-120557)
5 (PA-120993), 6 (PA-120926), 11 (PA-111226)
and to Mr and Mrs Martin Kelso for 7 to 10 inclusive

1 Group of children, Toronto, c 1900–10

2 J.J. Kelso and some of the CAS charges in 1900

3 A neglected boy just as he was received by Kelso in 1898

4 Entrance to the model playgrounds of the Playgrounds Association, Toronto, c 1900

5 Children on an outing sponsored by the Fresh Air Fund, Toronto, c 1905

6 Berlin Orphanage, Kitchener, June 1907

John and Irene Kelso
(*top*) 7 Christmas, 1909
(*bottom*) 8 in retirement, 1934

9 'Hard work and close study,' Kelso in 1883

10 Kelso in 1902

11 St Andrew's supervised girls' playground

In the Children's Aid

J.J. Kelso and Child Welfare in Ontario

1

Early Life

The Great Famine that engulfed Ireland between 1845 and 1849 was an over-whelming national calamity. In just five years almost one million people died of hunger and disease, and another million emigrated from 'the doomed and starving island.'[1] A population of eight and one-half million in 1845, most of whom were directly dependent on the land, was reduced by almost a quarter in half a decade. As in all economic crises, the burden of human suffering was unevenly distributed, and in the famine it was the impoverished agricultural labourers and small farmholders who were the worst affected. In the western and southwestern seaboard counties, where labourers and small farmholders formed a particularly high proportion of the population, the failure of the potato crop created starvation conditions throughout whole communities.[2]

In the more prosperous northern and eastern counties the famine had a far more limited impact. Many families, particularly those residing in the cities and small towns and engaged in commercial or manufacturing pursuits, were largely unaffected by the national disaster. Such a family was the Kelso family of Dundalk, County Louth, a small seaport on the east coast, midway between Belfast and Dublin. George Kelso, who was twenty-one years old in 1849, was the owner and operator of a starch factory in Dundalk. He was sufficiently prosperous to be able to take his young bride, Anna MacMurray, on a honey-moon to the Crystal Palace Exhibition of 1851 in London. The couple returned to a substantial, well-furnished, three-storey brick home, where they raised ten children. As each child was born, he or she was provided with a servant girl to look after his or her needs. One son died in infancy but the others apparently were healthy. To be born into the Kelso family was good fortune in the difficult economic and social circumstances of mid-nineteenth century Ireland.

The eighth Kelso child, John Joseph, was born in Dundalk on 31 March 1864. His early childhood was uneventful and much of his time was spent playing on the beach of nearby Dundalk Bay. He did not take easily to school, and later described his early education in Ireland as 'productive of little more than a cramped body and a rebellious mind.' At the age of eight he devised a system of truancy in order to spend as little time at school as possible. Not far from his home he discovered a secluded spot where he could hide his school books, calling for them on his way home in the late afternoon. From time to time, while the other boys studied their grammar and geography, John Kelso hiked to the countryside or more likely to the bay, to discover the crabs, fish, and other sea life left behind by the receding tide.

The Kelso family continued to enjoy its comfortable standard of living throughout the 1860s, a period of economic vitality for most of Ireland's townships. Late in the decade, however, the family's fortunes were suddenly reversed when a fire swept through their starch factory, completely gutting the building. The stone walls remained standing but the plant was not insured and the business was ruined. For George Kelso, then forty years old, this was a catastrophe. A fresh start was needed, and like many of his fellow countrymen his thoughts turned to America. In 1870, after settling his affairs as best he could, he set off alone for New York, promising to send word to the family to join him as soon as he was able to get established.

George Kelso's decision to migrate was typical of the means by which Irishmen in the second half of the nineteenth century sought to cope with distressing personal circumstances. The Great Famine activated a mass exodus which by the turn of the century removed almost four million people from Ireland. Kelso was part of this migration, but in almost all respects he was atypical of Irish emigrants of this period. The majority of the emigrants were agricultural labourers and the sons and daughters of small farmers, most commonly from the Catholic south and west of Ireland. They were predominantly young and unmarried, fleeing a land where social and economic circumstances offered little or no prospect of security.[3] Kelso's motivation and background were completely different. As a man of substance until the destruction of his factory, he was intent on regaining the status, possessions, and comforts from which he and his family had been abruptly parted. As a Presbyterian and a property owner, he shared more in common with the Protestant Irish who emigrated from Ulster to America in the eighteenth and early nineteenth century than with the Catholic Irish who composed the majority of his fellow emigrants in 1870.[4]

In his choice of North America, George Kelso followed the example set by most Irish emigrants. The relative closeness of the United States and Canada compared with other possible destinations such as Australia, the existence of a prospering Irish community in many North American cities, and the highly positive image of the United States as a land of opportunity combined to make North America the destination for some 90 per cent of Irish emigrants in the half century following the famine. Most of the new arrivals crowded into the large cities of the eastern seaboard, and it was in New York that George Kelso first attempted to establish himself. Failing to find suitable employment, he took the advice of friends and moved to Toronto, a major centre for Irish immigrants since the famine. Catholics constituted the large majority of Toronto's Irish immigrant population, but Protestant Irish were also numerous and played a conspicuous role in the life of the city, notably through the Orange Order.[5] After finding work as a clerk, George decided to stay. He sent a message to the family to join him and Anna and the children arrived in Toronto in the late fall of 1874.

Kelso's choice of Toronto as the new home for his family was defensible on economic grounds. For more than two decades Toronto had experienced rapid growth and development, and by the early 1870s the city was emerging as a commercial, industrial, and manufacturing metropolis of major importance.[6] Already well established by 1850 as the commercial capital of Upper Canada, Toronto during the 1850s and 1860s developed as a trading centre, linking the Ontario hinterland and the emerging settlements of the Canadian West to New York and British markets. Despite fierce competition from Montreal, Toronto by 1870 had become a major marketing and exporting centre, with its own banking and other financial institutions and an extensive network of railways. This growth of commercial activity was accompanied by the development of industry. By 1870 Toronto boasted almost five hundred manufacturing establishments employing 9400 individuals in a range of industries, including flour milling, brewing and distilling, metal fabricating, and the production of woollens and cottons. Given George Kelso's years of experience as the manager of a small factory, his decision to settle in a city experiencing rapid industrial expansion made practical sense.

Socially, too, Toronto held promise for the Kelso family. The Kelsos were accustomed to the facilities, comforts, and trappings of middle-class living and in such matters Toronto more than rivalled the small township of Dundalk. Toronto offered a wide choice of religious and educational institutions, a developing retail trade, and opportunities for the enjoyment of choral music, theatrical performances, and sporting activities. Physically, the city was taking on the appearance of a prospering metropolis with the erection of public buildings such as the Parliament, Upper Canada College, the Grand Opera House, and Union Station, along with cathedrals and churches and the new bank buildings in the business district. For a family with middle-class expectations and aspirations, Toronto was a prime location.

The growing class of merchants, bankers, manufacturers, professionals, artisans, and government officials in Toronto, together with their wives and families, were the main recipients of the benefits associated with the city's rise to metropolitan status. However, the growth of manufacturing in Toronto also created an industrial working class, comprised mainly of immigrants from England, Scotland, and Ireland, whose living conditions contrasted sharply with the comfort and security of those socially better placed. Extensive immigration during the late 1860s and early 1870s led to a worsening of slum conditions in several areas of the city. Unemployment and near starvation were widespread. The Kelsos' economic circumstances brought them into close contact with these conditions. They were by no means destitute when they arrived in Canada, but they lacked the means immediately to re-establish a middle-class life style. They were forced to begin their life in the new country amongst Toronto's poorer classes.

Both physically and emotionally it was a difficult transition for the whole family. Arriving in the fall, they passed their first Canadian winter in a badly-heated, dilapidated rented home. George Kelso made little progress in his employment, and his prospects were not enhanced by the economic dislocation which was experienced by Toronto in the mid-1870s. To supplement the income from Kelso's low-paid clerical position, the family was forced to sell many of the belongings it had brought from Ireland, including some fine household furnishings intended for the new home. Sadness compounded the misery and anxiety of the first winter when Elizabeth, George and Anna's twelve-year-old daughter, died after a short illness.

For the older members of the family the adjustment to a new economic and social status proved particularly galling. Anna Kelso, most of all, felt shamed by her new position in society. Two incidents during their first Canadian winter illustrate her attitude. The family had brought with it a number of letters of introduction to people who had emigrated from Ireland ahead of them and who had prospered in Canada. Anna called on one such Irishman, a wealthy businessman, to enquire concerning employment for two of the older children. She met with rebuff, and was humiliated by the realization that the businessman had assumed she was requesting charity. On another occasion, a former acquaintance from Dundalk arrived at the Kelso home in a fine carriage and, in a manner which Anna considered condescending, proffered a five-dollar note to assist the family. Anna refused the offer, explaining later to the children that she could never accept charity. Her attitude on these occasions was understandable. Brought up in Protestant, middle-class Ireland, she associated the receipt of charity with the stigma of Poor Law relief. The provision and distribution of food through the Poor Law authorities was a common occurrence in Ireland in the 1840s and 1850s, but the social gulf between the Kelsos and the Dundalk paupers must then have seemed unbridgeable. Unfortunately Anna's pride and inflexible self-reliance cut the family off from potential friends and supporters, and loneliness was added to their other problems.

Anna Kelso was at this time the dominant figure in the Kelso family. George Kelso rapidly became resigned to his reduced circumstances, and as he grew older he became increasingly dependent on alcohol. Much of the burden of responsibility for the family was consequently borne by Anna, a situation to which she was accustomed, having raised the children alone since George first departed for America. Motivated by ambition for her children, and by her sense of shame now intensified by George's alcoholism, Anna was the driving force behind the family's efforts to make its way in Toronto.

John Kelso, ten years old when he came to Canada, was deeply affected by his mother's sense of disgrace. Shortly after his arrival, he resumed his schooling, attending first the John Street Public School and then the Ryerson Public School. Ontario's school attendance laws at this time required that children between the ages of seven and twelve spend four months at school each year, but these minimal provisions were ineffectively enforced.[7] Aware of the family's hardship and of his mother's hatred of charity, and unattracted by Toronto's overcrowded public schools, the young boy decided to do something to help. In March 1875, not quite eleven years old, he saw a sign saying 'Smart Boy Wanted' outside the shop of James Bain and Sons, booksellers on King Street East. He entered the shop and, despite his youth, was given his first job. The pay was a paltry one dollar a week, but this amount could be doubled from tips earned by extra services, such as occasional errands, holding horses, and opening doors for customers. Despite his mother's sadness at such a young child working, she raised no strong opposition. Kelso's attendance at school was intermittent from this time onwards and when he was thirteen it ceased altogether.

The job with the bookseller did not last long as opportunities for more remunerative employment came Kelso's way. Late in the summer of 1875 he became a messenger for the Dominion Telegraph Company, located on the corner of Church and Front streets. There were about fifteen messenger boys employed in the office at a rate of two cents per delivery. This method of payment was open to abuse, since more money could be made by boys whose deliveries were closest to the telegraph office. Consequently, a pattern developed whereby the boys bribed the dispatchers with small articles stolen from the firms and offices to which they delivered the telegrams. Kelso did not participate in this system and thus had to make the longer trips. His scruples paid off as one day detectives entered the building and arrested three boys on charges of theft. Kelso was a spectator at their trial the next day, where two of the messenger boys were sentenced to three years each in the Ontario Reformatory for Boys at Penetanguishene. This episode, culminating in the imprisonment of his workmates, made a profound impression on Kelso, and in later life it remained as one of his clearest childhood memories.

The impact of the event was reinforced by a similar experience at Kelso's next place of work, the Barber and Ellis Warehouse. Walking along King Street one day Kelso was approached by a boy with whom he was acquainted and asked if he would like to buy a purse. It was a good quality purse of morocco leather and after purchasing it for fifteen cents, Kelso proudly showed his bargain to his friends. One of the men in the warehouse took it, saying he would find out what it was worth, but after several days he had still not returned it. In response to Kelso's insistent demands this man would say only that the boss, Mr Ellis, had the purse and that the best thing to do would be to say nothing about it. Instead, Kelso went to the manager's office and requested the return of his purse. The manager told him that the purse had been identified as one stolen from the store of Hart and Rawlinson. The purse had been returned to the store and the owners had agreed not to say any more about it. It was quite clear that everyone believed Kelso had himself stolen the purse while delivering a parcel. When Kelso explained the circumstances, a man was sent to accompany him in search of the boy, an employee of Hart and Rawlinson, who confessed to the theft. The boy was tried and for this and other thefts he received a sentence of three years in the reformatory. Kelso later stated that these childhood incidents influenced his decision as a young man to become actively concerned with the treatment of children in conflict with the law.

The incident of the stolen purse suggests that Kelso had developed early in life a capacity and inclination to pursue a course of action in which he believed. A further example of his determination occurred during his brief period in the employ of Timothy Eaton, which commenced in June 1876. Eaton, also an Irishman, arrived in Canada in 1868 and by 1875 his Toronto retail store was already firmly established. Kelso was attending the Ryerson Public School at this time and he responded to an advertisement for a boy assistant that he saw in the Eaton window one Saturday morning. He was hired after having answered in the affirmative Eaton's inquiries as to whether he was a good boy, attended Sunday school, and could read and write nicely. His salary was a dollar and a half a week and his duty was to assist the salesladies by taking the customer's money and goods to the rear of the store, securing the right change, and returning the parcel and money to the waiting customer. Everything was going well until a disagreement arose over responsibility for a broken window. Nobody would admit to the breakage and Eaton decided to deduct fifty cents from the salary of six employees whose involvement he suspected to pay for the window to be replaced. Kelso, who claimed innocence, was one of the six, but he felt that the deduction was unfair and refused to be one of those held liable. Despite a prolonged discussion with Eaton, who was not dissatisfied with Kelso's work, no compromise could be reached and Kelso resigned after only three months employment in the store.

For over two years Kelso continued this pattern of intermittent periods of employment as a messenger boy or sales assistant, interspersed by irregular school attendance. At the age of thirteen his life gained clearer and firmer direction by his engagement as an apprentice printer, firstly at the Ryerson Press and then at the Toronto *Mail*. He was steadily employed in this capacity for seven years, qualifying as a journeyman printer in 1884. He enjoyed the printing trade, but as he grew older he developed an interest in journalism, a profession which offered greater scope than printing for his growing ambitions. A casual glimpse one lunch hour at Union Station of George Brown, editor of the Toronto *Globe*, apparently set the seal on Kelso's desire to enter journalism. Brown was no hero to Kelso's fellow printers, and was widely perceived as an opponent of the Typographical Union as a result of his strong anti-union actions during the 1872 printers' strike.[8] However, Brown's imposing manner, and the interest and deference of the bypassers towards the famous man, made a strong impression on Kelso. The incident at Union Station, he later claimed, first sparked a youthful ambition to become a newspaper editor.

For an apprentice printer to plan to enter journalism was by no means an unattainable ambition. It was common at the time for a journalist to begin his career in the printery of a daily newspaper, and the wide range of newspapers and magazines in Toronto provided extensive opportunites for a young man who showed ability. Torontonians had the choice of four main daily papers in the early 1880s, in addition to numerous other periodicals catering to particular interests and tastes. First in prestige, circulation, and influence was the *Globe*, an established institution in Toronto's social and political life since 1844. Edited by George Brown until his death in 1880, the *Globe* was closely connected politically to the Liberal party. Largely to offset the influence of the *Globe*, the only Toronto daily of the early 1880s which could trace its history more than twenty years, the Conservatives established the *Mail* in 1872. This paper provided the main competition to the *Globe* during the 1870s and 1880s for Toronto's morning newspaper readership. The pre-eminence of these 'party' papers was challenged in the 1880s by the *Evening Telegram*, an afternoon paper first established in 1866, and the *World* which first appeared in 1880. The *Telegram* and the *World* contrasted with the *Globe* and the *Mail* in style, content, and readership. The *Globe* and the *Mail* provided sober, albeit partisan, news coverage, with a focus on political events – provincial, national, and international. They were designed to appeal primarily to well-educated businessmen and professionals. The *Telegram* and the *World*, aiming to attract a broader readership including Toronto's working men and clerks, provided a racier, more contentious, colourful, and satirical style of journalism with an emphasis on local events. Although other periodicals in Toronto employed journalists, it was on one of these four daily newspapers that Kelso hoped to begin his journalism career.[9]

While serving his apprenticeship Kelso devoted much of his spare time to self-education to equip himself for his chosen career. Self-improvement became a preoccupation, and he read widely although somewhat unsystematically. He kept a series of notebooks filled with quotations and other matters of interest, a practice which he kept up sporadically for the rest of his life. The contents of his notebooks indicated his wide range of interests. There were extensive quotations from Shakespeare, Byron, Ben Johnson, Milton, and Swift, interspersed with notes on history, biology, chemistry, geology, and economics. Dates of important events in British parliamentary history were recorded alongside such miscellanea as a description of the process by which fossils are formed, a note on the diameter of the sun, and the most recent estimate of the currency reserves in United States Treasury vaults. There were also Latin quotations and notes on English grammar. Nor was the Bible neglected. Kelso developed the habit of carrying tracts containing the Gospels and other scripture passages to read while travelling. He later said that this practice resulted in both spiritual and literary benefits. In 1883 he began a daily diary, which he kept with varying regularity for almost a decade. The total impression is of a serious, resolute young man.

To bring some order to his studies and to commence serious preparation for the matriculation examinations, Kelso in 1883 engaged the services of a tutor, Mr Sam Hughes, a teacher at the Collegiate Institute on Jarvis Street. At this time Kelso was attracted to the possibility of a university training. The printing trade brought him into daily contact with the world of writing and letters, and it was in this general sphere of activity that he now envisaged making his name. Deciding that a university degree would be a great advantage, he left the *Mail* in August 1884 to commence full-time matriculation studies at the Collegiate Institute. After years of part-time, largely self-directed studies, the opportunities provided by the institute were a delight. At the end of his first year of study Kelso wrote in his diary: 'The yearning desire of my heart was gratified, and I was able to give full scope to all the promptings of fancy or inclination.' He did well, gaining first place in his class in French and Latin, and an honourable mention in English. His tutor indicated that with continued good progress, he could expect to matriculate after another twelve months of study.

The decision to give up work for full-time study was not easy for Kelso since his family was now largely dependent on his income. During their first decade in Canada the Kelsos had enjoyed only moderate success, and their hopes of attaining in Canada the social position previously enjoyed in Ireland were still unfulfilled. The two oldest girls had married and left home. Alexander, the eldest son, had not settled into a career and made little or no contribution to the family income. Harry, a younger brother, was working for a bank and had been transferred to a branch outside Toronto. Gretta, three years older than John, was a sales assistant at Simpson's department store. Bella, Kelso's younger sister, was attending Whitby Ladies College, a major financial commitment for the family. Two other girls, Mary-Jane and Maya, were still at home. As George Kelso had by now largely abandoned his financial responsibilities towards his family, John Kelso was the only male member of the family living at home and bringing in a regular income. Thus, as soon as the academic year finished at the end of June, Kelso went back to work for the holidays. He found employment in the printing office of the Toronto *World*. This vacation job presented Kelso with his first opportunity to begin a career as a newspaper reporter.

During the first few weeks of his new job, Kelso was employed as a type-setter. It was work with which he was familiar and it presented little or no challenge. At this time the *World* was having problems with one of its proof-readers who was consistently turning up drunk at the office. The man was incapable of performing his work satisfactorily and, as a result, Kelso was asked to take on the duties of proof-reader. This was a promotion from type-setting and he was glad to accept the job. At first the position was temporary, and the newspaper management was evasive on the question of a more permanent one. The issue was shelved so often that he became discouraged, and for a while he went back to setting type, summing up his experiences as a proof-reader as 'poor pay and lots of blame.' Contributing to his frustration was the tardiness with which the *World* paid its employees. One day he waited at the *World* office nearly three hours for his wages, and he frequently wasted time in this manner.

On 31 August 1885 the Collegiate Institute reopened for another academic year. Kelso was not present as he had been working the night before and planned to keep working for a few more days in order to save enough to buy a new suit and overcoat. He also found the atmosphere of a newspaper office difficult to resist. At this time he made his first contribution to the daily press, a letter to the editor of the *Evening Telegram* proposing that 'the most awkward, inconvenient and unsightly' Toronto wharves be redesigned. He proposed construction of a wharf from Church to York streets and felt that the matter could quite easily be accomplished. 'Surely there is nothing unreasonable in this proposition, and if some of our influential citizens, backed up by an enterprising press, would only agitate the matter, all the inevitable difficulties would soon be overcome.' This was Kelso's first attempt to influence public policy. The tactics he proposed were those that he later used himself with great effectiveness in his career in social reform.

In the second week of September Kelso resumed full-time studies at the Collegiate Institute. He continued to visit the *World* office quite often, partly to see about the money which was owed to him. The *World* was still having trouble with its regular proof-reader and when Kelso was visiting one day in mid-September, one of the editors asked if he would fill in again. He agreed to do this, continuing to read proofs for the next week. In late September he was finally offered a permanent position as a proof-reader. He was now faced with a difficult decision: should he continue with his plans to matriculate and go on to the University of Toronto, or should he take this opportunity to gain valuable newspaper experience?

It was a major decision and for several days Kelso agonized over the best course to take: 'Perhaps never before in my life have I been called upon to exercise so great wisdom and discretion as at the present. Circumstances have conspired to place me in a position which seems to demand a sacrifice, no matter what conclusion I arrive at ... I am in a dilemma which will require all the wisdom and discretion I can bring to bear to extricate myself, so that I may never have cause for regret in the future.' He confided in two of his friends but each advised him differently. His tutor at the institute, however, suggested that he continue at proof-reading for the present and this was the course he finally took. For a month or so his feelings about his choice were mixed. The employees of the *World* continued to receive their salaries only haphazardly and belatedly, and Kelso noted that he found it 'rather discouraging to think of working for seven dollars a week, having to work in the afternoon for nothing, and then, to cap all, having to lose time hunting for my money.' By mid-October he was feeling truly depressed and was seriously contemplating a return to the institute. However, at this time Kelso persuaded W.F. Maclean, the editor of the *World*, to commission him to write a feature article for the newspaper on the subject of the public library, where Kelso was spending many of his afternoons. The chief librarian was Mr James Bain, Jr, the son of the bookseller who gave Kelso his first job. He was most obliging and gave Kelso every possible assistance. Early one morning, after arriving home from proof-reading, Kelso wrote up his manuscript and submitted it to the editors. On Saturday, 30 October, he had the pleasure of seeing it appear in print. This achievement restored Kelso's confidence in his decision to work for the *World*, and revived his resolution to make his way in the world. He wrote in his diary on the day his article appeared:

'My first success has rekindled the smouldering embers of ambition. I am determined that I shall succeed – the path may be rugged and the journey may be long, but the haven is sure at the end, and I will never rest until I have secured for myself a name and ... a position that will enable me to do a work equal to those brilliant lights who have gone before and whose memory men delight to honour. But this looks like brag and may one day make me blush, because unfulfilled.' Kelso's abilities as a writer were now apparent to the *World's* editors and before long circumstances again worked in his favour. In November one of the regular reporters for the newspaper took ill and Maclean asked Kelso to take that reporter's place for an evening. The position was shortly thereafter made a permanent one and by early December J.J. Kelso was busy reporting meetings, rushing to fires, getting acquainted with the other Toronto journalists, and 'gaining bushels of experience.'

Kelso experienced some regrets that his opportunity to matriculate for university had been forfeited, but he was compensated by his early successes as a reporter. His daily life now acquired a regular pattern. His routine began at about seven in the evening when he commenced work at the *World*. He returned home at four in the morning and usually wrote or read for a couple of hours before going to bed. He rose in the mid-afternoon, and the hours from then until returning to the *World* were his own for relaxation or study. Frequently, he spent these afternoons at the public library, studying his Collegiate Institute texts or other works of literature and history such as those of Disraeli, Spencer, and Coleridge. He was still prompted by a strong yearning to become more learned, more able, and more sophisticated. In his optimistic moods he believed himself to be making progress and expanding intellectually every day: 'My mind is growing broader and more universal. I am daily learning to observe more carefully, to think more deeply and to reason more accurately. There is still hope of my arriving in due time to the full and perfect stature of a man, and I may yet live to see the fruition of all the passionate longings and ambitions of boyhood.'

There was a further reason for Kelso's frequent visits to the library: the attractive young lady librarians. Kelso rarely missed an opportunity to make the acquaintance of young ladies and, next to his career ambitions, they were the major topic of his diary entries at this time. His later reputation as a ladies' man can certainly be traced to this time. Weekend excursions to Oshawa, visits to the circus and the exhibition, the Collegiate Institute games, and Sunday church services all provided opportunities to practise his charm. Those who attended the Collegiate Institute games in October 1885 particularly caught his imagination: 'The grandstand, as usual on this occasion, was one living conglomeration of beauty and femininity. I will not begin to acknowledge how completely these beautiful creatures fascinated my young and foolish heart. They were arrayed in all the finery of fashion, and nature, aided by art and all the bewitchments of coquetry was not to be withstood. The fair devils (if I may use that word elegantly) know their power, and they seldom scruple to use it ...' One young lady in particular caught his fancy and he escorted her home after church one Sunday in October. It was a passionate but prudent episode: '... we stood for a long time in the shadow of the porch at the door. Shall I ever forget those few moments of bliss as we looked deep into each other's eyes, and spoke in playful endearing banter. I held her hand in mine, and the soft white hand sent a thrill of pleasure through me, as I lovingly pressed it. I was longing to kiss those cherry lips and she knew it, and no doubt sympathized with the desire, but a calculating prudence which I can never wholly shake off restrained me, and sent me away without the blessing. Sweet Maude, my heart is in danger ...'

Living at home with four sisters provided further opportunities for meeting other young ladies, as the friends of Gretta, Mary-Jane, Bella, and Maya frequently made calls on the household. Kelso spent a considerable amount of time with his sisters, accompanying them on boat trips, weekend excursions, or visits to the exhibition. Often they would take a walk downtown together, chat with friends, perhaps eat an ice cream or enjoy a light meal, and then take the streetcar home. During winter, skating was a favourite family pastime. On other occasions he managed to get the *World*'s complimentary opera tickets and take his mother or one of his sisters to see the performance.

Kelso was also an active member of the Presbyterian church which the family had attended regularly since arriving in Toronto. Anna Kelso was a deeply religious woman, and she conveyed her strong Protestant faith to her son. He took on the responsibilities of Sunday school teaching, a task he performed with characteristic seriousness: 'I love the boys more each day I teach them and am growing more intensely anxious to do them good, and implant right principles in their young minds.' He was particularly appreciative of the rousing sermons of the Rev. D.J. McDonnell, the minister at one of the larger Presbyterian churches: 'He preaches to a wealthy and influential congregation and never hesitates to denounce their sins and shortcomings when he sees occasion.' Kelso's own piety was put to the test one Sunday afternoon when a friend suggested a jaunt in a 'two hossekerridge.' Despite his better judgment he accepted, and he suffered pangs of conscience as they drove past the Salvation Army who were conducting an open-air service at the side of the road. Nor did Kelso consider newspaper work a suitable Lord's Day activity, and it was only with extreme reluctance that he consented to work for the *World* on Sunday evenings.

Kelso was twenty-one years old when his career as a journalist commenced.

He viewed his appointment to the news staff of the *World* as the culmination and just reward for the decade of hard work since he arrived in Canada. He noted wryly in his diary that 'Providence has been good to me, but it has not given me all my blessings as a gift but rather as a wage.' This assessment was, in one sense, accurate. Since the misfortune of the starch factory fire in Dundalk, the Kelsos had been unable to rely on inherited privilege as the basis for personal advancement. J.J. Kelso had risen to this challenge, and by dint of long hours of work, application to study under difficult circumstances, and awareness of opportunity he had attained a modest but respectable position in Toronto society. At the same time, his diary entries showed him to be a young man not given to underestimating his talents and efforts. Imbued by his mother with a sense of shame at having fallen from bourgeois respectability, Kelso entered wholeheartedly into the struggle to restore his good name and that of his family. Moral rectitude and career success were his personal goals, and he was willing to work devotedly and unstintingly to achieve his ambitions. His experiences as a needy immigrant intensified his desire to succeed. Conventional in his religion and morals, serious concerning responsibilities and ambitions, he was proud of his accomplishments attained under difficult circumstances. The groundwork for a return to middle-class respectability had been established.

2

Young Reformer

During the 1870s and 1880s the pace of Toronto's industrial development accelerated; the population of the city grew rapidly, almost doubling between 1880 and 1890. Although new factories provided jobs for many newcomers, unemployment and poverty were widespread. In 1884 a Toronto police station received 495 applications in one month for shelter and during the winter two private agencies gave relief to more than 1800 families.[1] Goldwin Smith, a University of Toronto professor, estimated in 1890 that 4 per cent of the city's population depended on private charity.[2] Housing conditions deteriorated; squalid, unhealthy, and unsanitary slums became a growing source of concern.[3]

Public action to alleviate these conditions was impeded by prevailing social attitudes. The pioneer and frontier conditions in Upper Canada during the first half of the nineteenth century glorified self-sufficiency. And an expanding agricultural economy allowed many young poor people to hope for relative comfort by middle age. In these circumstances the dogma thrived that success came to all who lived respectably and worked hard.[4]

Conditions in Canada were often contrasted with those in Britain, where the existence of poverty was publicly recognized and provided for by the Poor Laws. In Canada, however, the prevalent attitude was that the poor should fend for themselves. Those who did not were considered lazy, weak, or immoral. This meant that there was no need to have permanent provisions for the poor.[5] As the *Globe* warned in 1874: 'Promiscuous alms giving is fatal ... it is the patent process for the manufacture of paupers out of the worthless and improvident. A poor law is a legislative machine for the manufacture of pauperism. It is true mercy to say that it would be better that a few individuals should die of starvation than that a pauper class should be raised up ...'[6]

At this stage of his career Kelso had little interest in the plight of the poor. He preferred to cover political events. The opportunities provided by police reporting for observation of the social and domestic circumstances of the poor were, in Kelso's view, less significant than the inconvenience of extensive travel between police stations and the boredom of routine stories.

Kelso's disinterest in poverty and the related social problems during this time was not shared by many of Toronto's social and business leaders. The consequences of urbanization and industrialization raised a challenge to the dominant views about poverty. The mass movement of population to new industrial cities such as Toronto created problems of housing, health, and employment. Family ties were perceived as weakening and individuals were left without resources to cope with distressing circumstances.[7] The plight of the sick, the poor, and the handicapped became more apparent in a closely settled city than in the country. Also, their problems impinged more directly on the lives of the more affluent city dwellers. As early as the 1830s it was recognized that public aid could not be wholly withheld from the sick poor because of the danger posed by the outbreak of cholera.[8] The developments in public health during the century were given impetus by the recognition that 'disease was no respecter of boundaries and that the slum dweller's illness was not his purely private misfortune which could safely be ignored by his wealthier neighbours.'[9]

Early in the century local governments were responsible for providing social welfare. However, as municipalities proved unwilling or unable to perform certain functions satisfactorily, the province stepped in with its own programmes. In 1859 the Board of Inspectors of Prisons, Asylums and Public Charities was created to oversee the range of provincial social welfare activities that had emerged. The board was given responsibility for the province's quarantine and marine hospitals, penitentiary, reformatories for boys, asylum, and local jails.[10]

During the twenty years after Confederation the provincial government became more active in the field of social welfare. The driving force for this development was J.W. Langmuir, provincial inspector of prisons, asylums and charities from 1868 until 1882. Profiting from Ontario's highly favourable fiscal position in the post-Confederation period, and supported by Sir Oliver Mowat, premier from the early 1870s until 1896, Langmuir undertook a vigorous programme of administrative reform. During his inspectorate the provincial mental hospitals were greatly expanded and improved, a special institution was established for the mentally retarded, a refuge for girls was created, and schools for the deaf and the blind were built. Considerable improvements were also made to the local jails, and intermediate prisons for men and women were formed.[11]

After Langmuir's resignation in 1882 the pace of administrative reform slackened, but the provincial government enacted further measures to cope with the social problems created by rapid industrialization. The Factories Act of 1884 outlined standards to be observed by manufacturers regarding safety and child labour. The act was poorly enforced, but it was an initial recognition of the need for protection of persons employed in industry. Similarly, the Workmen's Compensation Act of 1887 recognized, albeit tentatively, the need to compensate the victims of industrial accidents and their dependents. Legislation passed in the late 1880s and early 1890s provided for the maintenance of wives deserted by their husbands, the development of homes for the aged, and the establishment of houses of refuge for females. Despite considerable limitations, the measures enacted in Ontario during the two decades following Confederation recognized new problems and the need for government to assume new responsibilities.[12]

Private charitable organizations and institutions developed alongside the governmental social welfare services. Beginning in mid-century, churches and other non-governmental bodies established a wide range of welfare services throughout the province, including hospitals, orphanages, asylums, houses of industry, refuges, reformatories, and hostels. Organizations were established to aid prisoners, to encourage temperance, to prevent cruelty, to reform local government, to maintain the moral and religious well-being of young women, and to promote many other public welfare causes. Although these services commenced under private auspices, strong demands were made on the provincial government for funds, particularly to support extensive, institutional services. Prior to Confederation financial help was given on a piecemeal and unsystematic basis. However, during Langmuir's inspectorate the process became more orderly. The Charity Aid Act of 1874 established a funding formula for extending provincial grants to private organizations according to the amount of service provided. The act also laid down the principles that institutions receiving grants must accept provincial inspection and meet standards established by the province. The act further provided that the by-laws and regulations governing the operation of the institutions be ratified by the provincial inspector.[13]

The passage of the Charity Aid Act was a major step in the development of provincial government responsibility for social welfare services. It had the effect of encouraging the expansion of private institutions and services. During the two decades following its enactment, the number of hospitals receiving government aid rose from ten to thirty-two, state-assisted orphanages doubled from fourteen to twenty-eight, and houses of refuge increased ninefold to thirty-two in 1893. By the 1890s government-supported private institutions were an established feature of social welfare administration in Ontario.

The impetus for the development of private charity was varied. In mid-century the churches played a leading role in establishing health and welfare institutions. The Roman Catholic church took the lead in organizing institutions and programmes in centres with large Catholic populations. Women from prominent families also played a major initiating role. The private charities usually espoused strong moral, evangelical, and humanitarian aims. Their leaders were drawn principally from the social élite and the urban middle class, and the commitment of these groups to the values of respectability, Christian morality, established authority, and personal responsibility was reflected in the policies and programmes of the charities. Allied to these notions were ideas drawn from the experiences of social welfare programmes in the United States and Europe. Through bodies such as the National Conference of Charities and Correction and the National Prison Association, Canadians involved in social welfare became familiar with developments elsewhere on the continent.[14]

As a regular churchgoer, Kelso was likely aware of some charitable activities associated with his denomination, but the work of charitable and social reform agencies held little interest for him. However, his position as a reporter required him to follow Toronto's affairs closely. Municipal politics in 1886 were dominated by W.H. Howland, a businessman and prominent member of the evangelical movement within the Church of England in Toronto, who was deeply involved in philanthropic ventures in the city. He had conducted a mission to the poor living in the slums of St John's Ward and was personally involved in relief work and house-to-house visits.[15] He was also active in the Prisoners' Aid Association, formed to assist discharged prisoners adjust to community life, and the Industrial School Association, established to provide educational institutions for neglected, dependent, and uncontrollable children. In January 1886 Howland was elected mayor of Toronto representing a reform coalition of prohibitionists, trade unionists, militant women, Protestant clergy, and newspaper editors. He fought his campaign on a mixture of reform issues, including the enforcement of liquor licensing regulations, the exposure of corrupt contractors and officials, the removal of prostitution and gambling from the city, the combatting of cruelty to women and children, and the support of trade unions.[16] Howland's attempt to implement these pledges became the main concern of Toronto politics during 1886.

Through his work as a journalist Kelso became familiar with reform themes. He was regularly assigned to report meetings of the Canadian Institute, where reform issues were often discussed. The strike at the Massey Manufacturing Company that Kelso covered in February 1886 was the first occasion when Howland's claim to represent the working man's interests was put to the test. Later in the year Kelso covered the annual meetings of the Presbyterian Assembly and the Methodist Conference where temperance was a central concern. Reform matters were also frequently considered at meetings of the

Parkdale Council, another of his regular reporting duties. He was impressed by Howland, and in his diary he noted with satisfaction Howland's increased majority in the 1887 election.

Although he was an admirer and supporter of Howland, Kelso was not involved in social and political affairs during 1886. Throughout the year his major concern continued to be his newspaper career. He received many compliments from the *World* editors for his work, but he was impatient with his progress at the newspaper. Having tasted success, he was eager to proceed to greater achievements. His ambitions became a major source of anxiety: 'Lord, Lord, how hard it is to wait, to be patient. How unhappy is the lot of the ambitious! What fears, what strivings, what anticipation, what disappointments and sorrow. Do the joys and pleasures, successes and achievements, counterbalance these? No, no, they cannot begin to fill up the measure of trails that eat into the soul, like a burning, corroding poison.' From time to time he considered severing his connection with the *World*. He felt that he was not being paid enough and his application in May for a raise to ten dollars a week was refused. Furthermore, the *World* was not a high status newspaper. In June Kelso spoke to an editor of the *Mail* about joining their local staff and from that time he made continuing efforts to transfer to either the *Mail* or the *Globe*. In September he was promised 'the first opening' by both of these newspapers. But at the end of 1886 he was still employed as a general reporter at the *World*.

It was not only his connections with the *World* that Kelso considered breaking. From time to time he seriously entertained the idea of leaving newspaper work altogether. The ambition which he privately nurtured was to become a writer, and he felt that working as a reporter was not conducive to that end. Although his job on the newspaper was giving him worldly experience, the pace was too hectic. 'Everything flits past like a panorama,' he complained. 'I have no time to digest or assimilate, and often most instructive lessons are lost through want of meditation and reflection. That these two latter are essential, nay indispensable, to one who would be a great writer, and who would depict faithfully human thought and human character, must be admitted by all.' He wanted to devote some years to reading and study, but given his financial position and responsibilities to his family, this was not possible. He remained a journalist, successful at what he was doing but anxious to make his name in a more challenging field.

Kelso's first involvement in social reform began with a letter to the editor of the *World* by John Kidston MacDonald deploring the absence in the city of a society to prevent cruelty to animals. MacDonald belonged to a family of prosperous dry-goods merchants who were prominent in charitable activities. His letter was passed to Kelso with the suggestion that he might use it as the basis for a story. Kelso wrote a brief article on the theme of cruelty, and in response a small sum of money was sent to the paper to start a fund for the formation of a society to prevent cruelty to animals. Before long, seventy-four dollars had been collected. The strong public response to his article impressed Kelso, and he considered involving himself in the formation of such a society. A personal experience strongly influenced him. Walking along Yonge Street late one night in November 1886, he came across two sobbing children, a brother and sister. They told him that they had been promised a severe beating by their father unless they could beg at least twenty-five cents that night. So far their tally was only fifteen cents. Kelso took pity on them and searched for three hours to find a charitable institution willing to take them in for the night. The parents were charged the next morning in police court with neglect, but the case was dismissed by the magistrate who claimed there was insufficient grounds for prosecution. This event deeply affected Kelso. He began to envision a society oriented towards the prevention of all types of cruelty, encompassing children as well as animals.

A suitable opportunity to propose this scheme arose early in January 1887 at a meeting of the Canadian Institute that Kelso attended as a reporter. The question of a speaker for the February gathering was raised, and one of the members proposed half-jokingly that the young reporter be given a chance to speak. Kelso took advantage of the suggestion and at the meeting on 19 February 1887 he delivered an address on the topic, 'The Necessity of a Society for the Prevention of Cruelty in Toronto.' He proposed a general humane association with a broad set of objectives: preventing cruelty to children; rescuing children from vicious influences and remedying their condition; preventing the beating of animals, overloading streetcars, overloading wagons, working old horses, or driving galled or disabled animals; introducing drinking fountains; passing more effective laws prohibiting cruelty; adopting better horseshoeing methods; disseminating humane literature into homes and schools; teaching children to be humane; and encouraging everyone to practise and teach kindness to animals and others. The society would have a religious but non-denominational basis, and everyone could join. The address was practical, straightforward, clear, and well-received. At the close of the meeting a motion was passed: 'That in the opinion of the Institute, the formation in this city of a society for the prevention of cruelty would be conducive to the interests of the public morality, and this meeting desires to express its sympathy with the object contemplated.'

Encouraged by the support of the members of the Canadian Institute, Kelso proceeded to organize the establishment of a Humane Society. On 21 February he sent a circular letter inviting prominent Torontonians to a public meeting at

Shaftesbury Hall on the evening of the 24th. John MacDonald, president of the Toronto General Hospital and vice-president of the Industrial Schools Association, agreed to chair the meeting, and the speakers included Mayor Howland and Canon Du Moulin of the Church of England. Their support and that of other community leaders ensured a large and enthusiastic turnout. Kelso was on the platform and he gave a brief account of why the meeting had been called and what now needed to be done. He enjoyed this taste of public life: 'This was my first experience on a public platform and I trust it will not be my last.' The meeting agreed unanimously that a new organization be formed and that the title 'Toronto Humane Society' best expressed the broad humanitarian aims that were envisaged. A further reason for this choice of name was to avoid any possible confusion with the Ontario Association for the Prevention of Cruelty to Animals, an organization active in Toronto for a brief period during the 1870s before folding owing to lack of public support. An organizing committee was appointed which met a few days later to select the officers of the society. The lieutenant-governor accepted the position of patron and Mayor Howland consented to be named honorary president. The slate of vice-presidents included such well-known names as Samuel Blake, Goldwin Smith, George Hodgins, the Reverend D.J. McDonnell, and W.R. Brock. A council of twenty-four members was appointed, including ten ladies, to exercise overall control of the work of the society. Kelso was himself appointed to the influential and responsible position of honorary secretary.

The group of leading citizens who supported and encouraged Kelso in the formation of the Humane Society were no strangers either to one another or to public life. Blake, a businessman and a member of one of Toronto's leading families, was first associated with Howland in the Church Association of the Diocese of Toronto, the organization of the evangelical wing of the Church of England which flourished in Toronto during the 1870s. He worked closely with Howland in mission work to the poor, served as president of the Prisoners' Aid Association, and was an active member of the Industrial School Association. Dr George Hodgins, deputy-minister of education for Ontario from 1876 to 1889, was founding president of the Prisoners' Aid Association, and worked with Blake and Howland in both the Church Association and the Industrial School Association. Goldwin Smith and John MacDonald also belonged to the Industrial School Association. It was the support of this close-knit group of prominent Protestant businessmen and educationalists that enabled Kelso to launch the Toronto Humane Society successfully.[17] Kelso was deeply influenced by his contact with and acceptance by this group. It was flattering for a young man to be associating with leading members of the community, particularly those whose success, prosperity, education, moral and religious principles accorded so closely with his own beliefs and aspirations. His contact with these men also gave him further opportunities to become familiar with current views and opinions on social issues.

Leading public figures such as Howland and Goldwin Smith were prepared to give moral backing to the Humane Society, but it was soon apparent that the humdrum tasks of correspondence, fund raising, and establishing the organization were to be Kelso's responsibilities. During the spring and summer of 1887 he spent most of his spare time on Humane Society business. An office was established at 103 Bay Street and a clerk employed to deal with the routine work. During these early months the society concentrated on educational work; pamphlets, posters, and magazines describing the society's activities and aims were published and distributed to women's groups, temperance organizations, schools, and churches.

The society's first public campaign concerned the treatment of horses which pulled the Toronto Street Railway Company's streetcars. Horse-drawn cars had been in operation in Toronto since the early 1860s, but during the 1880s the street railway system was expanded on a large scale and by the end of the decade was being used by 50,000 to 60,000 passengers daily.[18] The Railway Company was the centre of a great public controversy in March 1886 when the drivers and conductors defied the company's owner, Senator Frank Smith, and joined the Knights of Labour as a step towards improving their pay and working conditions. Smith reacted by locking out his employees, receiving much of the blame for the subsequent public disorder and inconvenience.[19] However, the treatment of the company's horses, rather than the men, most concerned the members of the Humane Society. The horses worked long hours, carrying fifty to sixty passengers during peak periods; it was not unusual for a horse to drop down exhausted or even to die on the tracks. Soon after its formation the Humane Society set about to bring improvement to this situation. The poor treatment of the horses was stressed in the society's literature, and Kelso spoke about the problem with city aldermen whom he met in the course of his work. The result of the campaign was a decision by the city to erect water troughs for the horses. Although not a major breakthrough, this small success was important to the Humane Society as it sought to establish itself as an effective organization.

Of more long-term significance was the support of the Humane Society for the work of Inspector David Archibald of the Toronto City Police. Archibald was appointed a staff inspector in May 1886 by Howland to form a special squad to combat cruelty to animals, women, and children, and to oppose gambling, prostitution, sabbath-breaking, indecent exposure, and unlicensed drinking. Throughout 1886 Archibald's new section applied itself vigorously to closing brothels and enforcing the liquor licensing laws. However, combatting cruelty had scarcely got underway, despite pledges by Howland in the 1886 election that this would be a priority area for his administration. Early in the spring of 1887 the Humane Society offered to pay two months' salary for a police officer to be appointed to Archibald's section to handle cases of cruelty. In July the city agreed and the work was so successful that the society extended the trial period to cover the remainder of the year. In December 1887 the City Council acceded to a request that it appoint a permanent officer to work with the Humane Society in combatting cruelty. Its readiness to agree to this proposal was prompted in part by the fact that the fines which the anti-cruelty constable had collected were almost sufficient to meet his salary. At this stage the officer was mainly concerned with cruelty to animals, but he was to play an important role in the years that lay immediately ahead in the prevention of cruelty to children.

While engaged in establishing the Humane Society, Kelso continued to work energetically at his newspaper career. A considerable amount of his time in the early months of 1887 was spent reporting municipal affairs. He was chosen to cover the investigation into Howland's allegations of fraud in the Waterworks Department, one of the major initiatives of the reform group during Howland's second term in office. Such assignments were valuable experiences for Kelso in broadening his understanding of the workings of City Hall and the difficulties of implementing change. But he continued to be dissatisfied on the *World*'s staff, and when offered the position of police reporter on the *Globe* in late May he did not hesitate to accept. His new salary on the *Globe* was $14 a week, an increase of $2 over his remuneration at the *World*. Of equal importance was his rise in status. The *Globe*, with its established reputation, respectable readership, and temperate style, was more in keeping with Kelso's social aspirations and se-rious-minded nature than the maverick, iconoclastic *World*.

A further reason for Kelso's eager acceptance of the new job was that he was now keen to try his hand at police reporting, despite his dislike of the work during his early months with the *World*. He saw it as an opportunity to acquire a more thorough knowledge of human nature. On the *World* police reporting had meant waiting around the police stations in the early hours of the morning, or sometimes accompanying a constable on an investigation. By contrast, at the *Globe* Kelso worked during the day, and much of his time was spent in the police courts. At first he found this work among the 'scruff of the city,' as he described them, quite pleasant. The job gave him plenty of time to pursue his interest in the Humane Society, and he was able to confirm his reputation as a reform-minded citizen through his accounts of some of the more tragic cases which found their way into the courts. He gained knowledge not only from his contact with police and offenders, but also from members of the judiciary, such as Judge

McDougall of York County, with whom he had opportunities to discuss police systems in other parts of North America. But there were also disadvantages. The work was of rather routine and unchallenging nature. 'I learn practically nothing in composition as all my writing consists in chronicling police news,' he complained after less than a month on the job. Moreover, he was by no means sure that he enjoyed extensive close contact with the poor of the city. Certainly there were opportunities to learn about human character, but these were offset by his concern with 'the danger of being contaminated by the foul thought, language and action that literally fills the air.' This preoccupation with his own moral integrity, and distaste towards the way of life of the 'poor and criminal classes,' strongly shaped Kelso's attitude on social issues through these years.

During the summer months Kelso's dissatisfaction with his new job increased. On the *World*, a much smaller paper, the companionship was closer and the work more diverse. When he was transferred to night work in early August, Kelso decided once again to cast around for another position. He was offered the job of municipal reporter with the *Mail* in mid-August, but the salary was not good and mainly for this reason he declined the offer. He did manage to get some practice in composition by preparing some feature articles in addition to his regular reporting duties. 'The Chinamen of Toronto' was his subject for an article in July, and while on holiday in St Catharines he wrote an article on the Welland Canal. However, he could not shake off his malaise. 'I have great difficulty in concealing my dislike for the *Globe*,' he noted in late August. Had a suitable opportunity arisen, he would certainly have severed his association with the newspaper at this time.

Increasingly Kelso was gaining his deepest satisfaction from his work with the Humane Society: 'I believe I have done great good in Toronto by my efforts in the Humane line, and that thought is sufficient to compensate for every other sacrifice,' he wrote at the time. Apart from the campaign for drinking fountains and the appointment of the cruelty constable, little else of a substantial nature was accomplished by the society during its first six months. However, an office had been established, meetings were well attended, regular publications were being distributed, and the organization was financially sound. In October 1877 Kelso received a tangible reward for his efforts by being appointed a delegate to the American Humane Association annual convention in Rochester, New York. Several members of the Toronto society attended, but it was Kelso who organized the delegation and acted as its spokesman. The convention turned out to be a great success for Kelso personally and for the Toronto Humane Society. He delivered a somewhat embellished report on the Toronto society's activities that was well received. As a result of this speech and his enthusiastic participation in other conference proceedings, Kelso was elected assistant secretary of the

American Humane Association. He mentioned in his address that Toronto was most interested in hosting the next annual convention of the association. This was a rather presumptuous suggestion since Toronto was participating for the first time, the association had never previously met outside of the United States, and some American cities had indicated their wish to host the 1888 convention. Nevertheless, the Toronto delegation lobbied for its case, and when the vote was taken, Toronto was chosen. On his return home Kelso wasted no time in calling on Howland to tell him of the city's good fortune; the mayor promised every assistance in organizing the convention.

Kelso's initial interest in public affairs had been aroused by his observations of Howland's mayoralty, and through his experience and enjoyment of public life in the Humane Society. His Protestant, middle-class background and the strong moral influence of his mother led him readily to accept the precepts which guided Howland and likeminded reformers. As Kelso developed his interest in reform issues he began to devote his attention to the welfare of children. He was not alone.

In the late 1880s and 1890s many middle-class English Canadians were expressing concern with the manner in which children were being raised in Canadian society, including the implications of child-rearing practices for general societal well-being. Fundamental to this concern were new concepts of the nature of childhood and of the role of families and mothers. Children were seen as needing nurturing and tending, and there was new recognition of the emotional life of children. The importance of parents adopting a careful and systematic approach in dealings with their children was stressed, and there was a strongly developing belief in the influence of environment on children. Not only were the actions of parents crucial in determining a child's future behaviour, but also influences outside the home – education, entertainment, and physical surroundings – were seen as having a major impact. The importance of the mother's role in bringing up her children was stressed. The need for stable, secure, and loving families was viewed as paramount. Underlying these new beliefs was a deep faith in the ability of the home to shape society.[20]

Various factors contributed to the emergence of these notions in late nineteenth-century Ontario. The relative prosperity of the expanding urban middle class provided an opportunity for more attention to be given to the nurturing aspects of child-rearing than was possible in harsher rural settings where children played an important economic role. Workplace and residence were likely to be separate in the new cities and mothers assumed a greater share of the family's responsibility for raising youngsters. The mother's role assumed new importance. Social problems relating to the young were more visible in the cities and ideas developed elsewhere were assimilated more readily.

Whatever the reasons for their development, the impact of these new ideas on social and political life was profound. In education, public health, city planning, corrections, immigration, and many other areas of government activity and regulation, Canadians attempted to create the conditions to produce 'a new childhood for a new society.'[21] Of particular concern were the methods of dealing with neglected, dependent, and delinquent children. Prior to the 1880s public concern with these classes of children was limited. From the early nineteenth century the apprenticeship system was the primary means of disposing of orphans and children abandoned by their parents. Laws governing apprenticeship had been modified several times, but until the 1870s the apprentice's rights to fair treatment from his or her master were limited. The primary purpose of the system was the placing of the dependent child, and considerations of the child's subsequent welfare were secondary. The 1850s saw the development of special institutions for dependent children. Initially these orphanages adopted a policy of apprenticing out many of the children in their care, but the shortcomings of the system, particularly the difficulty in obtaining placements for young or handicapped children, led the institutions to develop programmes for the long-term care of dependent children. The other means of providing for children who lacked parents was by adoption. However, adoption had no clear legal status during the nineteenth century and an adopted child was without any special rights or protection.[22]

Some of the orphanages established in the latter half of the nineteenth century included neglected children in their overall responsibility, but their primary focus was on children without parental or other family support. Public interest in neglected children, those whose home lives were considered inadequate physically or morally, arose first in relation to juvenile crime. Separate institutions for young offenders were established in 1859. However, there was a widespread view that preventative as well as remedial measures were necessary to cope with the problem of delinquency. Youthful crime was linked to child neglect. Child beggars, hawkers, newsboys, habitual truants, other children of the street, and children whose parents allegedly instructed them in intemperance, vice, and crime were considered potential paupers, drunkards, and criminals.[23] Therefore, rescuing neglected children was considered as a measure to prevent crime.

The first legislation directly concerned with neglected children was the Industrial Schools Act of 1874, which gave public school boards the right to establish residential, custodial, and educational institutions for certain categories of problem children. Youngsters under fourteen found begging, homeless, or destitute could be committed by a magistrate to an industrial school, and a parent or guardian could apply for the committal of a child they found 'unable to control.' Most importantly, the act also established that a child 'who, by reason of the neglect, drunkenness or other vices of parents, is suffered to be growing up without salutory parental control and education, or in circumstances exposing him to lead an idle and dissolute life' could be sent to an industrial school. This broad clause was the first attempt in the province to legislate standards of child-rearing.

For ten years after the passage of the act of 1874 no school board exercised its right to establish an industrial school. In order to activate the legislation, the province in 1884 gave school boards the right to delegate their powers respecting industrial schools to any incorporated philanthropic society. At the same time a further category of children, those found guilty of petty crime, was added to the list of those eligible for an industrial school. These changes had the desired effect and in 1887 the recently-formed Industrial School Association opened the first of the schools, the Victoria Industrial School for Boys, at Mimico in Toronto. The Alexandra Industrial School for Girls opened five years later, also under the auspices of the Industrial School Association.

To the child-centred social reformers of the 1880s the establishment of industrial schools was a significant but inadequate response to the problem of child neglect. Apart from the very limited number of places in the Victoria Industrial School, the act's major weakness was that it did not specify who should be responsible for investigating cases of child neglect or for taking children into care from allegedly damaging surroundings. It was to remedy this particular failing of the provincial legislation that the Toronto Humane Society promoted, as one of its first actions, the appointment of a cruelty constable by the Toronto City Council.

The original impulse of the Toronto Humane Society was simply a conviction that human beings should behave kindly, rather than cruelly, to weaker creatures. However, its formation at a time when government policies regarding dependent and neglected children were undergoing reappraisal resulted in the society becoming involved in more complex and more political issues. The leaders saw the organization as a vehicle through which to promote their reform programme, as was apparent in the statement of aims issued in early 1888. As well as general aims such as 'the protection of children of drunken, cruel and dissolute parents or guardians' and 'the punishment of child-beaters and of heartless parents or guardians,' the statement proposed several specific new policies. These included the 'licensing and police oversight of bootblacks, and of vendors of newspapers and smallwares on the streets,' the establishment of a girls' industrial school and a 'temporary refuge for destitute and neglected children until they are disposed of or provided for,' and 'the desirability of having some officer specially entrusted with the duty of looking after the waifs and strays of the city.'[24] The general humanitarian outlook that characterized the early months of the society had been transformed into a specific programme of reform.

From the beginning of 1888 Kelso directed most of his efforts to the achievement of the policies outlined in the Humane Society's aims. During with winter months of 1887–8 he worked with Beverley Jones, a lawyer active in many charitable organizations, on a draft bill to extend governmental responsibility for neglected children. The bill was submitted to the provincial government on 12 February, and passed the legislature the following month. The Children's Protection Act, as it was titled, reaffirmed the authority of the courts to commit neglected children to the industrial school and to the Mercer Refuge, but also gave the courts new authority to send neglected children to authorized children's homes. It gave the homes the power to keep a child committed to their care until he or she attained the age of eighteen years, with the cost of care, up to two dollars a week, being borne by the municipality. The act was of considerable importance in that it provided the courts with many more potential institutional placements for neglected children, and also established public responsibility for the maintenance of neglected children in all recognized institutions. This was Kelso's first attempt to influence policy at the provincial level, and the success of the representation was a boost to his morale and an encouragement to the society.

The 1888 Children's Protection Act also contained a set of provisions which arose from Kelso's experiences as a police court reporter during the latter half of 1887. His involvement with the Humane Society had stimulated him to take a more critical look at the proceedings of the court. One aspect which he considered particularly inappropriate was the trial of young offenders in the same courts as adults. The need to separate juvenile from adult offenders in the prison system had been recognized for some time, but the situation of children being subjected to the same judicial processes as adults was still generally unquestioned. Kelso frequently observed 'little fellows eight or nine years old standing in the dock with old reprobates, and when the Clerk of the Court reads out the charge and asks the child to plead guilty or not guilty the whole proceedings are quite unintelligible to him.' In Massachusetts separate court hearings for juveniles had been held since 1869, and the idea of special courts to try children's cases was under discussion in the United States.[25] When Kelso and Jones were drafting their bill, they included a clause which provided that 'The Lieutenant-Governor may, upon the request of any municipal council, appoint a commissioner or commissioners, each with the powers of a police magistrate, to hear and determine complaints against juvenile offenders, apparently under the age of sixteen.' It was several years before any such juvenile courts were effectively established in Ontario, but the enactment of this provision was the first step in what became one of Kelso's major crusades.

The passage of the Children's Protection Act provided an auspicious start to 1888 for the Humane Society. A donation of $500 in late January by Miss Gwynne, an elderly lady who was its main benefactor, brightened its prospects even more. The society was by now well known. Several of Toronto's leading clergymen preached sermons praising its efforts, and Kelso's role was widely acknowledged. Indeed, he was gaining a degree of notoriety as a precocious youth attempting to reform the world single-handedly. An editorial in *Life Magazine*, a weekly published in Toronto, depicted him as a 'motley fool' striking out in all directions but essentially inexperienced in the ways of the world. There was an element of truth in this caricature. Kelso had not yet articulated a consistent social or political philosophy, and he was prepared to take action in a range of areas without detailed examination of all related issues. However, he considered the magazine's criticisms ridiculous, but welcomed the publicity. The main problem arising from the article was that his mother became upset and planned to write anonymously to *Life Magazine* defending her son's honour. Kelso managed to dissuade her from doing so, but he was touched by her concern which he saw as an example of 'the loving watchfulness and interest of a mother in the welfare and honour of her children.'

The three months which followed the passage of the Children's Protection Act in March 1888 were a quiet period for the Toronto Humane Society. Despite the enthusiastic start to the year, financial difficulties arose which resulted in the temporary abandonment of the society's office. Kelso was discouraged by 'everyone's great kindness in allowing me all the work without compensation of any kind.' A bonus of $100 paid to him in May in recognition of his services cheered him a little, but by June it appeared that the society was sinking into oblivion. Many people seemed to have lost interest in the movement. Kelso's explanation was that this simply reflected the tendency of people to be 'always running after changes and novelties,' but it is probable that there were also other reasons for this pause in the growth of the organization. Kelso's domination of the movement was not conducive to more involvement by others. The society was focussing its attention on children rather than animals, a matter of regret to some original supporters. Kelso began to consider other avenues through which to pursue his interest in deprived children. The idea which emerged was the formation of a Children's Fresh Air Fund, modeled on organizations in London, England, and New York.

The previous year Hugh Graham, editor of the Toronto *Star*, had launched through his newspaper a Fresh Air Fund to send poor women and children on excursions into the countryside during the summer months.[26] Early in May 1888 Kelso was given the opportunity of organizing the Toronto fund, and he accepted the challenge with characteristic energy and enthusiasm. On 18 May he sent out a circular letter to over two hundred citizens announcing a public meeting in Richmond Hall to establish the 1888 Fresh Air Fund: 'It is proposed to have several boat excursions, and a plentiful supply of refreshments, music and games. The good that may result from these excursions is almost incalculable. By a comparatively small expenditure, a ray of sunshine may be thrown into these young hearts that will remain through life.'

The support of all the Toronto newspapers ensured the success of the organizing meeting, at which a committee was formed and donations collected. The fund proved popular with the Toronto business community and many offers of assistance were received. The Toronto Ferry Company and the Toronto Street Railway Company both offered free transportation; local dairies and bakeries donated refreshments; printing firms offered to help in the production of handbills and tickets; and workers from the Christian Missionary Union volunteered their services as supervisors on the trips. The first outing took place on 27 June, and by all accounts was a great success. About four hundred children from St John's Ward, the poorest area of the city, were formed into a procession by the mission workers and marched down to the docks to a tune played by the Boys' Home fife band. Leading the procession were W.H. Howland and William Gooderham, a wealthy miller and distiller who was a supporter of the Industrial School Association and the Toronto Orphans' Home. The children were taken by ferry to the Long Branch Wharf, and after a picnic lunch made the return ferry trip home. The *Evening Telegram*'s reporter wrote:

It is impossible to describe the solid enjoyment of the children as the *Rupert* swept across Humber Bay and the low-lying groves of Long Branch came into view. Some gathered in little companies on the deck and sang their mission school songs, while others leaned over the rail and quietly watched the gleaming water. Others curiously watched the pilot, and many clustered around the boys of the band, doubtless with some envy. When the Long Branch wharf was reached, each child was given a bag containing a sandwich, a roll and a bun. The beautiful grove was made musical with the glad voices, and every available nook and spot was soon occupied. Some of the larger girls sat on the grassy bank, and looked out upon the blue waters; others explored the forest, gathering ferns and sweet wild flowers, while many joined in the different games, or congregated at the merry-go-round. At two o'clock the children were gathered in the pavilion and served with milk, buns and bananas; and at five o'clock they re-embarked and returned to the city without mishap of any kind.

Three further outings were held during the summer of 1888 and a total of 1600 children attended. At the end of the summer the fund had a surplus of over $200, an indication of the extent of the support for the scheme by Torontonians. More than ever before Kelso was in the public view. 'I am rapidly acquiring a reputation as the "children's friend" and I need hardly add that I am proud of such a distinction,' he remarked. He gained great personal pleasure from the excursions and wide popularity among children in the poorer districts: 'I shall never forget the happy faces of the youngsters and the thought of being able to give them so much enjoyment will follow me as a benediction all through life. Many of the children recognize me on the street and anxiously inquire when the next trip will be.' Fortunately, Kelso's reporting duties were slight during July and he was able to work almost full-time on fund activities. Children began to call in large numbers at the *Globe* offices requesting tickets for outings. When he distributed tickets on the streets he was mobbed with requests from children, and also from adults attracted by the crowd but unaware of what the tickets were for. It was an exciting and gratifying experience for Kelso, and a source of encouragement after the decline in support for the Humane Society.

Later in 1888 Kelso followed up his successes in the Fresh Air Fund with the establishment of a Santa Claus Fund to provide a Christmas party for poor children. Once again there was no lack of public interest. E.F. Clarke, Howland's successor as mayor, agreed to act as treasurer for the fund and mission workers provided voluntary help. Four hundred children were given a Christmas dinner at St James Cathedral Schoolhouse and were entertained by the Spadina Avenue Orchestra. Each child was given a bag containing cake, an orange, an apple, figs, and candies to take home. As with the Fresh Air Fund, the Santa Claus Fund was oversubscribed, an encouragement to Kelso and the other organizers to plan for a larger event the following year.

During the years 1889 to 1891 the Children's Fresh Air Fund grew in size and popularity. In 1889 twelve summer excursions were held, involving 3250 children. In the following year the numbers were more than doubled, twenty-nine excursions being undertaken for seven thousand children. A record was set in 1891, when nine thousand children attended Fresh Air Fund outings. Kelso and his fellow organizers were somewhat disappointed that plans to send city children to country homes for summer holidays did not eventuate. Nor did an idea to establish a poor children's vacation home in the country get beyond the planning stage. But apart from these setbacks the Fresh Air Fund excursions lived up to all expectations. The growth of the Santa Claus Fund was not as steady or spectacular, but in each year a party was organized involving between 600 and 1200 children. At no time was either fund undersubscribed, and the financial surplus achieved each year was used as a basis for the commencement of the following year's activities.

The continuing enthusiastic support for these two movements is not difficult to understand. During the summer many of the more prosperous Toronto families moved out of town to nearby summer cottages and resorts, and to provide the children of the poor with at least a taste of the joys of country life appealed to the imagination and the charitable instincts of many well-to-do Torontonians. The spirit in which contributions were made is captured by a poem which appeared in a Toronto newspaper in July 1891, beneath a cartoon depicting Kelso leading hordes of youngsters and mission workers 'To The Fresh Air Fund Boats':

> If you'd have bliss without alloy
> In your coming summer outing,
> And add an extra spice of joy
> To your fishing and your boating,
>
> Before you go, send in your mite
> For the Fresh Air Fund to Kelso,
> 'Twill help to make the summer bright
> For the waifs – each dollar tells so!

By contributing to the Fresh Air Fund and Santa Claus Fund many wealthy and middle-class Torontonians were also fulfilling what they believed to be their moral and social responsibilities towards the underprivileged. The *Empire* spelled out these obligations in its coverage of the 1889 Santa Claus party. Congratulating the people of Toronto on their support of the event, the newspaper sought to provide its readers with a broader understanding of the significance of the enterprise. It claimed that:

In [Toronto's] rapid development and growth happily there has been no downing of the afflicted and no turning of the cold shoulder to the oppressed. The heart of the city goes forth to all charities, and there has been none left without aid or sympathy, unless it be the absolutely undeserving. Christmas is an appropriate time in which to gauge the broad heart and beneficent tendencies of the people. There are poor and rich in the community. The poor predominate. The rich and middle-class help the lowly in the onward path and in the struggle for existence. The distribution of wealth may be unequal. The mob and the mass may growl under the voracity of the capitalists. But men of money as if by Divine edict, drop one by one into the ranks of charity, and become the

able upholders of the poverty-striken. Whether such is the divine implantation of
Providence or the happy whim of nature cannot be said, but at all events such are the
practical and happy evidences of modern civilization and of Toronto's growth. May it
year by year continue, widen and strengthen in its sphere.

As well as providing an opportunity for better-off citizens to help the children
of the poor, the activities organized by the funds were considered suitable
occasions for instruction of the children in religion, morals, and proper behaviour. The Christmas parties and summer excursions invariably included the
singing of such well-known children's hymns as 'Jesus Loves Me,' 'Stand Up!
Stand Up for Jesus!' 'There's a Land that is Fairer than Day,' and 'Shall We
Gather at the River.' At these gatherings the children were always lively, but
accounts stressed that their behaviour never approached noisiness or discord-
ance. If disorder did threaten, the helpers were quick to enforce better conduct.
The children were encouraged in mannerly behaviour and clean attire, and their
positive response was attributed to their appreciation of the efforts being made
for them. The instructional nature of the excursions and parties was at times
carried to an extreme. After one Christmas party, for example, the children
were given as their going-home presents a bag of fruit, some cake, and the
following verse neatly printed on a card:

FORWARD
Standing still is dangerous ever,
Toil is meant for Christians now!
Let there be when evening cometh,
Honest sweat upon thy brow,
And the Master shall come smiling,
At the setting of the sun,
Saying, as he pays the wages,
'Good and faithful one, well done.'

It seems doubtful that the card was widely read, understood, or appreciated by
the children as they made their way back to their slum dwellings.

The limitations of schemes which gave poor children a sampling of fresh air
and good food only to return them to their own deprived circumstances was not
widely recognized by those who sponsored the funds. Kelso, the chief instigator
and organizer, shared wholeheartedly in the euphoria which surrounded the
schemes, claiming in his diary that 'it is a grand work and does more for the poor
than all the missionary movements that have ever been devised.' He obviously
received a great deal of personal gratification from his own participation and was
touched by the happiness which he observed among the children. He accepted

unquestioningly the distinctions between the deserving and the undeserving poor made by newspapermen and others who commented on the funds, and stressed in his interviews with the press that few of the children at the excursions and parties were poor in the sense of being dependent on the community. He summed up his philosophy in a statement to the *Empire* in 1889: 'The children's fresh air and entertainment fund was established to give healthy enjoyment to the children of the poor, and those who know anything of its work cannot accuse it of pauperizing. On the contrary, it has fulfilled a noble mission in bringing happiness to the cheerless lives of many young people, and has given them a hope and ambition which before was wanting.' He also stressed the importance of the outings and parties as opportunities for mission workers and other comparatively prosperous helpers to learn about the difficult circumstances of poor families through direct contact with the children. In this way, he later claimed, 'the need for improved social conditions was made evident and hastened the many reforms that have since been brought about.' These various comments show the extent to which Kelso accepted prevailing notions relating to poverty and its causes. He did not question the widespread assumption that indiscriminate granting of relief to the poor would lead to dependency and 'pauperism,' but argued that the Fresh Air and Santa Claus funds catered to families who were undoubtedly 'deserving.' He did not hesitate to offer religious, moral, and social instruction to the children who attended fund functions, and clearly believed that the middle-class mores to which he personally subscribed were appropriate standards for all. He showed unbounded faith in the effectiveness of a day's outing on the moral fibre and physical health of slum children. In these attitudes Kelso reflected the orthodoxies of the reformers with whom he was associated. Personal integrity, concern for the less fortunate, initiative and hard work, and respectability according to prevailing social standards were the values by which Kelso judged his own life, and he saw no good reason to judge others differently.

Kelso's leadership of the Fresh Air Fund established his reputation as a popular and able leader in the child welfare sphere. His work in establishing the fund during the summer of 1888 distracted him temporarily from his duties as secretary of the Humane Society, but the slackening of public interest in the society during the early part of the summer passed, and by the fall Kelso was once again immersed in its activities. The most urgent matter requiring attention was the organization of the American Humane Association convention scheduled to be held in Toronto in mid-October. Kelso and the other officeholders of the society were kept busy during the preceding weeks making necessary arrangements. The meetings were held in the Toronto Normal School buildings, and everything proceeded quite smoothly. Kelso, as in the previous year, took a prominent part in the conference, and was elected to a position on the sub-executive of the association. The convention had two important consequences for the local reform movement and thus Kelso's career. In the first place it gave the Toronto Humane Society extensive publicity in the newspapers, resulting in a revival of interest in the society's activities. The press was unanimous in its praise for the work of the local society, as J.S. Willison explained in the *Globe* on 19 October 1888: 'Mr. W.R. Brock (president of the society) and his associates in the local movement are inspired by high motives, and are entitled to our generous sympathies. They are not cheap philanthropists, merely hunting for popularity by easy methods. They are not making a pretence of concern for the public welfare in order to make a living for themselves. It is a movement that has nothing in it for anyone except the children who are helped to clean lives and pure surroundings and the dumb animals that are protected from brutality and cruelty. We have hardly yet risen to a true appreciation of the value and dignity of this movement ...' Such glowing testimonials did much to boost the morale of the members of the society, and encouraged others to add their support.

The Toronto meetings of the American Humane Association also raised local awareness of current developments in child welfare in other parts of North America. Particular prominence was given to the work of the Children's Aid Society of Pennsylvania, which was active in placing neglected children in family homes. Accounts of the success of this approach were delivered by delegates, and received an enthusiastic reception. Willison wrote in the *Globe* that 'No discipline can be so potent as that of the family, and probably no better plan for the rescue of the little ones abandoned to the world has ever been devised than that of the Children's Aid Society of Pennsylvania.' This was not the first occasion on which the placing of neglected and dependent children in foster care had been advocated in Ontario. For many years the press had published reports of the work of Charles Loring Brace in New York, and Mrs Nassau Senior and Miss Florence Hill in England.[27] The foster home schemes operating in Massachusetts and Connecticut were extensively discussed the previous year when the National Prison Association met in Toronto. Some of Ontario's orphanages had engaged in extra-mural placement of children on a limited scale, and placement of children in family homes had been the accepted practice of the juvenile immigration agencies working in Ontario since 1868. The 1888 convention was Kelso's first opportunity to consider seriously the merits of foster over institutional care, a theme which later became central to his approach to child welfare.

The Toronto Humane Society capitalized on the publicity received from the American Humane Association convention by publishing a book entitled *Aims and Objectives*, its most ambitious venture in print to that date. The project originated early in 1888 when Miss Gwynne asked Kelso what humane activity he would embark on if he had five hundred dollars at his disposal. Kelso had been planning a book describing and explaining humane work and he responded with this suggestion. Miss Gwynne offered the money (and later contributed a further one thousand dollars) and the preparations began. Dr George Hodgins agreed to act as editor and, with Kelso's assistance, the volume was compiled. It was a substantial book, containing 242 pages of information on animals and children, including many illustrations. In the final months of the year Kelso and the other Humane Society workers were busy promoting the sale and distribution of the ten thousand copies which were printed. Although it was pleasing for Kelso to see another enterprise successfully completed, he was deeply disappointed that the editor did not see fit to acknowledge his contribution by naming him co-editor. His mother also felt her son had been cheated, and once again Kelso had to restrain her from intervening on his behalf.

Another project which took up much of Kelso's time and energy during the latter months of 1888 was the establishment of 'Bands of Mercy.' This movement, patterned after the 'Bands of Hope' of the Women's Christian Temperance Union, began in Middlesex, England, in 1875. By the early 1880s it had taken hold in several American cities, most notably Boston. The basic idea was to encourage children to form groups to assist in the work of protecting animals from cruelty. This notion appealed to Kelso and other Humane Society members, for the emphasis on developing humane attitudes amongst children corresponded closely with the society's educational and child-oriented approach. In late November the first Bands of Mercy were established in Toronto, two in Rose Avenue Public School and one in Given Street Public School. On 30 November Kelso addressed over one hundred children in the Rose Avenue School telling them how they might protect animals from ill-treatment and 'cultivate a spirit of kindness and thoughtfulness.' He was a popular speaker with children and throughout the winter months was in demand at various schools in Toronto. By March a large number of bands had been established in the city, and the Humane Society was planning to extend the work to surrounding areas. The movement spread so quickly that ten thousand copies of the society's pamphlet, 'Bands of Mercy Information,' were printed for distribution to school trustees and teachers. This pamphlet, prepared by Kelso, contained information on how to establish bands, a collection of suitable hymns and songs, and an 'Order of Exercises.' When a band was formed the children first decided on a name for their group, then elected officers and pledged to 'try to be kind to all harmless living creatures, and try to protect them from cruel usage.' Regular meetings were held at which the children gave recitations or related incidents in which they had tried to do a kind act or prevent

cruelty to animals. The Mercy hymns, such as this one sung to the tune of the
National Anthem, stressed the importance of strength of purpose and moral
commitment:

> God help our loving Band,
> Enable us to stand
> In Mercy's cause.
> Oh, give us great success
> In works of righteousness,
> Thy creatures all to bless,
> And keep Thy laws.
>
> Oh, all our hearts inspire
> With Heaven's own sacred fire,
> To make us strong.
> Thy spirit's power we crave,
> To make us true and brave,
> And aid us those to save
> That suffer wrong.
>
> God bless our growing Bands,
> Fulfilling Thy commands,
> At Mercy's call.
> Oh, grant Thy children grace
> Of every land and race,
> To join before Thy face,
> Love crowning all.

Kelso continued to be closely involved in this work throughout 1889 and 1890,
frequently taking time off from his newspaper work to address children in the
schools.

By the spring of 1889 the Toronto Humane Society was well established. An
office was functioning at 103 Bay Street, and thanks to Miss Gwynne and other
benefactors the financial situation was healthy. The accomplishments of the
society during its first two years were impressive. The Children's Protection
Act of 1888, drafted and promoted by the society, had been passed; a cruelty
constable had been appointed by Toronto City Council; improved conditions for
the city's horses had been achieved; and the American Humane Association
convention had been successfully hosted. In addition to these specific achievements, a large amount of promotional material had been distributed and an

educational campaign for schoolchildren commenced. For this list of achievements Kelso must be given most of the credit. Mr W.R. Brock, Canon DuMoulin, Beverley Jones, Inspector Archibald, and Dr Hodgins had contributed their support and skills at crucial times. Without Miss Gwynne's financial backing far less would have been accomplished. But Kelso was unquestionably the driving force behind the organization. His capacity for persistence and hard work sustained the society in periods when the interest of other members was low, and ensured that the many projects were seen through to a conclusion.

The work of the Toronto Humane Society extended into a wide range of areas during 1889 and the following years. Members become involved in efforts to combat cruelty in sport, abolish trap shooting, reduce overcrowding of street-cars, institute an ambulance for disabled animals, provide resting seats for assistants in stores, erect humane noticeboards, and encourage the study of entomology in schools. The 1887 campaign to provide adequate watering-places for Toronto's horses was sustained, and by 1891 the Waterworks Department of City Hall had erected some forty-two horse troughs. The society also became active in extending the humane cause throughout the province. By mid-1891 humane societies had been formed at Kingston, Galt, London, St Thomas, Peterborough, Stratford, Chatham, and Guelph. This latter activity was one in which Kelso took a special interest. The two campaigns of greatest significance to Kelso's career and personal development were, however, in the child welfare field. These were the attempt to enforce the licensing of Toronto's newsboys, and the work of the cruelty constable.

The large number of children who spent long hours on the streets of Toronto selling newspapers and peddling other inexpensive items was a cause of considerable concern to the members of the Humane Society and other reformers during the late 1880s. Most of these children lived with their parents or guardians, but others had no adults responsible for them and they resided in the Toronto Newsboys' Home, the St Nicholas Home, or cheap private lodgings. There were various reasons for the Humane Society's particular interest in them. The presence of so many poorly-clad, unkempt children on the city streets was an affront to the reformers' strong sense of order and respectability. Street trading was also closely linked in their minds to begging, pilfering, and exposure to more serious criminal and immoral activities. A large proportion of juvenile offenders had a background as 'street arabs,' as the children who roamed the streets were commonly called, and this seemed clear evidence of the link between neglect and crime. In response to this problem, Kelso, on behalf of the Humane Society, instituted early in 1888 a campaign for the licensing of newsboys and the prohibition of young girls from engaging in all forms of street trading. He gained an audience with Premier Mowat to raise the matter, and also addressed the legislation committee of the Toronto City Council. The result was the insertion of a clause in the Ontario Municipal Act giving Boards of Police Commissioners power to regulate street trading by children.

This measure lay dormant and largely unnoticed until the fall of 1889, when the Humane Society decided to press the Toronto City Council to pass the necessary regulatory by-law. The renewed interest by the society in this issue was a result of reports from the cruelty constable which showed increasing numbers of children involved in street trading, an estimated six to seven hundred boys and about one hundred girls being thus engaged in 1889.[28] The society was also involved at this time in enforcement of compulsory education for children and, as street trading was a full-time activity for many minors, the two campaigns were seen as complementary. Kelso led a deputation of members of the Humane Society to the Board of Police Commissioners in October 1889, after which the City Council agreed to adopt a by-law prepared by the society. This by-law provided that no child under sixteen could be employed as a newsboy or a bootblack without first obtaining a licence to engage in these activities. Boys under eight and girls of any age were not entitled to work as news-vendors under any circumstances. Every licensed child was required to wear a badge provided by the Police Commissioners, which could be revoked if the child was convicted of a felony or found associating with thieves. The penalty for violation of the by-law was a fine of up to two dollars to be paid, not by the newspaper or the parents, but by the child himself. If the child could not pay the fine, he could be committed to the Industrial School or to a charitable institution willing to receive him. Should the newsboy prove to be 'completely incorrigible,' provision was also made for committal to the common jail for up to two days, with or without hard labour.

Although the by-law was passed in October 1889, the Toronto police did not attempt to enforce it until July 1890. In part the delay was to give the newspapers and newsboys time to obtain their necessary licences and badges. But it was also caused by a vigorous campaign mounted by the newspapers. The *World*, the *News*, and the *Evening Telegram* rarely passed by opportunities to ridicule moral reformers wishing to impose their views on the community, and in this case their own interests were directly threatened. In April 1890 these newspapers began to advocate repeal of the by-law, arguing that it constituted unnecessary government interference, that the police had better things to do with their time than chase newsboys, and that most newsboys were well-intentioned, industrious children who were laudably assisting in the upkeep of their homes. The editorials used harsh and hostile language. The *Evening Telegram* was particularly biting: 'The juvenile population of Toronto can still breathe. The Police Commissioners have not yet passed a by-law to regulate the supply of air and sunshine to the boys of Toronto, but they may do so any day. A Board that will pass such an obnoxious, senseless, absurd, degrading and uncalled for set of resolutions is capable of meddling in almost anything.' The *World* mounted the most trenchant attacks of all, and Kelso was singled out as the object of the paper's criticisms. Dubbed 'The Tagger' for his desire to have all newsboys wear badges, he was portrayed in cartoons as a dog catcher with a huge net vainly trying to capture elusive newsboys. Every attempt was made to ridicule and embarrass him, and the editorialists pulled no punches in an onslaught of abuse against their former employee. The most blatant attack appeared in the *World* on 18 April 1890:

KELSO THE TAGGER

His Law to Tag Newsboys
Why Shouldn't Reporters Be Tagged
Humanitarians Run Mad

Mr. Fresh Blush Kelso, a young Irishman, blew into Toronto one day and set up as a reporter. Then he felt called upon to become a humanitarian, a guardian of children and a regulator of the people. He is self-constituted inspector-general of cruelty to: horses' tails, street cars (bob-tails), shoe-blacks, newsboys, sparrows and dickey birds and a sort of Humanitarian Pooh-Bah. He is still engaged in this lawful undertaking. He has a fondness for spouting from platforms, of having a lot of old ladies dancing about him, and still fonder of his own good looks. The Globe was made the organ of the humanitarians, and Fresh Blush lately got it into his head that it was time he undertook the regulation of the sale of the newspapers of Toronto; and to this end he and his society had a regulation issued by the police commissioners that hereafter the newsboys and newsgirls be tagged like dogs, that if caught without the tag they be sent to jail, and that the entire police force of the city be turned into a contrivance for catching all the untagged newsvendors found in the streets. Does Fresh Blush think if the children are driven off the streets they won't be engaged in something more discreditable than selling papers? Isn't his legislation, if it is effective, the best possible way for worthless parents to 'unload' their children on the city? 'Oh send out the brat to sell papers, the police will arrest him, send him to the Industrial School or somewhere else, and we will be rid of him.' Doesn't Fresh Blush think the police have got enough to do without chasing the newsboys? Why shouldn't reporters with good looks and smooth manners be tagged and something else as well as newsboys? Put a tag on Kelso and see how he'd like it.

The article was followed the next day by a piece of doggerel entitled 'Tag Town':

> This is the town where everybody must be tagged.
> The dogs are tagged.
> The letter carriers are tagged.
> The waterworks inspectors are tagged.
> The streetcar conductors and drivers are tagged.
> The firemen have tags.
> And now Tagger Kelso wants to put tags on the
> newsboys and cab drivers, the medical students
> and bank clerks.
> The tagger is thinking of a law to tag school
> children.
> Tag! Tag!! Tag!!!

Two days later the *World* suggested in an editorial that the Humane Society should change its name to 'The Society for Protecting Dogs and Worrying Children.'

It was a bitter campaign but it was waged unsuccessfully. On 1 July 1890 the licensing of newsboys was implemented and 592 badges were issued in the course of the year. Although problems of enforcing the regulations soon developed, in the short term the victory belonged to Kelso and the Humane Society. The publicity given to the issue directed attention to the large number of children roaming the streets of Toronto, and the licensing of newsboys was a step towards public responsibility for neglected children. Kelso followed up the campaign by working to improve conditions in the Toronto Newsboys' Lodging and encouraging the residents to learn trades so that they could give up the precarious existence of newspaper selling. The personal criticism he received during the campaign did not worry him unduly. He enjoyed press attention, and as he had no doubt that the licensing of newsboys was in the public interest he was able to dismiss as self-serving the whole press campaign. Self-assurance and readiness to impose and enforce his own standards on other members of the community now characterized Kelso's approach to social and moral reform.

The campaign to license newsboys was the most publicized activity of the Toronto Humane Society during its formative years, but the centrepiece of the society's activities was unquestionably the cruelty constable employed by the City of Toronto to assist the society in apprehending and prosecuting the inhumane. Constable Willis, who held the position from 1887 to 1892, was an industrious man who believed in the humane cause and who developed close personal and working relationships with the officers of the Humane Society. His activities constituted the main interest of the society during its first five years. Willis divided his attention between cruelty to animals and cruelty to children. Cases of cruelty to animals covered a wide range of offences including flogging and kicking of horses, beating of horses with a pitchfork, working horses which were suffering from sore shoulders or lameness, overcrowding of poultry in coops, starving animals, and overcrowding cattle trains. Willis received annually some three hundred complaints of such actions, and of these almost two-thirds were brought to court. Over 80 per cent of those charged with animal cruelty were convicted. The constable's work in combatting cruelty to children involved more complaints but far fewer prosecutions. Over 1900 complaints of cruelty to children were made to Willis between 1887 and 1891, and although these resulted in 250 children being committed to the industrial schools or other institutions, prosecution of parents was rare. Willis also dealt with many complaints of ill-treatment or desertion of women, but again there were few successful prosecutions.

Throughout this period the focus of Willis's work against child cruelty was on prevention rather than prosecution. The 1891 Humane Society Report stressed this point: 'The work consists largely of warnings, suggestions and counsels, and the wholesome moral effect of the presence actual, and expected, of the Constable. Both Staff Inspector Archibald and Constable Willis have assured the Society that the purely preventative service performed ... occupies a large portion of the time of the officer engaged and cannot be put into the definite form of arrests and convictions.' The apologetic tone of this report was an indication of the frustration felt by the Humane Society with their limited powers to intervene in situations involving neglectful or cruel parents. In some extreme cases of parental cruelty Constable Willis was able to secure a prosecution under existing criminal law, and such cases were widely publicized as illustrating the need for stronger legislation to protect children. The following newspaper account, for example, caught the imagination of the Humane Society workers and was reproduced in the Annual Report:

The charge of aggravated assault preferred against ... by Inspector Archibald was investigated in the Police Court yesterday [7 Feb. 1890]. The evidence was very strong against the woman, and Police Magistrate Denison committed her to The Mercer for six months. The victim is her step-daughter, a child not yet seven years old, who looks less than five, so thin and starved does she appear. On information received through the Humane Society, Constable Willis went up to the house on Monday to see what truth there was in it. He found the house locked up and could not get in, and after remaining for an hour, left and returned again at four o'clock. When he went in the morning the child was at the window with her head bandaged up, and in answer to the Constable's question said her mother had locked her in and gone out. When he went back he heard the prisoner swearing and asking the child if she had given her away to the teachers at school, the mother adding 'You can stop there till your hand rots off you.' The Constable then went to the door and in answer to his knocks the woman opened the door. He told her his mission and she immediately ran upstairs addressing the child thus, 'if you tell on me I'll cut your heart out.' Three teachers from an adjoining school testified to having seen the bruises on the child, and had several times heard her compalin of her step-mother's treatment. Several neighbours were also witnesses. They said they had from time to time heard the child crying and receiving a thrashing. The day when the little girl was locked up during the mother's absence, the neighbours had put a child on the roof of a house to hand food to her. On Monday the child said she had had nothing to eat excepting a crust until the police had taken charge of her. Such things as these were of frequent occurrence. The Magistrate, in sentencing the prisoner, said it was an exceedingly bad case and the evidence was very strong against her.

Opportunities for decisive action such as this were not frequent, and the limited accommodation in industrial schools and orphanages, and the lack of authority to protect children in situations where action was resisted by the parents, were major impediments to the constable's work. Together with his colleagues in the Humane Society, Kelso was convinced by observation of Willis's work that greater powers to protect children from neglectful and cruel parents should be granted to responsible members of the community, and this became a key element in his emerging view of necessary reforms in the child welfare system.

Kelso's deep involvement with the Humane Society and the Fresh Air Fund did not lead him to neglect his own family duties. His ties with his family continued to be close. His father was now in his sixties, and the prime responsibility for the family passed to Kelso, the only son still living at home. He took his family commitments seriously and came into frequent conflict with his sisters over his attempts to regulate their activities. He spent much of his now infrequent spare time in various social activities with the family, and a good deal of his money on their upkeep, a fact frequently mentioned in his diary: 'All the money I have ever earned has gone to make those around me happier and I have found the proverb true that it is more blessed to give than to receive.' On his twenty-fourth birthday on 31 March 1888 he found himself nearly $200 in debt, but he was not worried as his prospects appeared bright. Looking ahead, his spending priorities included a piano, an insurance policy for the family's household effects, a family plot in the cemetery, a pony and carriage for his mother and sisters, and a house in which his parents could spend their last days. His first major investment was made in the summer of 1889, when he purchased a building lot at Long Branch, near the summer cottage that the Kelsos rented each summer. He paid $225, and the following February negotiated a bank loan of $500 to construct a cottage. In the summer of 1890 the family enjoyed the luxury of living in their own dwelling for the first time since arriving in Canada. The fortunes of Kelso's brothers and sisters were mixed. George was making a steady but unspectacular career in banking. Alexander was without regular employment. Martha, Kelso's eldest sister, gave birth to her first child at Christmas 1889. The younger girls were still attending college, except Maya who, after a long illness, died in April 1889. She was buried in the same plot as Elizabeth, Kelso's sister who passed away during the family's first harsh Canadian winter.

Family cares and public responsibilities had by no means dampened Kelso's ardour towards the young ladies of Toronto. No subject, including reform, received as much attention as they in the pages of his diary during 1887 and 1888. Maude continued as his favourite companion during much of 1887, but she was displaced late that year by Myrtle, a girl only sixteen years of age. For a while her mother forbade Kelso to call at the house, an instruction which did not prevent the couple from continuing to meet and correspond. After a while a college friend of his sister Bella became his main interest, although she too dropped out of his life after a few months. 'Why is it,' he pondered, 'that my heart is so disturbed by every pretty face, by the pressure of a little hand, the glance of a pair of eyes, the utterance of a few words? Every day my heart is torn and lacerated afresh with a pleasure that is almost pain in its deliciousness.'

Kelso's heavy involvement in Humane Society work during 1888 had been made possible by his relatively light workload at the *Globe*. In early January he achieved his wish of being taken off police reporting and was appointed municipal reporter. This was daytime work and the hours were short, a convenient circumstance as Kelso's reform activities were begining to interfere with his responsibilities to his newspaper. At this time he became a member of the Toronto Press Club, and a successful newspaper career seemed to be within his grasp. However, his ambitions were now strongly focussed on a desire to be wealthy, a theme which at this time took precedence over his interest in social reform. 'I often get discouraged to see people all around me growing rich and buying fine houses, while I am as much behind as ever and see no prospect of immediate advance,' he complained. 'I think I could be contented if I did not see so many instances of men amassing wealth in a year or two.' On occasions such thoughts led him to consider once again leaving newspaper work for more profitable activities. In his diary on 4 April 1888 he proposed a means of combining his interests and talents for public and personal gain: 'I make this entry tonight because I have just come to a decision that I think will affect my whole future life. I have come to the conclusion that dreaming and philosophizing will not help me on in the world, nor toiling hard for the enrichment of others. Therefore, I have decided that so soon as the way is clear I will start a small printing business and publish a humane journal on my own account. This may take two or three years preliminary arranging, but I write now under the firm conviction that it will come sooner or later. Then, with God's aid and blessing, I will become prosperous and hold up my head – a man among men!' Kelso frequently expressed this interest in a business career in the following two or three years, but he never took practical steps towards that end. This was probably due in part to lack of capital, but also his career in journalism continued to show promise. For three months in early 1889 he was interim city editor on the *Globe*, and he enjoyed these increased responsibilities. Appointment to a permanent senior editor position on the *Globe* appeared imminent.

During these years of his early and mid-twenties Kelso was continually torn, as he was throughout his life, by three competing desires: to achieve success in his career, to be rich, and to provide leadership on social issues. At various times one or other of these ambitions would dominate, but the tension was always present. For Kelso, the need to choose amongst competing goals contradicted his idealized picture of the role of the social reformer. The community leaders with whom he associated applied themselves to their careers, acquisition of wealth, and charity, and viewed these as complementary activities for public-spirited citizens; Kelso admired and aspired to this model, but his involvement in charitable work at an early age, with career and fortune yet unmade, forced him to make decisions which Howland, Blake, Gooderham, and the like did not have to face. For Kelso the choices were acutely difficult. His desire to re-establish the social and economic standing of the Kelso family and achieve personal success had motivated his efforts to advance himself since arriving in Canada, and considerable progress to this end had been made. His achievements in the sphere of charity and social reform threatened this progress, but offered other considerable rewards. He enjoyed his contacts with members of Toronto's social and political élite, and the publicity which surrounded his activities. The Humane Society and the Fresh Air Fund gave him scope to exercise his considerable talents as an organizer and publicist. The contacts with the slum children and the chances to influence legislation and administration provided a sense of mission which he did not find in his work as a journalist.

There were times in the years ahead when he seriously reconsidered this commitment, but the attractions of charitable work were too great. His successes as a reformer during the late 1880s made him more committed to this career and distracted him from other avenues of endeavour. On balance he was satisfied with his choice. As he wrote in his diary on Christmas Day 1889: 'My consolation is that I have tried in some degree to improve the passing moments and leave behind me a record of good deeds. My sweetest and most precious reflections are the bright and eager faces of the children to whose hearts I have been permitted to bring a little happiness, and into whose lives I have perhaps been able to infuse a higher and nobler ambition than they knew before. Also, that through my efforts thousands of dumb animals have been protected from cruelty in multitudinous forms, and hundreds, perhaps thousands of persons, interested in humane and charitable work. I have long since learned that happiness comes from unselfishness, and I would not today exchange my hours of toil and self-denial for thousands of dollars.'

3

Laying the Foundations

Eighteen-ninety was a turning-point in the history of child welfare in Ontario. Largely as a result of pressure from the Prisoners' Aid Association, led by Samuel Blake and W.H. Howland, the provincial government appointed a Royal Commission on the Prison and Reformatory System of Ontario.[1] The commission's central task, according to its terms of reference, was 'to collect information regarding Prisons, Houses of Correction, Reformatories, Industrial Schools, etc., with a view to ascertaining any practical improvements which may be made in the methods of dealing with the criminal classes, so far as the subject is within the jurisdiction of the Provincial Legislature and Government.' The five-man commission, chaired by the retired inspector of prisons, J.W. Langmuir, interpreted this mandate broadly, defining its primary objective as the determination of the main causes of crime in the community. This ambitious goal led the commission to pay particular attention to child welfare and juvenile delinquency, as well as the adult correctional system. Langmuir's prestige, widespread concern about the incidence of crime, and the commission's vigorous and thorough approach created extensive public interest in the inquiry. 'All the moral forces of the community,' Kelso wrote later, 'actively united in the demand for intelligent and progressive legislation for the prevention of crime.'[2]

Kelso was not personally involved in pressuring the government to appoint the Royal Commission, although he was aware of these moves through his contact with the leaders of the Prisoners' Aid Association in other activities. His first reaction on hearing that the commission was to be established was to lobby for his own appointment, either as a full commissioner or as secretary. His hopes for a position on this prestigious body rather exaggerated his own standing in public life, and he was greatly disappointed when told he was considered too young for the post. His role was thus restricted to reporting its proceedings for the *Globe*, and presenting a brief on behalf of the Toronto Humane Society. This latter event took place on 14 November 1890 and provided an opportunity for Kelso to describe in detail his analysis of existing deficiencies in child welfare legislation and his proposals for reform.[3] He began his account with a description of the campaign to license newsboys. The system of young boys selling newspapers he described as 'pernicious right through. There is no system of dealing with those engaged in it so as to bring out their moral nature.' He dwelt at length on the moral decadence of the newsboys and newsgirls, and the high proportion of boys who became criminals and girls who entered prostitution. Existing measures to reform these children he considered totally ineffective. The Newsboys' Home, despite its 'nice clean beds' and 'texts on the wall or over the bed, and appropriate mottoes,' could not attract the newsboys, who objected to the regulation of their behaviour in the home and preferred life in the 'low dives.' 'There is no training these boys to habits of industry. They will neglect their work, run away, and throw themselves out of a situation without the slightest regard of what is to become of them. My idea is that we ought to endeavour to do away with this system altogether, to stop entirely a large number of these boys from pursuing this occupation.'

Kelso then proceeded to describe the programs and policies he would implement to deal with newsboys and similarly neglected children, to keep them from criminal careers. First he advocated a 'truant school' to cater for those children who were not complying with the school attendance laws. Together with Beverley Jones, Kelso had pressed the local school board to establish such an institution and the matter was under official consideration. The mission school established and organized by W.H. Howland was Kelso's prototype for a 'truant school,' and he attributed the apparent success of Howland's school to the 'consecration' of the woman in charge. 'She was interested in it so much that she dressed the children, washed them even, got them to school with her, gave contributions of food to children in order to gather them and encourage them to go to the school. Those who are engaged in it must give their whole heart to this class of work, or it will not be a success.' In addition to the 'truant school,' Kelso proposed the immediate implementation of the provisions of the 1888 Children's Protection Act relating to the separate trial of juveniles. He explained to the commissioners that the Toronto City Council had refused to establish separate hearings for juveniles on the grounds of expense, the result being that children continued to be 'systematically manufactured into criminals. There is no other term can be applied to it.' In conjunction with this proposal, Kelso advocated the establishment of a children's shelter to which arrested children could be taken pending their trial. This would ensure that children were at no stage brought into contact with hardened adult criminals, and avoid 'habituating a child to this kind of thing' and thus 'breaking down the instinctive dread that every child has of a prison.'

Kelso next discussed the moral and physical surroundings of many neglected children. He was particularly concerned with the number of children who regularly attended theatrical performances in Toronto. 'The class of plays the boys go to see is Irish comedy and Irish drama of the most sensational sort ... there are a great many full of the worst kinds of villainy, and the villain is held up always as a most heroic character ... the desire to attend these places is sometimes the means of leading youths into crime. They have no money, and they resort to thieving in order to gratify this desire.' In terms of the physical environment, Kelso spoke out strongly in favour of more playgrounds for young boys. 'Everyone knows that if a boy does not get a chance to develop himself physically, to work off his animal spirits, these spirits will find vent in some direction.' He and Beverley Jones had been active during the previous twelve months in successfully persuading the Toronto School Board to convert the Jesse Ketchum Park in North Toronto into a children's playground, and he now advocated further developments of this kind.

The matter which Kelso stressed above all in his evidence to the commission was the need for stronger powers to protect children from neglectful or cruel parents. This theme, a central concern of the Humane Society based on the experiences of the cruelty constable, recurred frequently in Kelso's address. He expressed some reluctance at relieving parents of their responsibilities and duties, but felt 'that as a matter of protection it must be done very often.' He spoke approvingly of the powers given to philanthropic organizations in the State of New York. 'When they find a parent is neglecting to bring up his child properly the law enables them to sever altogether the connection between the parent and child.' Even in England, according to Kelso 'the most conservative country in the world,' the necessity for such powers had been recognized. In Ontario the acceptance of this principle would mean changes to a number of policies. Kelso proposed that neglected children sent to an industrial school should in many cases be permanently separated from their parents. 'We might just as well throw money into the bay as educate a child at an industrial school and allow the parents to take it back again after it has been educated and trained.' He strongly supported the committing of children to industrial schools on indeterminate sentences, to provide the authorities with maximum control over their future. Kelso did not, however, favour long periods of residence in the industrial schools. He expressed the view that children were placed at a disadvantage by being kept in an institution 'with the same companions, the same cast iron regulations, getting up at a certain hour and wearing a certain uniform.' Placing of children in good homes, particularly in the country, was

Kelso's proposed solution, the industrial schools to serve merely as temporary residences. Central to Kelso's conception of a reformed child welfare system was the establishment of a new type of voluntary society to work with neglected children and 'prevent children from becoming criminals.' In addition, he envisioned the appointment of probation officers to examine the complete circumstances of children brought before the courts and advise on the course of action to be taken in each case.

Kelso's submission to the Royal Commission provides a clear statement of the beliefs and assumptions which were to guide his activities as a reformer in the years ahead. He accepted the commissioners' assumption that the prevention of crime was the central problem, and that the neglect of children was the major cause of juvenile and adult crime. Kelso considered that children were deeply influenced by their environment, and consequently that modification or complete alteration of a child's surroundings was the key reform strategy. All measures should be taken to keep children from harmful moral influences. If a child's family, the most potent of all influences, failed to meet established standards of child-rearing, the authorities should firmly and unhesitatingly remove the child and place it in wholesome and kindly surroundings. Only if such measures were adopted could the nation hope for a crime-free and stable future.

The Report of the Prison Reform Commission was presented to the provincial government on 8 April 1891. On the basis of a wide literature review, visits to many correctional institutions in the United States, and numerous interviews, the commissioners called for a complete reform of the correctional and child welfare systems. The prevention and curing of juvenile delinquency was highlighted as a primary task. To achieve this, the commissioners stressed that the 'baneful influence of bad homes' would need to be countered, and they argued that traditional parental rights should be forfeited if this would result in saving a child from crime. The commission's recommendations included preventive and remedial strategies. Included amongst the former were proposals that school attendance laws be strictly enforced, that more playgrounds and gymnasia be provided by the authorities, that a curfew be introduced for boys and girls, and that day industrial schools be established in all parts of the province to train and control truant and disorderly children. As for children who had already committed offences, the commission favoured the use of special children's shelters for their detention prior to trial, and closed hearings in which every effort was made to avoid the committal of the child to the jail, refuge, or reformatory. The use of probation officers and suspended sentences was strongly supported. When children had to be confined, the commission recommended they be sent to an industrial school on the understanding that as soon as possible the schools should place them in the care of a private family, either as apprentices or boarders. The province-wide network of industrial schools proposed by the commission would also have responsibility for supervision of those children placed with family homes in their area. In this task of supervision, the schools' officers were to be supported by local voluntary associations 'who shall take upon themselves the important but delicate duty of looking after and caring for these children.' The commissioners thus suggested an expansion of both institutional and non-institutional arrangements for neglected and delinquent children.

The recommendations of the Royal Commission accorded closely with Kelso's own stated views of necessary reforms to the child welfare system. He was particularly pleased to see that support was expressed for his suggestion that a new type of voluntary child welfare society be established. The idea of a province-wide system of voluntary child welfare associations appealed to Kelso for a variety of reasons. His experiences in the Humane Society had convinced him that much could be achieved for neglected children through an organization of voluntary workers. The activities of the Humane Society, however, had been frustrated by limited powers in cases of child neglect and lack of official authorization for their child-saving work. Voluntary organizations backed by official sanction seemed to him a logical solution. Kelso was also beginning to feel that the Humane Society was no longer a suitable vehicle either for the child-saving movement as a whole or for his own personal ambitions. This stemmed first of all from the persisting conflict within the society between those who wished to focus on cruelty to animals and those who believed that children should be the priority. This tension had been present since the very beginning of the organization, Kelso being closely identified with those who wished the society to be first and foremost an organization for child-saving. He was frequently urged to take a firm stance on this issue, as many of the child-savers were unsympathetic to the animal lovers. A letter typifying this attitude, directed at Kelso, appeared in *Life* magazine in November 1888: 'Now in common sense, wouldn't it be more consistent with the spirit in which your Society was formed if its members devoted all their time and money to relieving the destitute men and women around them, and left the dogs to scratch for themselves until the outcasts and destitute, who are made in God's image, are all helped? Think it over Mr. Kelso, and if it strikes you as a good idea, let it furnish a theme for your eloquence at the next meeting of the Society.'

Kelso did not react strongly to such urgings, as he felt then, and throughout his life, that the prevention of cruelty to animals was a worthwhile endeavour. This aspect of his work brought him considerable favourable publicity. The *Mail's* women's columnist in May 1891, for example, praised Kelso for his work with animals: 'I do not think anyone has helped to promulgate the gospel of kindness to animals more widely than Mr. Kelso. Toronto owes that gentleman a great deal for his services in the cause of overworked and cruelly treated animals. The city has benefited by his untiring efforts to elevate the people of Toronto towards kindness to the brute creation, and no appeal made to him on behalf of suffering and ill-treated animals has ever been made in vain.' Nevertheless, the persisting tensions within the Humane Society were a source of anxiety to Kelso. 'The difficulty is cropping up of keeping the animals and children from clashing, the two having their separate and distinct friends,' he commented early in 1890 and the problem continued to annoy him. By April 1891 he had arrived at the conclusion that to advance the aims of the child-saving movement a separate organization devoted solely to that purpose was required.

There were also more personal reasons for Kelso's dissatisfaction with the Humane Society. He clearly wished to have control of the organization, and he complained about the 'constant interference' in the affairs of the society by other members, particularly those ladies who were chiefly interested in rescuing animals. He was also disgruntled by what he saw as the illiberal manner in which he had been treated. His devotion to duty as secretary of the Humane Society was unquestioned, but he was disappointed that his rewards had taken the form of plaudits rather than remuneration. In fact, he did receive gifts from time to time from Miss Gwynne, the society's benefactor, including forty dollars at Christmas 1890 and a hundred dollars a few weeks later for the simple task of finding her some verses which had been published in the *Globe* in 1881. These substantial bonuses, however, were not considered by him to be adequate financial reward for his effort. In addition to these concerns, he was increasingly aware of the need to consolidate his various activities and ration his time. As well as his involvement in the Fresh Air Fund and the Humane Society, he had also accepted the position of secretary of the Toronto Public Places Association, an organization formed to establish parks, squares, and playgrounds in the city, and to plan other civic improvement projects. This was all becoming too much of a burden, and by summertime 1891 Kelso felt a strong need to sort out his priorities.

The publication of the Royal Commission report gave Kelso the opportunity to embark on a new venture aimed at overcoming his problems within the Humane Society, and at the same time providing fresh impetus to the child-saving movement. His proposal was the establishment of a new child welfare organization in Toronto, which could serve as a prototype for others to be established elsewhere in the province. 'When the Royal Commission report was published the time seemed opportune for the organization of a Children's Aid

Society, to wisely direct the trend of legislation that was sure to follow,' he wrote later. Taking advantage of the publicity given to the report, Kelso opened his campaign with a signed letter to the Toronto *News* which was published on 15 April 1891:

I happened to be at the Police Court the other day and the first thing that caught my attention was the presence before the bar of no less than seven boys, not one of whom was eighteen years of age. They were charged with larceny in various degrees, and one had even gone so far as to have served a term in Kingston penitentiary. The number of boys who come up in the Police Court from day to day is a problem that calls for the most careful inquiry and the application of remedies calculated to effect a decided change. The police report for the past year gives the number of boys arrested between the ages of ten and fifteen to be 653, while the number between the ages of fifteen and twenty was 971, a total of 1,624. Should we not organize at once a society that will rescue children from such unfortunate conditions and afford them the opportunity to grow up good men and women?

This message was followed three days later by a long front-page article in the *Globe* entitled 'The Waifs of the Street.' In this piece Kelso outlined in detail his analysis of the need for reform, and the direction reform should take. More clearly than ever before he stated his reasons for selecting the child as the object of reform:

If we wish to counteract in any measure the suffering and injury brought upon humanity by the criminal and outcast portion of the population we must begin with the child. This rule prevails in every department of nature, and nature's laws as we well know can never be violated with impunity. In the child we see the future citizen, and carrying the same principle farther we see typified in his expanding intellect the future State and Nation. Is it not therefore reasonable and natural to suppose that no effort will be spared by the municipality or State to see that every child, no matter what his or her misfortune of birth or environment, shall have opporunity and assistance to develop into an honest, useful and industrious citizen? The mind of a child is the tenderest and holiest thing on earth, for it is begotten of heaven, not earth. To misrule and misguide this heaven-born mind is to rob it of its promise and purpose, is to cripple its powers of being and doing, is to extinguish its latent virtues and graces, and is an injury and a sin that may never be forgotten nor forgiven.

The article concluded with a list of proposed reforms to 'prevent children from growing up to swell the criminal classes.' Heading the list of reforms was 'the organization of a Children's Aid Society to superintend the work of child-saving.'

There was no immediate positive response to these articles, and for a few weeks afterwards Kelso was preoccupied with the organization of the 1891 Fresh Air Fund activities. He did, however, discuss the idea of a Children's Aid Society with a number of community leaders, and he secured endorsement for the scheme from W.H. Howland, Beverley Jones, Inspector Archibald, J.W. Langmuir, and Dr Rosebrugh. With this prestigious backing he felt confident to proceed. On 23 June he sent out two important letters, which together constituted a complete redirection of his reform efforts. The first was a letter of resignation as secretary of the Humane Society:

Dear Mr. Brock, Owing to the fact that my active connection with philanthropic work militates seriously against my private interests, I am compelled to place in your hands my resignation of the office of Secretary of the Toronto Humane Society. I need hardly tell you that I take this step with the greatest reluctance, and with the earnest hope that this action may not in any way retard the progress of a work which I believe is much needed in Toronto, and to which I have given for the past four years my best thought and energy.

The second was a circular letter sent out to about two hundred citizens inviting them to a public meeting on July 3 to discuss the advisability of organizing a 'Children's Aid Society and Fresh Air Fund' combined. The circular stated that 'the need of a strong society to deal with all matters affecting neglected or criminally-disposed children has impressed itself upon many,' and went on to list the various issues in which the society could become involved. With these two pieces of correspondence, Kelso simultaneously ended his leadership of his first reform movement and initiated the movement with which he was to be associated for the remainder of his life.

The letter of resignation drew a more immediate response than did the circular proposing a Children's Aid Society. The president of the Humane Society called a special meeting of the society two days later at which the resignation was received and accepted. The president spoke highly of Kelso's work, commenting that as he was still a young man having to make his way in the world it was only fair that he be relieved of the responsibility and duties of the secretaryship. There was a touch of irony in this comment. Most of those present at the meeting were aware that Kelso had started to organize a new society which would be taking support away from the Humane Society. His stated reason for resignation, to devote more time to private rather than philanthropic activities, thus appeared rather flimsy. Nevertheless, Kelso was thanked for his efforts, wished well for the future, and unanimously appointed as a vice-president of the society.

There were, unquestionably, some members of the Humane Society who were glad to see Kelso step down as secretary. He had opponents within the organization, particularly amongst those who saw the society's mission mainly in terms of animals. This group now saw their way clear to dominate the society. There was speculation in the newspapers that Kelso's resignation was a consequence of disagreement with the animal lovers, but statements that he had left the Humane Society 'at the mercy of a few zealots who might not improperly be termed brute worshippers' were exaggerated, as Kelso continued to be active in the Humane Society after his resignation as secretary. In particular, he became closely involved during 1892 in the organization of a conference to form a Canadian Humane Association. Continent-wide humane activities also continued to hold his interest. In 1891 he was still treasurer of the American Humane Association and he was deeply disappointed when, rankling after his resignation, the Toronto society members refused to send him as a delegate to the October 1891 American Humane Association convention in Denver. Kelso continued throughout his life to support campaigns against cruelty to animals, and he rarely missed the monthly meeting of the Toronto Humane Society right up to his death. His resignation was not a case of abandoning the cause of humane treatment of animals. It was, rather, a decision that there were other higher priorities.

The initial response to the letter inviting citizens to form a Children's Aid Society was somewhat disappointing to Kelso. Only about seventy-five people assembled in Association Hall on 3 July in response to his circular, and amongst those absent were some reform leaders, most conspicuously J.W. Langmuir. Many of Kelso's long-standing associates did attend, however, and the meeting was described by the *Globe* as 'thoroughly representative of the public-spirited philanthropy of the city.' Those present included Dr Rosebrugh, Beverley Jones, and W.H. Howland. The warden of Central Prison, the city relief officer, and Inspector Archibald attended as official representatives. After the meeting was opened with prayer, W.H. Howland was elected chairman and he proceeded to outline the reasons for the formation of a new society. He stressed that at present there was no organization which dealt with all aspects of the care of neglected children. There was a need for a strong and vigorous organization to give its whole time and thought to the cause of poor children. Such a society, he suggested, would deal with all questions affecting neglected children, including the cruelty and indifference of parents, reforms in police procedures, and pressing for improved laws. He then invited Kelso to speak in more detail about the various matters with which the society would be concerned. Kelso briefly outlined his reform programme, by this time no doubt familiar to his listeners. As preparation for the meeting he had obtained statements from several community leaders who were unable to attend, and he read these to the meeting.

The letters expressed agreement with the need for a new society, stressing the themes of crime prevention and economy in administration as well as humanitarian concern. The letter from Langmuir stressed the urgent need for reform: 'The recent investigations of the Prison Reform Commission have convinced me beyond all doubt that until some measures such as those proposed in your circular are generally adopted in large cities we can never hope to stem the ever-increasing volume of vice and criminality in the community; moreover, no time should be lost in organizing the work, as the increase which is going on in all city populations will render the initial proceedings, if long delayed, all the more difficult. I shall be glad to render all the assistance that I can in attaining the desirable object that you are seeking.' The Honourable S.H. Blake, a long-time supporter of Kelso and a leader of the Prisoners' Aid Association, wrote in similar terms: 'I need hardly say that I most heartily sympathize with any movement that is made for the looking after our neglected children. They are a most dangerous element, recruiting the ranks of criminals and leading astray other children with whom they mingle. We are not a rich enough community to be able to sustain the criminal class, and we should therefore seek to "nip it in the bud." ' A somewhat more positive note was sounded by Inspector Stark of the Toronto City Police, but he too was primarily concerned with reducing the numbers in the criminal class: 'The task of saving the boys and girls is more congenial, more likely to be productive of good results, and cannot but be more satisfactory in every way in the end than reforming them. Criminals are nearly all made before they reach the age of twenty. Keep the boys on the right track till they reach that age and the chances are all in their favour.'

Several other speakers followed Kelso on the platform. Then, in accord with the protocol governing the formation of a new organization, a member of the audience rose and proposed that a new society be formed to 'deal with all matters affecting the moral and physical welfare of children, especially those who from lack of parental care or other causes are in danger of growing up to swell the criminal class.' As expected, the motion was passed without opposition. A further motion was then proposed naming J.J. Kelso as president of the new organization, supported by an Executive Committee of about twenty people. The meeting again unanimously supported the motion. Kelso, who had expressed some reticence prior to the meeting about taking the leading position, then thanked his friends and associates for conferring this new honour upon him, and the proceedings were terminated with the doxology. Kelso now had his child-saving organization and, for the time being, he was in control.

Although Kelso was appointed president of the Children's Aid Society, during his first few months in office he assumed many of the functions of organizing secretary. He spent much time attending to the mundane but necessary tasks of finding an office, employing staff, organizing a committee structure, raising funds, and facilitating good public relations. Within a few months the society was in a sound organizational position. An office was provided free of charge by the Confederation Life Insurance Company, and a full-time secretary and agent employed. Incorporation of the Toronto Children's Aid Society as a charitable body was successfully applied for in October, its objectives defined as being 'to care for and protect neglected children; to secure the enactment and enforcement of laws relating to neglected children or juvenile offenders; to provide free summer excursions and other means of recreation or pleasure for poor children; and, generally, to advocate the claims of neglected children upon the sympathy and support of the public.' Committees were appointed to deal with different aspects of the society's work. A legislation committee began to prepare proposals for submission to the provincial government, and a children's temporary shelter committee set itself the task of establishing a shelter in Toronto as a matter of urgency. Another committee supervised the Fresh Air and Santa Claus funds, and a fourth was responsible for the finances and administration of the society. As president, Kelso was closely involved in the activities of each of the committees.

Kelso's most important contributions during these early months were in the areas of fund-raising and public relations. In September he prepared and distributed a pamphlet entitled 'Reasons Why Businessmen and All Lovers of Children Should Liberally Support the Toronto Children's Aid Society.' Under the society's newly adopted motto, 'It is wiser and less expensive to save children than to punish criminals,' the pamphlet contained statements from a dozen community leaders stressing that sound economy and Christian charity would both be served by speedy and liberal contributions. To press home this message, Kelso went to pains to ensure that the first annual meeting of the society, held on 6 December 1891, was a social and political success. The Academy of Music was hired for the occasion, and its pictures and electric light provided a bright and cheerful setting for the meeting. Powerful addresses from Kelso and other speakers were interspersed by musical items and poetry readings. The evening did much to consolidate the position of the society, which by the end of the year was in a healthy condition, both financially and in terms of community acceptance.

Although the formation of a Children's Aid Society in Toronto was Kelso's main objective during the latter half of 1890 and the first few months of 1891, once this was accomplished he began to regret this new investment of time and energy. Indeed, in late 1891 he became deeply dissatisfied with his life and work. In the first place, he was finding it impossible to dominate the Children's

Aid Society in the manner which he had envisaged and intended. A number of young, talented, and energetic people had been attracted to the organization, and Kelso's leadership was continuously challenged and questioned. This was not interpreted by Kelso as a healthy development. He had founded the society with certain specific objectives in view, and he was impatient with discussion, disagreement, and compromise. His method of operation, developed during his years in the Humane Society, was personally to undertake the tasks that he believed necessary; the role of the organization he saw as one of assistance, support, and legitimation. This approach was most effective during the early years in the Humane Society, but even there it caused strain with other members which was, in part, the cause of his resignation as secretary. In the Children's Aid Society, already by the end of 1891 a larger, more structured body than the Humane Society, Kelso's approach was unworkable. Leading members of the society, such as J.K. MacDonald, the Reverend J.E. Starr, and Dr Rosebrugh, each had their views on the way the society should proceed, and the energy and commitment to press for the acceptance of their viewpoint.

Kelso's low spirits at this time also resulted from uncertainty regarding his future. Although the reform movement had come to dominate his life, he still viewed his charitable work as a diversion from the important tasks of establishing a career, making a fortune, and fulfilling family responsibilities. In these three areas Kelso felt strongly that he was failing, and although his resignation from the Humane Society was primarily a strategic decision, the statement in his letter of resignation that philanthropy was interfering with his private life was accurate. His career in journalism had not progressed since his appointment as interim city editor of the *Globe* in January 1889. He was reappointed, after some dispute, to this position in January 1890 but the return of the regular city editor a few months later resulted in his demotion once again to the rank of municipal reporter. The city editorship fell vacant in the fall of 1890 and Kelso expected to be given the job. He was passed over, however, and informed that the reason for the decision was that he was too involved in philanthropic work to be able to devote the requisite time to the paper. This decision by the *Globe*'s editors was most understandable. Although Kelso's ability as a reporter was undisputed, he was frequently taking time off during the day to attend meetings and to speak to various groups, and from time to time was attending conferences out of town. The Bands of Mercy work in particular conflicted with his reporting duties, as he had to visit the schools during the day. At one point he seriously considered taking an official leave of absence from the *Globe* to devote himself to this work. An appointment as assistant city editor in January 1891 was welcomed by Kelso, but it was little consolation for missing out on the main position. There was no improvement during 1891. 'My position on the *Globe* is stationary,' he wrote in December; 'I cannot look for advancement nor can I hope for an increased salary. In fact, I must confess that the outlook is decidedly gloomy.'

Kelso's failure to progress as a journalist caused him to be concerned with his family life. He was anxious during these years to see the Kelso family gain acceptance and a place of respect in Toronto society, and this was difficult to accomplish on a reporter's salary. He was deeply concerned by the fact that two of his sisters were working in order to maintain the family's living standard at an acceptable level: 'All the success that has attended me in my public charitable work has been dampened by the thought that it has involved our little household in much privation and sorrow. My neglect of number one has proved a sad mistake.' Although most of the family were actually prospering well enough, Kelso's older brother had not found regular employment and he and his wife were in difficult circumstances. Kelso spent much time worrying about these family matters, and he felt that his comparatively low salary was a major cause of the family's problems.

Kelso had a further reason for concern over his limited financial resources. At the various conferences he attended and in the course of his reform work in Toronto he came into contact with many young single women, and he made the close acquaintance of many of them. With the exception of his limited means, he was a most eligible young man and his bachelorhood was a subject for mild amusement in Toronto reform circles. Canon Du Moulin drew laughter by mentioning the subject at the 1891 annual meeting of the Humane Society: 'It is a great pleasure to see Mr. Kelso in his place, discharging so efficiently his duties as secretary. One thing astonishes us, that some amiable young Jemima is not interested in him, he is so good-looking, and so amiable, and so humane.' While Kelso did not view marriage with any urgency in 1891, he was aware that he was not financially able to support a wife, and that the prospects of being able to do so in the foreseeable future were not great. This by no means deterred him from encouraging the affections of young women who showed an interest in him. One such woman was Irene Martin, whom he met while attending the American Humane Association convention in Nashville, Tennessee, in October 1890. Irene was the daughter of a prominent cotton heiress in Nashville, and Kelso met her when he was taken by some American friends to dine at her home. He was attracted by Irene, who had a reputation as a 'southern belle,' and she in turn was interested in the 'sparkling speaker from Canada,' as her sister, who attended the convention, had described Kelso. They began to correspond regularly, and four months after returning home from Nashville Kelso wrote in his diary of the 'many sweet and tender recollections' of their short acquaintance. Although Kelso had no definite plan to marry Irene Martin or any other woman in 1891, his financial inability to do so even had he wished was a concern and an irritation.

Kelso's misgivings about his private life and his dissatisfaction with his position in the Children's Aid Society resulted in a decision in February 1892 to resign from the presidency of the society. He had been president for only eight months, and his resignation signalled a firm intention to focus on personal rather than public concerns. His resignation was accepted at the society's monthly meeting, and a resolution was passed 'that while regretting the retirement of Mr. Kelso from the Presidency of the Children's Aid Society, this meeting desires to place on record its high appreciation of his philanthropic efforts on behalf of neglected children. As founder of the Children's Fresh Air Fund, and also of the Children's Aid Society, he has rendered distinguished services to the community, and has inaugurated a work the good results from which in the future it would be impossible to estimate.' In appreciation of his services Kelso was then elected an honorary life member of the society. For the first time in five years he held no position in any society which entailed official duties, and he was thus free to pursue his personal ambitions.

In the months following his resignation as president, Kelso concentrated on rebuilding his journalism career. Early in 1893 he was elected president of the Press Gallery of the Ontario Legislature, but the more important goal of promotion to an editorship on the *Globe* remained unfulfilled. During 1892 he also took on two paid part-time positions with the provincial government. While Parliament was in session he worked as official stenographer to the Public Accounts Committee, and in March 1892 he received an appointment as member and secretary of a commission appointed to investigate the practice of dehorning cattle. This was an issue on which the Humane Society had expressed concern, and it was largely on account of Kelso's association with that organization that he was given the position. He received eight dollars a day plus expenses while working for the commission, almost twice his rate of pay on the *Globe*. The commission met over a three-month period and travelled extensively throughout Ontario. These part-time positions enabled him to increase his income during 1892 by almost 50 per cent. They also brought him into further close contact with government ministers and senior officials, a matter which shortly had an important bearing on his future.

Despite Kelso's firm resolve in early 1892 to minimize his involvement in reform, he found it impossible to break his ties with the child-saving movement and during the year he reluctantly became active in a number of Children's Aid Society projects. Although he did not organize the Fresh Air Fund in the summer of 1892, he did sit on the 'Christmas Treat' committee and initiated the establishment of a 'Santa Claus toy shop' on King Street. The idea of the store was to give the citizens of Toronto the opportunity to donate presents to poor children for Chistmas, and in this respect the scheme was a success, with over five thousand presents being distributed. He also became involved in a campaign to bring about changes in the Criminal Code relating to the separate trial of juvenile offenders. The most time-consuming activity, however, was his membership on the children's shelter committee. Kelso had stressed the need for a shelter for several years, and after resigning as president he decided that his main continuing contribution to the work of the society would be in this field. A shelter was opened by the society on 7 March 1892 in a small house at 18 Centre Avenue, and during 1892 a total of seventy-five children were given temporary refuge. Kelso's experiences as a committee member supervising this work confirmed his conviction that far greater powers to intervene between parents and children should be granted to 'child-saving' organizations: 'Our hearts have often been made sad by having to return children to parents who we knew would not bring them up in the ways of truth and righteousness. We shall welcome the day when the law is so amended as to allow the Society to put such children under guardianship.' The shelter's main problem during its first year was that the children admitted on a temporary basis often ended up staying for weeks and even months, until a decision about where to place them was made. Kelso, whose strong reservations concerning institutional care for children were well known, opposed this tendency and successfully pressed for the passage of a set of rules that no child could be kept in the shelter for longer than one month. He continued to take a close interest in the operation of the shelter despite his resignation from the committee in 1893.

Kelso's continuing involvement in the Children's Aid Society during 1892 conflicted with his efforts to devote himself to career, family, and fortune. Indeed, within a few weeks of his resignation from the presidency of the Children's Aid Society it was clear that, despite his intentions, he would continue to play a leading role as a 'child-saver.' This was in part simply a consequence of his having invested so much time and energy to the cause over a period of some six years. His whole life had been oriented around reform for those years and to disentangle the ties abruptly which bound him to the movement proved impossible. His resolve to retreat into private life was also weakened by political developments which opened up new possibilities for child welfare reform. The presentation of the findings of the Prison Reform Commission in April 1891, and the subsequent formation of the Toronto Children's Aid Society, stimulated Sir Oliver Mowat's Liberal government to give consideration to the passage of a new Children's Protection Act to implement the proposed reforms. During Kelso's presidency the Toronto Children's Aid

Society pressed strongly for such a measure, the Legislation Committee being established in October 1891 specifically for that purpose. In November 1891 the society sponsored a Prison Reform Conference in Toronto to discuss the recommendations of the Prison Reform Commission and urge their speedy implementation. The conference was well attended and resulted in a deputation to the premier urging new child welfare legislation. The Reverend J.E. Starr, one of the most active members of the Children's Aid Society, was appointed chairman of the Legislation Committee and during the winter of 1891–2 was active in urging Mowat to commit the provincial government to action. Other individuals and organizations supported the campaign. Lady Aberdeen, wife of the governor general of Canada, spoke to Mowat on the matter on behalf of the Women's Branch of the Ottawa Humane Society, and this organization also issued a report advocating new laws. The outcome was that early in 1892 the premier requested J.M. Gibson, the provincial secretary, to investigate the possibility of introducing a bill during the parliamentary session then in progress. Gibson, who had had little or no previous interest in child welfare, was somewhat intimidated by the prospect of preparing a major piece of legislation on such short notice. After devoting a night or two to studying the question he proposed to Mowat that the matter should be postponed for a year to enable the government to give the matter sufficient thought and study. Mowatt concurred and it was agreed that Gibson should spend considerable time during 1892 preparing a bill for submission during the 1893 parliamentary session.

Kelso was a member of Starr's Legislation Committee during 1892 and was aware of these developments. Late in the year he received an invitation from Mowat to discuss the proposed bill, and was told in confidence that the government was planning to appoint a superintendent of neglected children who would be responsible for implementation of the new act. Mowat asked Kelso if he would consider accepting this position. This forced Kelso to reappraise his earlier decision to concentrate on reviving his journalism career. However, given his gloomy prospects at the *Globe* and his commitment to reform, he did not take long to decide that he would accept the superintendency if it was officially offered to him. Such an appointment seemed an ideal solution to his problem of choosing between charitable activities and personal career. Kelso provided Gibson with a good deal of the written material he had collected over the years, particularly the laws of other countries pertaining to child neglect, and discussed the proposed bill with Gibson on several occasions. When Gibson introduced the bill 'for the Prevention of Cruelty to, and better Protection of Children' into the Parliament in February 1893, Kelso listened from the Speaker's Gallery fully expecting that the measures which Gibson was describing would soon be his to implement. The Toronto newspapers also anticipated

Kelso's appointment as superintendent. The *Star* described him listening to Gibson's speech: 'He wore a happy smile upon his bearded lips and his heart beat high with many a conflicting emotion, for today is the greatest day of his life, the crowning point of his career.' A number of editorials appeared also assuming that Kelso would become the first superintendent.

In fact, Kelso's appointment was not yet completely secure. Gibson, who became the responsible minister when the act was passed in May 1893, received a number of applications for the position, including one from the Reverend Starr. In Kelso's favour was his extensive experience in child welfare, his considerable knowledge of provincial government structures, and his proven leadership qualities. These had to be weighed against his youth and the difficulty he had shown on occasion in getting along with fellow workers. Although Gibson pondered over the appointment for several weeks, it would have been difficult to decide against Kelso. His associates in the provincial government were pressing for his appointment, as were the Toronto newspapers and most of the reform organizations. In June he received official notification that the position was his, and he commenced duties as the first superintendent of neglected and dependent children in Ontario on 1 July 1893. The *Globe*, although it would now lose Kelso's services, expressed the general approval which greeted the government's decision: 'This is an appointment made solely on the ground of merit, and it is one that meets with the hearty approval of the various philanthropic organizations with which Mr. Kelso will be thrown into contact. Judging from his past record, Mr. Kelso is more likely than anyone we know of to wisely and cautiously, yet zealously, work out the details of a particularly difficult problem.'

Kelso's pleasure on receiving the appointment was somewhat soured by a dispute over salary. He had earned over fifteen hundred dollars the previous year, and assumed that as superintendent his remuneration would be at least that amount. He was dismayed, therefore, to learn that his new salary had been fixed at only one thousand dollars. The Kelso household had permitted itself the luxury of a maid in the previous year, but she now had to be dismissed and the family also contemplated moving to a smaller house. This represented a major setback to Kelso's personal ambitions. The superintendency was seen by him as an opportunity for increased social standing as well as public duty, but this relatively low salary was a damper to his social aspirations. After a few weeks in the position he raised the matter with Gibson, and received a raise to twelve hundred dollars a year. 'With this meagre income,' wrote Kelso, 'I struggled along as best I could.'

Kelso's ready acceptance of the offer of the superintendency was a reflection of his satisfaction, and that of his fellow reformers, with the provisions of the

Children's Protection Act of 1893, which became widely known as 'The Children's Charter.' The act adopted many of the proposals advocated by the Toronto Children's Aid Society and allied reform organizations in the preceding years.[4] Central to the new legislation was an emphasis on the protection of children through the punishment of those found guilty of neglecting or exploiting them. Fines up to $100 and imprisonment up to three months could be imposed. Children found to be neglected, and those without parents or guardians, could be placed under the charge of 'any duly authorized Children's Aid Society.' Such a society was given wide powers, including the apprehending of children, their 'supervision and management' in children's shelters, and the status and prerogatives of legal guardians respecting children committed to their care by a court. The Children's Aid Societies were also to work closely with another class of organization established by the act, children's visiting committees. These committees were to select foster homes for children under the control of the Children's Aid Societies, to visit children in foster homes in their area at least once every three months, to remove children from one foster home to another should this prove necessary, and generally to promote 'a philanthropic sentiment on behalf of neglected, abandoned and destitute children.' The promotion, establishment, and supervision of Children's Aid Societies and visiting committees throughout the province was the central responsibility of the superintendent of neglected and dependent children.

The provisions in the 1893 act granting broad powers to authorized voluntary societies to remove children from allegedly neglectful parents, and accepting the foster care method of raising neglected children, represented a major triumph for Kelso and his colleagues in social reform. Despite his reluctance during the early 1890s to remain active in 'child-saving' endeavours, public acceptance of his views provided opportunities for reform work which Kelso found himself unable to resist. His strong views on the need to save neglected children from crime and immorality were now shared, at least in part, by the provincial government and many community leaders. The superintendency and the broad powers granted under the Children's Protection Act could not be refused.

4

The Superintendency

Kelso's main responsibilities during his first years as superintendent were to establish Children's Aid Societies and visiting committees throughout Ontario, and supervise their development. These responsibilities took up most of his time in the years 1893 to 1900. The 1893 Children's Protection Act became widely known throughout Canada, and Kelso was closely involved in promoting the development of similar legislation in the other provinces. His official duties were extended in 1897 when he was appointed inspector of juvenile immigration agencies for Ontario, in addition to the superintendency. Official duties did not, however, curtail Kelso's role as publicist and reformer. He used his official position to challenge existing child welfare policies, in particular the continuing practice of conducting the trials of juveniles in adult courts.

Kelso started duty as superintendent under strained circumstances. Arriving at the Parliament Buildings on 1 July 1893 he discovered that arrangements had not been made for him to start work. Although the establishment of the superintendency had been planned for more than half a year, Kelso began his public service career without an office, desk, chair, or stationery. It was several weeks before his basic needs were provided, making it difficult for him to work effectively. He used the office of the provincial secretary, who was temporarily absent from Toronto, but this arrangement came to an end when Gibson returned in early August. Finally, he received grudging permission from some clerks to put a second-hand desk in a corner of their room. This became his office. It was not until a year later that he was given his own space on the first floor in the north-east corner of the Parliament Buildings. The government's tardiness in providing adequate accommodation was matched in other matters. Kelso was not given secretarial or clerical assistance until two years after his appointment and during this time he conducted his correspondence by hand. The first records were kept in a ledger discarded by another office. Legal assistance was not provided for the drafting of the first official forms. During the first two years the superintendency was strictly a one-man show.

These stringent circumstances reflected the parsimonious attitude of the Ontario government to the provision of social welfare services, despite the enthusiasm which surrounded the passage of the Children's Protection Act. The budget for Kelso's office in the first year was only four thousand dollars, including his salary. The manner in which this money could be spent was strictly circumscribed. During his first month as superintendent he was asked to take charge of a thirteen-year-old girl whose mother had been committed to the women's reformatory. The girl badly needed new clothing. Kelso purchased the clothes for her, forwarding the bill to the provincial auditor. It was returned with an explanation that such spending could not be authorized and that the monies appropriated for the branch should be used solely for office expenses, publicity, travel, and related costs. The auditor did, however, contribute five dollars from his own pocket towards the girl's clothing expenses, and a further donation was made by a government minister to whom Kelso unsuccessfully appealed the auditor's decision. With these contributions Kelso started a benevolent fund for use in similar circumstances. Limitations of this kind vexed him throughout his career as a public servant. In these early days the restrictions were particularly acute, as the government's commitment to its child welfare policy was tentative, wavering, and uncertain. Kelso later attributed his early difficulties to the government's fear of criticism from the parliamentary opposition.

The limited resources granted to Kelso contrasted with his extensive responsibilities. Under the terms of the Children's Protection Act he was responsible for the establishment and encouragement of the new Children's Aid Societies and visiting committees, the inspection of industrial schools, infants' homes, and children's shelters, and the maintenance of records about children committed to the care of the Children's Aid Societies. For one man, operating under severe financial constraints and without assistance, this was a formidable list of responsibilities.

Characteristically, Kelso began his work by mounting a vigorous public relations campaign. He wrote letters and articles to the press and sent circular letters and copies of the act to judges, magistrates, children's institutions, police, clergymen, and teachers. The amount of material prepared by him during his first few months in office was remarkable. On 20 July, for example, his articles were published in the *Educational Journal*, the *Mail*, the *Empire*, the *Week*, the London *Advertiser*, and the Toronto *News*. The next day there were follow-up articles in three of these papers, as well as a piece in the *Presbyterian Review*. These and other writings created widespread public response to the new

legislation. By September Kelso was flooded with requests for further information and for assistance with child neglect cases. This required the preparation of
guidelines for those considering the establishment of Children's Aid Societies
and visiting committees, and extensive correspondence in response to specific
questions. Kelso was also in great demand as a speaker and in the early months
he spent considerable time travelling in the province. His cause captured public
imagination; laudatory articles in the press became common. A poem published
in the Toronto *News* appearing beneath a cartoon of Kelso holding hands with
two young children was typical of press reaction:

> You'd hardly think, to glance at his
> Nice boyish-looking features,
> That this young man directs the fate
> Of many fellow creatures.
>
> The poor, neglected little waifs,
> Whose parents scarcely knew them,
> May pick up heart and come to him –
> He'll be a father to them.

Kelso became personally involved in handling individual cases of child neglect within days of taking up his appointment. This involvement was partly a
result of personal inclination. He had enjoyed his previous contacts with
children in activities such as the Fresh Air Fund and the Santa Claus Fund, and
saw continuing direct involvement with neglected children as an integral part of
his work. Dealing with specific cases of neglect or cruelty provided a welcome
change from tedious office work. But in fact, Kelso had no real choice but to
investigate personally cases referred to him. It was not until 20 October that the
Toronto Children's Aid Society was incorporated under the Children's Protection Act, and for a considerable time after that there were large areas of the
province without incorporated societies. In the interim Kelso was the only
person with powers under the act, and the success of the publicity campaign
ensured that many requests for service were received. On 10 July the first entry
was made in the new register of 'Complaints of Cruelty to or Neglect of
Children':

1 Mrs. J.F.
   from Corresponding Secretary of Toronto Girls' Home re: Daisy W., placed at service
   with a farmer in Wellington County, not properly treated and her return refused.

ACTION – visited the place and brought back the girl, charging the farmer $10 for expenses.

Kelso also received requests for children to work on farms and in homes. Like many of his contemporaries, he believed in the virtues of rural living and consequently encouraged families from non-metropolitan areas to foster neglected children. In his first annual report he stressed this aspect of his work:

Adult labour is scarce, and even when attainable is expensive, while growing lads, after a little experience, can do much of the required work for half the pay. When treated kindly and not overworked they usually enjoy their occupation and develop a healthy and robust physique. A great evil, to which public opinion has frequently been directed, is the steady gravitation of population to large cities, robbing the smaller towns of their importance and business activity, and leaving the rural districts with a force insufficient to develop the resources of the soil. If this be true, should it not be the constant aim of those engaged in juvenile rescue work to deport to rural districts as many dependent children as possible, at such an age as will enable them to acquire a taste for their new surroundings, and if we are not ourselves able or willing to meet the demand, should we exclude other children from these benefits?

The first entry in the 'Requests for Children' register was made on 11 July:

1 Mrs. M.A.B., Niagara Falls, little girl eleven or twelve – supplied from Girls' Home.

Kelso's personal involvement in child protection cases led him into several awkward, embarrassing, and amusing situations. One day in July he received a telegram asking him to meet a child that was being sent to him by train. When the train arrived, a woman handed him a baby, saying that it had been abandoned in the village and the reeve had decided to send it to Kelso. The woman then disappeared and Kelso was left holding the child. It took him an evening of travelling around Toronto, carrying the infant, before he managed to find a woman willing to provide temporary care.

On another occasion Kelso brought back to Toronto a five-year-old girl who had been living in the Hamilton Infants' Home. No one wanted to adopt her. Kelso intended to find a home for the girl in Toronto, but having no place arranged, decided temporarily to take her to his own home, much to the surprise of his mother and sisters. The family became very fond of the little girl and there was much sadness in the household when the time came for her to leave. Kelso had to promise not to bring any more children into the family circle.

Another awkward situation arose from the boarding of a pretty sixteen-year-old girl. The girl confided to the woman with whom she was placed that Mr Kelso was going to marry her. The news spread quickly. Two prominent ladies called on Kelso in an attempt to persuade him to change his mind. The situation was then explained – with embarrassment to all parties.

In his early child rescue work Kelso worked without clear guidelines. His decisions were based on the provisions of the 1893 act and on his knowledge of the practices of other jurisdictions. The act's definitions of neglect, dependency, and cruelty were phrased in broad terms. Kelso had considerable discretion in deciding whether or not to initiate court proceedings for removing children from their parents or guardians. In some instances there was little doubt that charges should be laid. For example, in early July 1893 twenty residents of the Don Mills area complained to Kelso that a couple were constantly beating and ill-treating their children. The evidence presented seemed so overwhelming that Kelso secured a warrant. With two police constables he helped arrest the parents. The children were placed in the Children's Aid Society shelter, and the parents were brought to trial.

Another case in which there was little doubt that intervention was required began with a letter from a clergyman alleging gross neglect and ill-treatment of a slightly mentally handicapped eleven-year-old boy living with his parents about twenty miles from Toronto. After investigation, Kelso discovered that the boy was forced to sleep outside. His clothes were sewn together so that he could not take them off and for two months he had been a wanderer in the village, getting a meal where he could and sleeping in stables and outhouses. Kelso told the parents that unless they signed an agreement to pay for the boy's board, he would prosecute them for cruelty. A placement was arranged for the boy. The foster parents received eight dollars a month from the natural parents. This case and others like it were used by Kelso in his speeches and reports as evidence of the good work being done under the 1893 act.

Other situations not involving obvious cruelty proved more difficult for Kelso to assess. However, his bias in this early period was clearly in favour of removing a child from parents or guardians if there was suspicion of ill-treatment or neglect. In April 1894 he investigated a complaint concerning a girl who had been living for five years with a farming couple. It was alleged that the couple had not made payments to the girl in accordance with an apprenticeship agreement. Against the wishes of the couple, Kelso moved the girl back to the Toronto Girls' Home: 'The child I considered had been overworked and unjustly treated, although the farmer's wife wept a good deal at the idea of her going away.' Subsequent entreaties from the farmer's wife for the return of the girl were denied. In another situation Kelso agreed to remove a twelve-year-old girl from her home on the grounds that she did not get along well with her new stepmother and 'a change was considered best for all concerned.' Decisions such as this represented a broad interpretation of Kelso's legislative mandate to combat child neglect. However, these decisions were consistent with his view that decisive action was needed in removing children from homes that fell below acceptable standards.

Although Kelso kept busy with child protection work, the most urgent task facing him in the first months after his appointment was the establishment of a network of Children's Aid Societies throughout the province. The 1893 act provided that such societies, duly incorporated, would have powers to act as police constables in enforcing the Children's Protection Act and the Industrial Schools Act. Officers of the societies would have the power to apprehend children without warrant and bring before a judge children under fourteen whom they considered to be neglected or dependent and in need of substitute care. If the judge considered that the child was neglected, dependent, or cruelly treated, he could make the child a ward of the Children's Aid Society. The society was responsible for arranging temporary care for the child and placing him in an approved foster home. The Children's Aid Society would be given legal guardianship until the age of twenty-one, unless the guardianship order was rescinded by a judge. The granting of these powers to Children's Aid Societies was complete fulfilment of the desire of the Ontario child-savers that strong powers be granted to voluntary societies to intervene in families where neglect or cruelty to children was suspected. Kelso soon set about organizing the societies and ensuring that these new powers were put into effect.

The first organization to become approved as a Children's Aid Society under the 1893 act was, not unexpectedly, the Toronto Children's Aid Society, which was already two years old. Its structure and purpose were readily adaptable to the requirements of the Children's Protection Act. The Reverend J.E. Starr, Kelso's rival for the position of superintendent, was appointed full-time secretary of the Toronto Children's Aid Society in September 1893, ensuring capable and knowledgeable leadership. Two other full-time staff were appointed shortly after Starr. One was an agent to investigate complaints of cruelty and neglect and the other was a superintendent for the children's shelter. The society's incorporation under the Children's Protection Act in October 1893 was celebrated at the annual meeting held late in September. The governor general, Lord Aberdeen, was present, ensuring an impressive attendance by Toronto notables. Addresses were delivered by J.K. MacDonald, president of the society, J.M. Gibson, and the governor general. It was moved 'that having regard not only to the work which has already been done by the Children's Aid Society of Toronto, but also to the possibilities for increased usefulness afforded by the

Children's Protection Act, this meeting commends the Society to the hearty and generous support of the public.' The first accredited Children's Aid Society was thus successfully and enthusiastically launched.

The Reverend Starr and his co-workers applied themselves with vigour to their new responsibilities. During its first year as an accredited society the Toronto Children's Aid Society investigated 414 cases of suspected cruelty and gave 181 children temporary refuge in the shelter. It went even further than Kelso in its readiness to remove children from their parents, and Kelso was forced to complain about its policies. He had two concerns. Firstly, the large number of children being removed from their families was causing severe overcrowding in the children's shelter. Secondly, the board of the Toronto Children's Aid Society had begun, in its enthusiasm, to adopt the practice of making children wards by simple resolution of the board, a method clearly not sanctioned by the act since this was the court's responsibility. Conflicts with the Toronto Children's Aid Society continued throughout Kelso's career as super-intendent, and in future years debate and negotiation with many of the Children's Aid Societies concerning interpretation of the act, methods, and standards became a major and time-consuming aspect of his work.

The accreditation of the Toronto Children's Aid Society took little of Kelso's time since the society was already established and had full-time staff to promote the organization and undertake child protection work. Similar organizations did not exist elsewhere in the province. Kelso had to begin by arousing the interest and concern of local citizens. His publicity campaign was undertaken with this object in mind. One circular letter distributed in September 1893 to community leaders contained testimonials from businessmen and leading community figures who had been involved in the formation of the Toronto Children's Aid Society. It concluded with a plea from Kelso for citizen involvement: 'No city or town in Ontario should be without an active and vigilant Children's Aid Society, well-organized and equipped, to look after the interests of ill-treated, neglected or orphaned children, thereby seeking to stay the curse of evil which is so often perpetuated by the failure to apply simple remedial measures in the period of childhood. To all friends of friendless and ill-treated children this circular letter is therefore sent, in the hope that they will be led to unite in this most essential and charitable work.'

Kelso received many responses to this and other letters. He followed up this correspondence with a series of tours in the province, addressing meetings and helping to establish organizing committees. His first trip, in late September 1893, was to Ottawa, where interest in the formation of a society was already strong amongst the members of the Ottawa Humane Society. He first called on the leaders of the Humane Society to discuss a course of action. It was agreed to arrange a public meeting for the following day. Kelso visited the editors of the major daily newspapers, obtaining favourable press comment. About thirty or forty people attended the public meeting where Kelso was the main speaker. In his address he stressed the themes of economy, reduction of crime, and the paramount importance of an upbringing in a good Christian family home. He explained the provisions of the new act and his own role, urging the Ottawa community's participation. Considerable discussion followed, and it was agreed to call a meeting of the city's charitable organizations to form a society. Kelso returned to Ottawa on 8 December to attend the meeting. As in Toronto the Ottawa inaugural meeting was a vice-regal affair, and Kelso dined with Lord Aberdeen prior to the meeting which was held in the City Council Chambers. After Kelso's address the meeting resolved to form a Children's Aid Society and the first officers were elected. The city sheriff was appointed founding president.

Between his first and second visits to Ottawa, Kelso undertook a two-week organizing tour to Peterborough, London, and Guelph, and in each of these centres a nucleus for a society was established. The first stop, on 2 November was Peterborough, where a Society for the Prevention of Cruelty to Children was already in operation. This society had difficulties in its anti-cruelty work arising from inadequate powers to intervene between parents and children. As a result it was highly receptive to Kelso's message. At the public meeting called to consider the formation of a Children's Aid Society, Kelso stressed that he should be viewed 'more as a friend of helpless, ill-treated and dependent children than as a government official.' He explained his function as one of 'removing all obstacles in the way of effectively looking after children who need looking after.' His speech in Peterborough, as elsewhere, downplayed the role of government and stressed the overriding importance of voluntary effort: 'The responsibility for the care of neglected and otherwise unfortunate children rests largely upon the Christian community in which they are to be found. The government has furnished the means in the shape of legislation by which the matter can be systematically and authoritatively attended to.' Officers for the Peterborough society were elected at this first meeting and, as in Ottawa, the local sheriff was chosen the first president. After Peterborough, Kelso travelled to London where he made contact with the Protestant Orphans' Home. He stayed in London for a week, addressing a public meeting and a second meeting called by the City Council. At this latter meeting it was agreed to establish a Children's Aid Society. In early 1894 the London Society was formed. On his way back to Toronto Kelso stopped over in Guelph for a day. At a public meeting in the City Council Chambers a decision was made to establish a society. The network of Children's Aid Societies envisaged by the framers of the 1893 act was beginning to take shape.

Further organizing trips were undertaken by Kelso in the second year of his superintendency. The development of the societies continued at a good rate. By the end of 1895 twenty-nine societies were formed and Kelso was personally involved in establishing all but a handful of these. The formation of new societies continued as one of Kelso's main tasks throughout the 1890s; by 1899 the number in Ontario had risen to thirty-five. After the first few trips Kelso established a set routine for organizing new societies in the smaller communities of the province. He first contacted the reeve or mayor, asking for support in forming a society. With this backing, he then arranged a meeting at which he explained the nature of child-saving work by means of lantern slides. These slide shows, consisting mainly of pictures of neglected children 'before and after' the intervention of Children's Aid Societies, were very popular. For many years Kelso used this method to publicize his work. The Guelph *Mercury* described the pictures shown by Kelso at a promotional meeting in 1898: 'They were nearly all of children, and showed clearly the transformation wrought in the appearance and lives of the children by taking them from their evil surroundings and giving them a chance in decent homes. The contrast between the children when taken in charge by Mr. Kelso and the Children's Aid Societies, and afterwards, was very striking, and the audience testified to their appreciation of the good work being done by repeated applause.'

Despite the rapid growth in the number of Children's Aid Societies, at the turn of the century there were still some large areas of Ontario in which no society had been organized. These unorganized areas were recognized as a problem by Kelso as early as 1894. In his report for that year he wrote that 'some of the worst cases of moral depravity that could well be imagined have occurred in small villages and lonely country districts, where this class of people feel themselves somewhat secure from molestation.' While Kelso may have exaggerated the deterrent effect of the 1893 act, there was still the practical problem that powers of apprehension and guardianship of neglected and dependent children were granted only to Children's Aid Societies. Consequently, in unorganized areas there was no institution to carry out the task of protecting such children. A considerable number of neglected children from these areas were sent to Kelso, who had to deal with them as best he could. In 1895 he managed to bring this anomaly to the attention of the provincial government. An amendment to the Children's Protection Act was passed which conferred on the superintendent the powers of Children's Aid Societies in areas where no society was formed. As a consequence Kelso, and later his agents, continued to be active in direct child-saving work until 1914, when a network of societies finally covered the province. Although this child rescue and protection work gradually declined, in the 1890s it was still a major responsibility for Kelso. In 1895, for example, he was personally involved in arranging the boarding of over half the children placed in foster homes in the province, a major commitment of time given his extensive administrative and supervisory duties.

For Kelso the establishment of the Children's Aid Societies represented his most important achievement during his early years as superintendent. He envisaged that as the societies became firmly established they would combine both the functions allotted to them under the 1893 act and a more general child advocacy role, such as that played by the Toronto Children's Aid Society in its early stages. In the draft constitution he circulated to prospective societies in 1893 he proposed the adoption of objectives relating to both roles:

To protect children from cruelty, to care for and protect neglected, abandoned or orphaned children; to provide such children as may be lawfully committed or entrusted to the Society with suitable homes in private families, and to watch over and guard their interests and promote their happiness and well-being; to secure the enforcement of laws relating to neglected and dependent children or juvenile offenders; and to take the part of a friend towards any child accused of offences against the laws of the Province or Dominion; to provide free summer excursions, temporary residence in the country, or other means for benefiting poor children; and generally, to advocate the claims of neglected, abandoned or orphaned children upon the sympathy and support of the public.

This broad view was too ambitious. The societies found the fulfilment of their statutory obligations a sufficiently challenging aim for at least their first decade. And, although occasionally criticized, they generally received praise in the press and elsewhere for carrying out their statutory responsibilities. Many would have shared the opinion of the *Globe* reporter who wrote in December 1894: 'Since the passage of the Gibson Act rescue work among children has taken a very different standing. What was before done sporadically is now performed with the regularity and continuity sanctioned by law. Preventive measures for the treatment of crime are of vastly more importance than the merely punitive; therefore, viewed apart from the humanity which would prompt the rescue of neglected children, the work may be regarded as proleptic economy, for which another generation may be thankful.'

Most important to Kelso's vision of the Children's Aid Societies was their voluntary, non-governmental nature. This, he felt, was crucial to their success. He emphasized this point on all possible occasions. In his 1894 report he stressed that the outcome of the government's policy towards neglected children 'rests entirely with the Christian and philanthropic people whether or not they will engage in the work, since there is not, and could not in the nature of things be, any compulsion in forming an organization which depends so entirely upon voluntary service, actuated by the very highest motives of compassion and benevolence.' Later he wrote that 'benevolent societies have a tremendous advantage for good since they can draw largely upon the zeal, cooperation, and liberality of Christian people while, in a direct state work, all these powerful agencies are completely alienated.' Throughout his career Kelso continued to oppose excessive involvement of government in social welfare, including child welfare. He strongly believed that neglected and dependent children should be aided only from the motivation and perspective of Christian charity.

One result of the establishment of Children's Aid Societies was an increase in the number of people working with neglected and dependent children in Ontario. At the time of passage of the Children's Protection Act the province had many full-time and voluntary workers in child welfare employed in twenty-five children's homes, two industrial schools, the reformatory for boys, the refuge for girls, the homes for handicapped and feeble-minded children, and seven British agencies bringing children into Ontario. In addition to these people there were many others in the professions, the judiciary, and the clergy engaged in child-saving. The response of these groups to the Children's Protection Act was crucial. The fledgling Children's Aid Societies were working in areas that overlapped with the responsibilities of many well-established institutions and agencies. The societies were dependent on the co-operation of judges, municipalities, police, and others for their success. With these considerations in mind, Kelso proposed in mid-1894 a provincial conference of those involved in the care and protection of neglected children. In late July he sent out a circular letter asking for response to the idea of a two-day conference 'at which methods of child-saving work might be considered, and a general understanding arrived at.' He proposed for discussion such topics as existing provincial and dominion laws for the care and protection of children, the child and the institution, the foster home method, the supervision of boarded children, the industrial school and reformatory system, and the importation of British waifs. The reaction to the proposal was favourable. Kelso proceeded to organize the Ontario Child-Saving Conference that was to be held on 18 and 19 October 1894 at Confederation Hall, Toronto.

The conference attracted a large attendance. Many delegates attended from the newly-formed Children's Aid Societies and the older established institutions and agencies. The main population centres of the province sent delegates; the province-wide nature of the gathering was emphasized by the appointment of a Brockville judge as chairman. The prevailing mood at the commencement of the conference was one of optimism about a united child-saving movement. Kelso expressed this feeling in his address early on the first day with his claim that 'with the present laws, and a vigorous prosecution of child-saving work, there need be no hesitation in saying that fully half the vice, crime and pauperism of the present day would be swept away.' However, when the delegates began to discuss the means by which to pursue this grand objective, their varying approaches surfaced and it became clear that there were important issues yet to be resolved.

The first contentious issue was raised by the provincial secretary, J.M. Gibson, in the opening address to the conference. He complained that municipalities and local magistrates had adopted an unsympathetic attitude to the placement of neglected children in foster homes. The 1893 act made municipalities liable for the maintenance of children in foster homes at the rate of one dollar per week and also provided that municipalities were responsible for the expense of maintaining children's shelters. Gibson claimed that municipalities were not making these payments and that police magistrates were being influenced by local councils not to place children in the care of the Children's Aid Societies owing to the expense involved. Other speakers agreed and the president of the Toronto Children's Aid Society made specific reference to the unsympathetic approach of the Toronto City Council.

A related issue was the continuing role of children's institutions. Many administrators of children's homes were aware that the system of Children's Aid Societies and foster care envisaged by the Children's Protection Act challenged the role of their organizations. Gibson was asked if the government intended to phase out orphanages and similar institutions. His reply was noncommittal. However, the delegates from the Children's Aid Societies made no secret of their understanding that the government's policy was to reduce the role of institutions. The Reverend Starr proclaimed that 'all homes and institutions, if this Act is properly worked, will be empty in five years.' Others claimed that the institutional care of children was outdated. The conference did little to resolve the disagreement. On the contrary, it resulted in the battle lines being more clearly drawn.

The conference also brought to light a number of administrative problems arising from the Children's Protection Act, particularly those relating to the visiting committees. The Children's Protection Act provided for the appointment of a children's visiting committee in each electoral district of the province. A committee consisted of six persons, including at least three women, appointed by the county judge, sheriff, and mayor. The legislation stated that the committees were to assist in the selection of foster homes, to visit children placed in foster homes, to report on these visits to the superintendent, to inspect children's shelters, and to 'promote and encourage a philanthropic sentiment on behalf of neglected, abandoned and destitute children, and to adopt such methods as thought best for securing voluntary subscriptions of money to be used in carrying out the objectives of the Act.'

Other matters discussed at the conference included separate trial for juveniles, industrial schools and reformatories, the immigration of British waifs, and the efficacy of whipping boys who had committed offences. Discussion ranged from broad philosophical questions such as whether or not the 1893 act interfered with parental responsibility to detailed reports about progress being made in particular cities. The conference served an important educational function in clarifying for delegates the act's implications, and brought Children's Aid Society workers from across the province together for the first time. It also made Kelso more aware of problem areas which he would have to address. However, in his final speech to the conference Kelso did not dwell on the disagreements and problems which had been aired. He emphasized the delegates' common cause and the potential benefits of the 1893 act:

It may be said with confidence ... that the State, with its official machinery, cannot, singlehanded, do the work of child-saving which is so greatly needed in every civilized state. It is one of the most pleasing, as well as one of the most hopeful, facts in the history of the Ontario Act that it was framed and passed largely at the instance of those who had gained their knowledge of the necessity for such an Act, and the shape it should take, by experience in the work of child-saving by voluntary effort, and that, instead of taking the work out of the hands of the voluntary organizations, the Act aims at utilizing to the utmost the agency of all such workers. Its main purpose is, in fact, to remove obstacles, otherwise insurmountable, out of the way of the voluntary agencies, and to aid in making their efforts more effective.

Although the major disagreements at the child-saving conference were between the representatives of the institutions and the advocates of Children's Aid Societies, some conflicts among those working to implement the 1893 act were also evident. The main issue provoking this conflict was the role of the visiting committees.

Kelso had initially great expectations for the visiting committees, and considered them of equal importance to the Children's Aid Societies. Their primary task, in his view, was to ensure that the foster home system functioned efficiently. In his first annual report he wrote: 'Having adopted the foster home system as the most desirable plan, it was necessary to provide machinery for ascertaining suitable homes and for maintaining some degree of oversight when children were placed out. In Australia, the appointment of committees of ladies and gentlemen, interested in this cause and desirous of aiding in the alleviation of the misfortunes of the children, proved very effective, and this plan has been incorporated in the Ontario law. When fully organized, it is easy to see what a powerful network agency these committees may become ... the children's

visiting committee is the most natural, effective and at the same time economical plan ... two or three postage stamps will often accomplish as much in the way
of finding good homes as could be accomplished by a salaried official travelling
at considerable expense ... I have no doubt but that in this enlightened province
many good people will freely volunteer their services.' In August 1893 he sent a
circular letter to judges, sheriffs, and mayors urging the rapid appointment of
visiting committees. He recommended that those appointed be 'church members, well-known in the district and possessed of some influence among neighbours.' From the start Kelso experienced difficulties in getting the visiting
committees appointed. Only six were in operation at the end of 1893, and,
although this number had grown to twenty-six a year later, he still considered
this to be unsatisfactory progress. At the child-saving conference the effectiveness of the committees was questioned and Kelso was placed in the position of
defending their operation. He told the conference that the visiting committees
were 'almost exclusively a part of the machinery of the central office, each
member being a local correspondent and visitor representing this office, and
altogether guaranteeing that the children placed out under the Act by the
Children's Aid Societies are doing well and are kindly treated.'

There were several reasons for the difficulties experienced by the visiting
committees. Firstly, their role as defined by the act overlapped with that of the
Children's Aid Societies, causing some confusion and animosity on the part of
the nascent societies. Secondly, their method of appointment was inappropriate. Since Kelso was not personally responsible for choosing the visiting committee members, it frequently happened that those chosen had little understanding of what was expected of them and little enthusiasm for their task.
Their contact with Kelso was impersonal and irregular, and he had great
difficulty maintaining contact with them and supervising their work. Thirdly,
and perhaps most importantly, the use of voluntary workers for supervision of
foster homes proved difficult to implement. In part this was simply a matter of
expense. There was no provision in the 1893 act for the payment of travelling
expenses to visiting committee members who frequently had to travel long
distances to visit foster homes. A greater problem was the sensitive nature of
supervision. Writing several years later Kelso claimed 'those Societies that have
tried visiting committees find that the volunteer visitor is not experienced or
tactful enough, is spasmodic in service, and is liable to do as much harm as good.
They do not, as a rule, study the work sufficiently to be experts, nor do they
know the homes where great care has to be exercised to avoid giving offence.
Foster parents object to a local visitor, perhaps a neighbour, calling to see the
child as an inspector, whereas someone coming from a distance and knowing all
about the work is received on an entirely different basis.'

In recognition of these difficulties amendments were made to the Children's Protection Act granting the superintendent a more prominent role in the appointment of the committees. The amendments also clarified the relationship between the committees and Children's Aid Societies. After 1897 the visiting committees were essentially auxiliary committees of Children's Aid Societies, and their importance, which was never great, gradually declined. The function of supervision of children in foster homes could not, however, be ignored. In April 1896 Kelso appointed J. L. Harvie, a woman with experience on the Board of Management of the Hospital for Sick Children, as the first paid visitor of the office of superintendent of neglected and dependent children. Harvie was Kelso's first salaried assistant. Her appointment was an indication of the importance Kelso attached to effective supervision of foster homes. It was also his first concession to the notion that there could not be complete reliance on voluntary effort.

The task officially allocated to Harvie was to visit children in foster homes and generally to assist in the supervision of more than 300 foster children scattered throughout Ontario. Between April and December 1896 she personally visited sixty-two children. In the process she travelled some 1500 miles by rail and over 100 miles on rough and muddy roads. The following year she extended this to 250 visits, travelling well over 2000 miles. In as many homes as possible she arranged to stay the night, or at least to take a meal, in order to become acquainted with the members of the household and observe the home surroundings and the influences being brought to bear on the child. After each visit she wrote a brief report, and if there were any difficulties or problems she wrote to Kelso recommending appropriate action. Her reports provide a clear picture of the criteria she used for deciding whether or not a foster home was satisfactory. She described two homes that made a favourable impression on her in the following manner:

Called to see W., a fine boy of 10 years old, at the farm of Mr. A. The boy was at school, and his foster mother reported him as clever with his studies, and affectionate in disposition. He attends church and Sunday School regularly, and is regarded with much affection. There are no other children in the house, which is a very comfortable and pleasant one.

Visited the residence of Mr. A., in a town in eastern Ontario, the adopted home of a little boy about four years old, was delighted with the appearance of everything within and around the house. The rooms were airy and pleasant, comfortably furnished, with many evidences of taste and refinement visible. J. is a merry, playful little fellow, calls his foster parents mother and father, and is the pet of the household.

Other homes she found less pleasing:

Called at the home of Mr. L. to see J., a girl of twelve. The surroundings were somewhat comfortless, the child not at school, and apparently not receiving much moral or spiritual instruction. Reported to this effect.

Drove to the farm house of Mr. Y., who two years ago adopted a little boy of five. The home is a good one but the foster parents, naturally kind hearted people, had been over-indulgent and the boy, a clever and strong-willed child, had become rude and disobedient. The foster parents were urged to be more firm in dealing with their charge.

Went down to H. to inquire into the surroundings and treatment of M., a girl of fourteen. The home, in some respects, was a good and pleasant one, but the difficulty was that the girl was at times wayward and troublesome, and the foster mother quick-tempered and inclined, when occasion required, to punish with unnecessary severity.

In addition to Harvie, Kelso early in 1896 appointed Reverend James Lediard as part-time children's agent for Grey County. Lediard became one of Kelso's most valued co-workers. He inspected foster homes in the Owen Sound region and undertook many speaking engagements on Kelso's behalf. A similar role was played by Mr S.M. Thomson, a tailor from Brantford. He was appointed as an agent in 1898. Thomson supervised foster home placements arranged by the Brantford and other nearby Children's Aid Societies. Gradually he became a full-time child welfare worker, although he never received a salaried appointment. Some of the larger Children's Aid Societies, such as Toronto, London, Ottawa, and Hamilton, employed full-time agents shortly after their formation. The combined efforts of these agents, Harvie, Lediard, Thomson, and the visiting committees ensured that by the turn of the century almost all children in foster homes were receiving some form of supervision.

Kelso's insistence on the supervision of foster homes reflected his strong public commitment to the foster home concept and his determination to ensure that the Ontario experiment with foster care was a success. Although he had advocated foster care for several years prior to 1893, his appointment as superintendent under an act which made the foster care method mandatory for Children's Aid Societies prompted him to take an even stronger stand on the issue. His support for foster care was based on his belief in the worth and beneficence of a loving, Christian family environment. He wrote to the visiting committees in 1893: 'Remember that these little ones have been wronged, that their forlorn condition does not arise from any fault of their own, that they crave affectionate and forebearing treatment, and that they have a right to receive at the hands of the community a home and a chance to develop their capabilities. Seek for them an entrance into a warm motherly heart and into a home where morality, temperance and industry prevail.' Kelso believed that married couples should accept children from philanthropic and charitable motivation and that their compensation should be viewed in non-material terms. In a brochure issued in 1893 entitled 'Home Wanted,' Kelso stated: 'Experience conclusively proves that to give a homeless child to a Christian couple who have no little ones of their own is to confer a positive blessing upon them. The home is made so much brighter and happier that they never regret the day they threw open their heart's door to the forlorn child in need of love and protection. Therefore we earnestly and confidently appeal for homes for these children. We would like every Christian man and woman to see in the person of each homeless child the blessed Master pleading with them for active personal service. You may not be wealthy, but are you so poor that you cannot give affection to a trusting and loving little heart? God will surely bless those who from pure motives seek to serve Him through these children.' As a corollary to these views, Kelso held strongly to the belief that foster parents should not receive payment for their service, although he conceded that in some circumstances a small sum for expenses was appropriate. However, he considered it quite proper, and indeed desirable, for foster children to help with housework and farmwork, provided they were not overworked and school attendance was regular.

Kelso also insisted on strict enforcement of the rules that natural parents should not be told where their children were placed and that they should not be permitted to visit them. In defending this policy he explained that 'the parents who have to be dealt with are not as a rule the sort of people who could be trusted with the address.' Kelso believed that natural parents, as a consequence of their neglect, forfeited their rights to their children and that strict separation was in the child's best interest. From experiences of having children visit their natural parents he came to the conclusion that the children would again become exposed to the detrimental influences from which they were originally rescued. For these reasons he strongly advocated that full guardianship be secured by Children's Aid Societies for all children cared for in foster homes.

Kelso's enthusiastic support for the foster home method was matched by his vigour in denouncing the institutionalization of neglected and dependent children. In the first two years of his superintendency Kelso was relatively restrained in his opposition to the orphanages and children's homes of the province. On such occasions as the 1894 child-saving conference he was careful not to offend unnecessarily the administrators of the orphanages. However, he did not conceal his view that institutions were a totally inappropriate means of caring for neglected children. In an address to the 1893 World's Congress of American Humane Associations in Chicago he had asserted 'the real happiness of childhood is a quality that is not and cannot be developed in the institution. The rules which are made necessary by the presence of a large number have a stupifying effect on the children, suppressing their natural exuberance of spirit, and making joyousness and light-heartedness practically an offence against the order and dignity of the establishment ... the maintenance of children in public institutions is expensive and on the ground of economy alone a change to the foster home system is desirable.'

As he became more confident in his position as superintendent, and as the Children's Aid Societies became better established, Kelso became even more strident in his criticism of the institutions and unequivocally advocated their closure. In his 1897 annual report he bluntly accused the defenders of the institutions of placing their own interests above those of the children: 'It would certainly be rejected as a most absurd position that the welfare of the building should be placed before the welfare of the children, for whom all the philan-thropic effort is supposed to be expended, and yet I fear that in many instances the children are lost sight of, and the rules, regulations and plans for the aggrandizement of the institution placed far above the interests of the little boys and girls whose hearts crave for a real home, a real mother and a real, instead of artificial, system of work and play.'

Kelso's criticisms, and the work of the Children's Aid Societies, were some-what effective. In 1895 an amendment to the Children's Protection Act was passed permitting the transfer of children from institutions to the care of Children's Aid Societies. Two years later the societies were given supervisory power over adoption placements made by maternity boarding homes. However, there was little decline in the number of children maintained in institutions during the 1890s. Institutions continued to play a major role in accommodating neglected and dependent children at the turn of the century.

By 1900 Kelso had cause for satisfaction with his progress in carrying out his duties under the Children's Protection Act. By that year thirty-two Children's Aid Societies had been established in the province and during the period from 1893 to 1900 a total of 1318 children had been placed in foster homes. Despite the failure of the visiting committees, a comprehensive system of supervision and inspection of foster homes had been established. All this work had been organized almost single-handedly by Kelso at minimum expense. The annual expenditure on his office prior to 1900 never exceeded $6000 – an economy which brought him praise in the legislature but which he strongly resented. Kelso's record was not completely unblemished. He failed to persuade the municipalities to meet their obligations under the 1893 act to finance temporary shelters. Toronto was the only city to establish a shelter during the 1890s. The continuing role of the orphanages was a further disappointment. But overall Kelso's reputation as an energetic administrator was now established. When Sir Oliver Mowat retired as premier of Ontario in 1896 he wrote to Kelso praising his efforts: 'I have no doubt that the success achieved has been largely owing to the zeal and tact with which you have discharged the duties of Superintendent, for which you are entitled to the acknowledgement of all concerned.'

Mowat's views were not shared universally. Although Kelso was widely acknowledged as the leader of the child-saving movement in Ontario, he was not without critics. His main opposition came from the children's institutions and, to a lesser extent, from the municipalities, groups he had severely criticized for their lack of support for his work. His relations with the Toronto Children's Aid Society, never happy since his resignation as president, also remained lukewarm. Although Kelso generally received good press, the *World* and the *Mail* became increasingly critical, adopting the viewpoint that the Children's Aid Societies were infringing on the rights of parents. These newspapers made capital out of instances when disputes arose between natural parents and societies over the custody of children. The *Mail* commented after one case that 'we are unfortunately afflicted with a band of goody-goodies who, if they could only enforce it, would allow no one any liberties but themselves, and think that their individual views are to be enforced at any sacrifice to others.' Kelso, in reply, stressed that his goal was to assist rather than break up families: 'Personally, I do not suppose that anyone who knows me would imagine me likely to steal away anyone's child or do other than help and encourage poor mothers to maintain their children themselves. During the twelve years in which I have been engaged in child-saving I have invariably advocated the improvement of the home life by timely intervention, so that it might not be necessary to have children removed.' This statement made in 1898 represented a modification of his earlier emphasis on the need to separate children decisively from neglectful parents. The *Mail's* criticisms were certainly not without foundation in the light of earlier statements and practices.

Kelso's experiences during the first years of implementing the Children's Protection Act provided him with the opportunity to clarify and refine his views about child welfare methods. He took his task of preparing an annual report about the execution of his duties very seriously; these reports had an average length of over one hundred pages. The reports, described by the *Globe* as 'no ordinary jejune government pamphlets,' conveyed Kelso's deep interest in developing new approaches to child welfare work. By 1900 his views on child care had set into an established pattern. He favoured foster care over institutions, volunteers over paid officials, and measures to ensure the best interests of children over the rights of their parents. He was beginning to stress the value of supporting families and keeping children in their natural home. However, he was adamant that if it was decided to remove a child from its family, separation should be absolute. The parents should give up all rights to communicate with the child or to influence the child's future. Underpinning his whole philosophy was a deep faith in the restorative and enriching influence on young children of an upbringing in a loving, Christian family. For their own benefit, and for the benefit of the community, Kelso's fundamental aim was to place all neglected and dependent children in Ontario with such a family.

Fulfilling his responsibilities as superintendent was in itself a challenging undertaking. However, Kelso continued to take an active interest in a wide range of child welfare issues for which he had no direct responsibility under the Children's Protection Act. He unhesitatingly involved himself in matters beyond his official jurisdiction, using his new position as a platform to press for reforms and to assert his leadership of the child-saving movement. During his early years in office his time was divided between his official duties and other reform activities. Chief among these was the campaign for a separate trial of juvenile offenders.

The 1888 Children's Protection Act, passed by the provincial government at the instigation of Kelso and Beverley Jones, provided for the appointment of special commissioners to hear charges against children under sixteen on behalf of, and in place of, the regular magistrates and judges. The act also provided for the private trial of children in premises other than the courtrooms used for adult criminals. The passage of this act was one of Kelso's first successes. However, it also provided him with his first experience in the difficult task of implementing new legislation. Adoption of the new procedures was not mandatory, and Toronto was the only municipality that showed interest in the appointment of special commissioners. And even in Toronto the provision of separate trials for juveniles was strongly opposed. A motion in November 1889 to appoint com- missioners was defeated. The only progress at this point was the agreement of one of the city magistrates to hold a separate court for children after the adult court adjourned. Those councillors who supported separate trials resubmitted their motion for the appointment of a commissioner in January 1890. This time they were successful and later that month Alderman John Baxter was appointed by the provincial attorney-general as a commissioner to hear children's cases. However, the major flaw of the 1888 legislation now became apparent. The most common charge against children was larceny, an offence under the dominion Criminal Code. After a period of uncertainty it was concluded that the commissioner had no jurisdiction over cases involving dominion law, and thus could deal with only a small minority of juvenile offenders. Kelso and his colleagues consequently redirected their efforts towards amending the dominion statutes to allow for the separate trial of juveniles, regardless of the offence.

The campaign for federal government action began in March 1892 under the auspices of the Toronto Children's Aid Society. On March 29 Kelso submitted a lengthy document to Sir John Thompson, minister of justice, proposing the introduction of separate trial facilities for children and the federal government's active involvement in matters relating to neglected and delinquent children. The letter received only a formal acknowledgment, but later in the year the minister visited Toronto and received a deputation from the Toronto Children's Aid Society. Thompson expressed his support for a separate trial for juveniles, promising federal action. The result was the insertion some months later of the following clause in the Criminal Code: 'The trials of all persons apparently under the age of sixteen years shall, so far as it appears expedient and practicable, take place without publicity, and separately and apart from that of other accused persons, and at suitable times to be designated and appointed for that purpose.' It thus appeared that the constitutional impediment to the separate trial for juveniles had been overcome.

When Kelso became superintendent he made regular visits to Toronto's police court to determine the new federal law's effectiveness. Strictly speaking, this matter was not within his jurisdiction. The 1893 Children's Protection Act reaffirmed the 1888 provision for separate and private trial of young offenders with respect to provincial laws, but gave the superintendent no mandate to enforce these provisions. Nevertheless, this was one of Kelso's long-standing concerns and he spent many mornings during July observing the police court proceedings and discussing the trial of children with police magistrates. He was disappointed with what he found. The Toronto magistrates had all decided that it was not 'expedient and practicable' for them to try children separately. Most children charged with offences continued to be treated in the same manner as adults. Without feeling in any way constrained by his official position, Kelso began a press campaign to expose this practice. During July he contributed articles to many newspapers and magazines describing the events which were taking place in the courts, pointing out that the legislation was not being followed. He stressed the need for reform. In the Toronto *Mail* on 8 July 1893 he recounted the trial of a fourteen-year-old boy charged with stealing firewood: 'There was not a soul in that court to interest himself in that boy. No enquiry was made as to the home surroundings; the magistrate did not know and did not enquire whether he had a home or not; no parent or guardian was asked to become sponsor for his future good conduct, nor was there anything in the trial, so far as I could judge, that would act as a deterrent, except, perhaps the threat of gaol. For adults I am not so much concerned, but for children who are not able to plead their own wrongs, for young girls whose virtue and un-smirched name means their whole life, I would plead for consideration. Give them a chance to grow up honestly. Why should not the law and officers of the law be towards them as a parent, shielding their innocence, reproving their faults, and helping them to improvement without subjecting them to defilement and public exposure?'

Kelso's agitation in the press was not immediately successful. During the next two months he could not maintain his campaign for the separate trials of juveniles owing to the heavy demands and direct responsibilities of the superin-tendency. However, an opportunity to advocate separate trials arose when he visited Chicago in October 1893. The World Columbian Exposition was in progress; in one week Kelso attended the International Humane Congress and the Waif Saving Congress of America. At the latter he was invited to give an address on the progress towards separate juvenile courts in Ontario. In his speech he conveyed the impression that separate courts for children were an accomplished fact: 'The Ontario Children's Law provides for a Children's Court which is in every sense of the word a private court. This court is presided over by a Judge of the Court of record, and every time the child is brought in its parents or guardians must be there also. In case any person has reason to believe that any child is being ill-used all he has to do is to report his suspicions to any person competent to sit in the Children's Court, who thereupon issues a warrant upon which any policeman or county constable or officer of the Children's Aid Society may investigate the matter and summon the parents or guardians to Court.' This was somewhat misleading. The 1893 act did envisage a children's court system and the 1892 amendment to the Criminal Code provided for the separate trial of juvenile offenders. But these provisions had not yet been implemented to the extent that he implied. Nevertheless, Kelso's address received extensive and acclamatory coverage in the Chicago press the following day. At the congress Kelso made the acquaintance of Harvey B. Hurd, who later drafted juvenile court legislation in Illinois and was subsequently appointed as founding judge of the Illinois Juvenile Court. This court, established in 1897, was the first such institution in the United States. Kelso claimed that the publicity surrounding his address and correspondence with Hurd had a decisive influence on the enactment of juvenile court legislation in Illinois and elsewhere in the United States.

On his return to Toronto Kelso resumed his efforts to secure the enforcement of the 1892 amendment to the Criminal Code. On 21 November 1893 he wrote an article for the *Globe*, calling on philanthropic workers and charitable orga-nizations to support a campaign to make separate trial of juvenile offenders mandatory for all police courts. 'The trial of young children in open court on the same footing as adults is one of the greatest wrongs that could be perpetrated, and is a blot upon nineteenth-century civilization,' he wrote. 'Let the agitation become so definite that a remedy may be provided before another session of Parliament ends.' Kelso's strategy was to apply pressure simultaneously at the local level on the police court magistrates and at the federal government level on the minister of justice. The local campaign reached its high point in March 1894 when Kelso, accompanied by the honorary solicitor of the Humane Society, attempted to intervene in the trial of two young girls charged with larceny. This case was used by Kelso as a test case of the 1892 amendment. He graphically described the treatment of the girls in a *Globe* article the following day: 'Two young girls were up in the Police Court yesterday morning charged with larceny. One was thirteen years of age and the other sixteen. They had never been in a police cell or Police Court before. Both were arrested on Saturday night at their homes and were locked up in the station all night. On Sunday morning they were taken in the van with a crowd of adults to the gaol, where they were placed in the same corridor as the women now awaiting trial for abortion. After spending a day and night in the gaol, they were bundled into the "Black Maria" this morning, with about forty others, and were carted to the Police Court to stand trial. They were placed on trial at 11 o'clock in the midst of over 100 men, who had gathered to take in all the interesting features of the show.' As expected, the magistrate refused to accede to Kelso's request that the girls' cases be heard privately and apart from the adult court. The magistrate's argument was that he was only required to treat juveniles differently when it was 'expedient.' In this case he had decided that a special trial was neither convenient nor necessary. Kelso publicized this refusal in articles for the press. The newspapers' reaction was favourable to his campaign. The *Star* commented in an editorial: 'It is not in the interest of good morals that young girls, retained, perhaps, for some misdemeanor should be made to associate, even for a few hours, with convicted thieves and worse criminals. Superintendent Kelso was right in the action he took in the matter.' Taking advantage of this publicity, three days after the trial Kelso drew up a petition to the federal minister of justice. Circulating from his office, and bearing his official letterhead, it read: 'We, the undersigned petitioners, being impressed with the great importance of preventing children – future citizens – from drifting into crime, would humbly pray that legislation may be introduced during the present session of Parliament, making it obligatory upon all courts and municipalities to provide for the separate trial and confinement of youthful offenders, and the establishment in large cities of the probation system of dealing with such children.' The response was encouraging. Over 1000 signatures were collected. These were promptly forwarded to Ottawa for consideration by the minister of justice.

It is difficult to determine the influence of the petition since there had already been some discussion of this matter in Ottawa. However, a few months later Senator G.W. Allan introduced a bill which provided, among other matters, for the 'separation of youthful offenders from contact with older offenders and habitual criminals during their arrest and trial.' This bill was enacted in July 1894 as the Youthful Offenders Act. To ensure that the government's intent was clearly understood and would be implemented, the Criminal Code was amended. The 1892 clause concerning juvenile offenders was replaced with this section: 'The trials of young persons apparently under the age of sixteen years shall take place without publicity and separately and apart from the trials of other accused persons, and at suitable times to be designated and appointed for that purpose.'

Even with these enactments the struggle for separate trial of juveniles in Ontario was far from over. Magistrates and judges throughout Ontario generally ignored the federal laws, claiming the failure of the municipalities to provide proper facilities for separate trial. Throughout the 1890s Kelso continued to press unsuccessfully for implementation of the 1894 legislation in Ontario. As late as 1898 he was still urging that the legislation establishing separate trial 'be constantly brought to the attention of the magistrates and court officials and every effort be made to secure observance of the spirit as well as the letter of the law.' It was not until the next decade that separate trials for juveniles throughout Ontario became an established policy.

By the mid-1890s Kelso was widely recognized as Canada's leading expert in child welfare matters. Ontario was the first Canadian province to implement legislation to deal with neglected and dependent children; Kelso's experience and success as superintendent was unmatched by anyone else in the country. Consequently, when the Manitoba government decided in 1898 to introduce new child protection laws, it was to Kelso that it turned for advice. Early in that year the Hon. J.D. Cameron, attorney-general of Manitoba, invited Kelso to visit Winnipeg to assist in the drafting of a Children's Protection Act. For Kelso it was an opportunity to visit Western Canada for the first time and to spread his views on child welfare in another province. On 22 March he left Toronto for the western trip – an opportunity for work and pleasure.

The railway route from Toronto to Winnipeg passed through Detroit, Chicago, and St Paul. Kelso used the trip as an opportunity for sight-seeing and for making contact with colleagues. In St Paul he called on Mr H.H. Hart, a leading figure in the United States child-saving movement, and visited the Minnesota Board of Charities and Corrections. He arrived in Winnipeg on Friday, 25 March, where he was met by J. L. Sifton, the inspector of public institutions, and D. McIntyre, inspector of schools. His first speaking engagement was on

Sunday evening when he spoke to six hundred children at the Grace Methodist Sunday School. This was followed the next morning by the most important function of his trip, an address to the members of the Manitoba legislature. In his speech he outlined the work which had been accomplished in Ontario, stressing the superiority of foster homes over institutions, the economy of Ontario's approach to child-saving, and the success which had been achieved in 'transforming incipient criminals into good citizens.' The address was well received. The *Winnipeg Free Press* commented that all that would be required after passage of a Manitoba Children's Protection Act would be the appointment of another Kelso to direct its operation. After his address he spent several hours conferring with legal officers from the attorney-general's department about a draft of a proposed Children's Protection Act for Manitoba. The next few days were spent meeting and talking with various groups interested in child protection work. Kelso visited schools and churches and spoke with the administrators of children's homes and provincial government officers. Between Monday and Thursday he gave fifteen addresses in addition to interviews and conferences. Two public meetings held in the evenings were particularly well attended. Kelso's slide lecture on 'child-saving' was as well received in Winnipeg as it had been throughout Ontario. Manitobans were evidently impressed by Kelso's message. Shortly after he left Winnipeg a Children's Protection Act was introduced into the provincial legislature. The act, which was closely modelled on the 1893 Ontario act, was assented to on 27 April 1898. Two months later the Children's Aid Society of Winnipeg was organized.

During his week in Winnipeg Kelso received a telegram from the Hon. J. Baker, the provincial secretary of British Columbia, inviting him to extend his western tour by coming to Victoria to consult with the British Columbia government about child-saving work. This was further recognition of Kelso's knowledge and experience; he accepted the invitation with enthusiasm. He left Winnipeg on 31 March, arriving in Victoria after a three-day train journey through the Dakotas, Montana, and Washington. He was treated as a celebrity. Premier Turner suspended the business of the legislature to permit Kelso to address the members in the legislative chambers. The speech was a great success, receiving prolonged applause. No immediate action was taken by the British Columbia government to pass child protection legislation, partly because of an impending provincial election. However, the groundwork was laid and contacts made. In 1902 British Columbia enacted a Children's Protection Act closely modelled on the Ontario legislation. While in British Columbia Kelso also visited Vancouver and addressed a public meeting about the need for a Children's Aid Society in that city. Three years later such a group was formed. Now that he was on the west coast Kelso decided to take advantage of the opportunity to visit California. This trip was undertaken primarily for pleasure, but Kelso spent some time studying the local system of caring for neglected children. While there his criticisms of the state's children's institutions were widely quoted in the press. After a few days he travelled back to Toronto exhilarated and refreshed by his six-week trip.

Kelso's success in implementing the Children's Protection Act resulted in the Ontario government extending his duties. In 1897 the new position of inspector of juvenile immigration agencies was added to his responsibilities. This appointment thrust Kelso into the centre of another controversial issue, involving the welfare of children and the economic and social development of Canada.[1]

The importation of British waifs into Canada began in 1869 when fifty young girls from a workhouse near Liverpool were brought to a receiving home at Niagara-on-the-Lake, Ontario, by Maria S. Rye, who had previously organized the emigration of domestic servants to Canada and Australia. The girls were placed with families in various parts of Ontario. The scheme received favourable publicity within Canada and further parties of workhouse children were sent to Rye from England during the following years. By 1875 Rye had brought 202 boys and 1102 girls to Canada, ranging in age from six months to fourteen years. Other British child-saving organizations became involved and by 1874 more than a dozen British agencies were sending over 1000 children to Canada each year. By 1897 28,945 children had been brought to Ontario in this way, and at least a further 10,000 had been placed in homes in other parts of Canada.

Three-quarters of the children who arrived in Canada by this means were from private or church orphanages and rescue homes. The remainder were wards of the Poor Law workhouse. The movement reflected a mixture of economic and humanitarian concerns. The juvenile immigration agencies viewed the project as an effective means of rescuing dependent children from their deprived surroundings in the British industrial cities. At the same time, the immigrant children undoubtedly helped to meet a strong demand for farm workers in Ontario. It was generally recognized and accepted that most households which applied for British children were motivated to do so by the need for farm labour. Between 1870 and the turn of the century the demand for child workers continued to outstrip the supply of British children.

The overseas placement of waifs came under strong criticism in Britain during the 1870s. In response, the British government sent Mr Andrew Doyle, an experienced official of the Local Government Board, to Canada in 1874 to report on the issue. Doyle's report, published in 1875, severely criticized the juvenile immigration agencies, claiming that children were often poorly treated in the receiving homes and family homes in which they were placed. He expressed doubt about the value of the juvenile immigration and recommended that if the schemes were continued, the receiving and adoptive homes should be regularly inspected by persons independent from the immigration agencies. His views were sharply challenged by Canadian authorities who, in the 1870s, strongly supported the work of Rye and her colleagues. This support, backed by public opinion in Ontario, reflected the shortage of labour in rural areas in a period of generally declining immigration.[2] These children were viewed as valuable help on the farms. However, in the late 1880s attitudes began to change. The new concern about the social and moral surroundings of Canadian children created opposition to child immigration. It was claimed that the immigrant children, 'the offal of the most depraved characters in the cities of the old country,' as one Ontario member of parliament described them, corrupted other young people with whom they associated. It was also feared that the young immigrants were most likely to grow up to be criminals. The case against the continued immigration of waifs was put forcibly in the report of the 1890 Ontario Royal Commission on the Prison and Reformatory System. After hearing the views of many witnesses, the commissioners concluded: 'The importation of children taken from the reformatories, refuges and workhouses of the old world is fraught with much danger and calculated, unless conducted with care and prudence, to swell the ranks of the criminal class in this country.' They recommended that if juvenile immigration continued, precautions should be taken to prevent the immigration of children of known criminal parents and of children who had 'spent their whole lives in an atmosphere of vice and crime; who are so saturated with evil and know so little of good.' Opposition to the immigration of waifs also came from the labour movement, particularly the Toronto Trades and Labour Council, which was concerned that juvenile immigrants would flood the Canadian labour market and drive down wages.

Kelso's first extensive contact with the issue was during his reporting of the 1890 Royal Commission for the *Globe*. He was initially inclined to support the commission's opposition to juvenile immigration. He shared the concern that a criminal class was being imported into Canada but he also felt that too little attention had been paid to the problems and treatment of the children involved. Prior to 1890 the welfare of the immigrant waifs received scant consideration in the Canadian debates. When Kelso became superintendent in 1893 he made it clear that he interpreted his responsibility for neglected and dependent children as including those children boarded out by the immigration agencies. He told the meeting held in Ottawa in September 1893 to organize a Children's Aid Society that 'some of the worst cruelties perpetrated in this country are in the case of children brought out from Britain and placed in houses where there is no one to protect their interests and where they are shamefully overworked. Many of these children are nothing but white slaves, made to get up long before daylight and to work until late at night and deprived of the pleasures and advantages of childhood.' Later in 1893 he corresponded with several juvenile immigration agencies and read their reports and statistics. He also visited a number of farms where British waifs were placed. These investigations led him to review his initial opinions. In his first annual report he claimed that 'the benefit to the province, generally, of juvenile immigration far outweighs the attendant evils.' On the basis of his investigations he concluded very few of the immigrant children became criminals, stating that the wide publicity given to a few cases had blinded the eyes of many people to 'the immense number of children who have done well and are now useful and respected members of society, saved from the degradation in which they were born and lifted to self-respecting citizenship.' The only criticisms made by Kelso were the inadequacy of the supervision of the children once they were placed in homes and the general need for greater government regulation of the work.

These views were reinforced by Kelso's visit in April 1894 to the reception centre for immigrant children run by Dr Barnardo's Homes. A party of 185 boys had just arrived from England. Kelso's notebook records that he was 'favourably impressed with their appearance and manner. Most of them seemed a good class, healthy and strong, and I think they will do well.' Later in the year he made a similar visit to the Dr Barnardo's Home for English Girls where eighty-five girls had recently arrived. Kelso's impression was once again favourable: 'Some of them seemed to bear in their faces the inherited seeds of vice, but the majority appeared to be happy and well-dispositioned children.'

The immigration of British children was one of the most controversial matters raised at the child-saving conference in 1894. Kelso did not take a leading role in the debate. The strongest statements came from D.J. O'Donoghue, a leading spokesman for organized labour, and the delegates from the immigration agencies. O'Donoghue argued that Canada already had enough dependent children of its own to look after. He also claimed that immigrant children frequently became criminals, involving governments in considerable expense, and that immigrant children were competing with native men and children for jobs. According to O'Donoghue many men in the labour movement were brought to Canada as British waifs and 'their stories of the treatment they received in the country places before they reached the age of manhood are of a character to make an ordinary Christian's blood curdle.' Other speakers presented information refuting the claim that the waifs typically became criminals. The immigration agencies claimed that their children turned out 'as well, if not better than the average Canadian-born child.' The agencies received support from other delegates who appealed to charitable motives: 'We should not, because they are little waifs and strays from beyond the sea, get a platform of excitement against them. Do not let us turn our faces against them, but let us do all we can to save them and build them up as they go along.'

Kelso regularly discussed the juvenile immigration issue in his reports and speeches between 1893 and 1897. At this time he was attempting to develop an adequate system of supervision over the children in the care of the Children's Aid Societies. He was concerned that similar supervision be provided of immigrant children in their new homes. He continued to support juvenile immigration but now stressed the importance of government regulation of the work of the juvenile immigration agencies. This was the theme of his discussion of juvenile immigration in his 1896 annual report. He advocated government inspection of the immigration agencies, guarantees by the agencies that only healthy and normal children would be brought into the country, and the employment of sufficient staff to supervise the children in their new homes. He also proposed that any expenses incurred by the provincial government as a result of an immigrant child becoming a public ward should be met by the immigration agency concerned. These views were consistent with Kelso's growing belief in the need for government regulation of voluntary effort on behalf of neglected and dependent children.

The Act to Regulate Juvenile Immigration, passed by the Ontario legislature in 1897, adopted these proposals. The act required the licensing of persons or agencies engaged in juvenile immigration and stipulated that agencies be inspected four times a year. The agencies were ordered to maintain records of children they brought to Ontario and to supervise the children until they reached the age of eighteen. They were required to maintain a proper reception centre that could also be used in circumstances in which children were returned from their foster homes. It was made an offence for any agency to bring into Ontario 'any child who, from defective intellect or physical infirmity, is unable to follow any trade or calling, or any child of known vicious tendencies or who has been convicted of crime.' Moreover, if any child became dependent upon a municipality or the province within three years of arriving in the country the agency could be required to pay the cost of maintenance. The families receiving children were also regulated by the act. It was made an offence to turn a child adrift if the placement was not satisfactory. The rights of immigrant children to attend the province's public schools were affirmed. The agencies were given the duty of promptly investigating reports of ill-treatment and overwork and of laying charges against foster parents guilty of these offences. Finally, a post of overseas examiner was created to examine children before they left Britain to ensure their suitability.

Kelso's first task after appointment as inspector of juvenile immigration agencies was the preparation of a special report on the issue. This report, presented to the provincial government on 15 December 1897 was the most comprehensive study of juvenile immigration prepared in Canada since 1876. In the report Kelso stressed his belief that much of the opposition to the immigration of waifs was based on prejudice and sensationalism: 'In the absence of any law on the subject, or any government officer holding direct control of the work, isolated cases, vague reports and hearsay stories, become settled beliefs, until today there are thousands of good people united in condemnation of the whole movement, who base this condemnation entirely on what they have heard or read in the newspapers.' He stressed that the campaign against juvenile immigration had been 'tremendously hurtful' to the children involved, 'many of whom are handicapped in their desire to live uprightly by the wholesale abuse and misrepresentation to which they have been subject.' Kelso made clear his support for the new act. He stressed the importance of supervision of foster homes, claiming that 'children have gone astray in the past and others had been abused, who would probably have acted and been treated all right had a close supervision been maintained by those responsible for them.' He saw no objection to children working for the families with whom they were placed, expressing his belief that 'farm work should be healthful and enjoyable employment for young people, if the employers are reasonable and kindly disposed.' He concluded:

It is with some hesitation that I have prepared this report knowing, as I do so well, the strong feeling of hostility to child immigration that prevails in many sections of Ontario. Nevertheless, I have regarded it only right to set forth the conclusions that formed themselves in my mind after reviewing this work from all standpoints. Those conclusions are, briefly, that child immigration, if carried on with care and discretion, need not be injurious to the best interests of this country. There has been some poor work in the past, and some undesirable features, but there has also been much that was good and commendable. If the present Ontario Act is faithfully observed by the various agencies, and properly administered by the officials having it in charge, many of the objections now urged should be removed. The children in their persons should be free from disease or taint of criminality, and their treatment here should be such as to surround them with every desirable safeguard, and thus ensure them becoming good citizens.

This assertion of the value of juvenile immigration and of the wisdom of the new act placed Kelso in the position of chief apologist for the Ontario government's policy. Criticism of the policy came from many quarters, including organizations as politically diverse as the Toronto Trades and Labour Council and the Hamilton Canadian Club. The immigration agencies felt that the 1897 act would seriously hamper their work. Their objections were well publicized in the British press and even in the British House of Commons. In defence, Kelso wrote to one English critic: 'There are now some ten agencies extensively engaged in the work of bringing orphan and abandoned children from Great Britain to Ontario, and surely we are justified in taking steps to ascertain that the work is honestly and legitimately carried on. We know from experience that all the children brought here do not turn out well, and this we believe to be partially the fault of those who, in their desire to emigrate a wayward or erring child, do not altogether consider the interests of the country to which he is sent ... It is not our desire or intention to debar any healthy, respectable child from the privileges of citizenship, but it is our aim to prevent in any way possible the deterioration of our people by the introduction of diseased or vicious children, and neglect of supervision on the part of those engaging in the work.'

After several years of observing the effectiveness of the 1897 act Kelso's belief in the value of properly regulated juvenile immigration was unwavering. In a newspaper article written in 1905 he reiterated the view that juvenile immigration was advantageous for the child, the foster parents, and, ultimately, Canadian society. 'Our greatest need is population,' Kelso's article concluded. 'We have a great country, with vast resources, and it would be a grave mistake to shut out these young people who, in a few short years, will become industrious men and women, thoroughly Canadian and British, and doubly valuable because of the moral tone and industrious habits acquired on our Canadian farms.'

In the early years of the twentieth century Canadian interest in juvenile immigration declined, and defending government policy in this area ceased to be a major concern for Kelso. In 1900 the dominion government established a special division to supervise these children and in his 1907 report Kelso noted that juvenile immigration had become the responsibility of the dominion government. The issue became prominent again after the First World War but by that time the Ontario government had repealed its legislation and Kelso was no longer a key figure.

Kelso's achievements between 1893 and 1900 were the most lasting and fruitful of his career. He took full advantage of the broad responsibilities conferred on him by the Children's Protection Act. The network of Children's Aid Societies he established remained as the basis of Ontario's child welfare system into the twentieth century. Supervised foster homes, placed on a firm footing by Kelso, also became a permanent feature of child welfare policy in Ontario. Kelso's important role during these years was to implement the policies arising from the changing conceptions of childhood adopted by many Canadians in the late nineteenth century. His own views reflected these new notions. He viewed children as impressionable creatures, whose potential was dependent upon the care with which they were raised. Apart from a small minority who had 'inherited the seeds of vice,' children were potentially upright and productive citizens if the correct influences were brought to bear. The best environment, in Kelso's view, was a loving, Christian home 'where morality, temperance, and industry prevail.' He believed that if neglected and dependent children were provided with such homes future generations would experience sharply reduced rates of crime and pauperism. For Kelso child protection was a major strategy of social reform.

Kelso's views on specific child welfare policies stemmed from these basic beliefs. He opposed institutional care of children because institutions were artificial and could not substitute for a 'real home.' He advocated decisive and permanent removal of children from 'unsatisfactory' homes because he was convinced this was the way to save the child from a criminal or immoral life. He campaigned for separate trial of juveniles to ensure that children charged with offences were not subjected to further pernicious influences. He supported juvenile immigration provided the waifs were carefully placed with good families and were properly supervised.

Despite his successes as superintendent, Kelso was never completely reconciled to the role of government official. He was well suited to the task of promoting and encouraging the formation of Children's Aid Societies but routine administration and the need to observe bureaucratic procedures and guidelines were not to his liking. He preferred the image of 'Children's friend' to that of 'government official.' He did not let his official position restrict his activities as a social reformer but rather used the superintendency to further promote his campaigns. He remained wary of government involvement in charitable work. He was committed to the view that child-saving was the responsibility of private citizens. Government, he believed, should assist, but never supplant, voluntary organizations.

5

Rescuing Juvenile Offenders

In 1900 the main features of the child welfare system outlined in the Children's Protection Act were established. Kelso's work as superintendent was settling into a routine pattern. While in Toronto his office hours – ten until four – were light, but this was not the full extent of his work. His duties also involved extensive travel around the province, inspecting the work of the Children's Aid Societies and addressing public meetings about child welfare work. He enjoyed these opportunities to see the countryside, meet friends, make new acquaintances, and exercise his talents as a speaker and organizer. Office work was less enjoyable. January and February were especially trying since he was obliged to concentrate his efforts on the preparation of his annual report. He complained about the difficulties of this task in a February 1899 letter to Irene Martin: 'Getting up a report is quite an undertaking for it requires a lot of wise thinking to decide what to say and what not to say. One has to use so much policy in this world to try and please everyone and at the same time to adhere to what you believe is the right course.'

Kelso's correspondence with Irene Martin, the Nashville woman who had impressed him at the 1891 American Humane Association Convention, resumed at the beginning of 1899 after a break of over five years. The two had met again in 1894 during one of Kelso's visits to the United States, and this meeting had rekindled their friendship. But after a brief flurry of letter writing, they both became distracted by other events. After their resumption of correspondence Kelso visited Irene in early summer 1899, and the couple planned a rendezvous in Detroit later in the year, and a possible engagement.

Kelso's renewed interest in the prospect of marriage stemmed in part from dissatisfaction with his complete absorption in public life. His private affairs had for some time been static and uninteresting. He was still living at home with his mother and had little social life other than that arising from his public position. The strains of official duties and the problems he observed in his work made him occasionally depressed. He longed for other outlets. He told Irene early in 1899: 'My work has many advantages and is the means of greatly benefitting both children and the community but there is also much responsibility and many heavy cares and anxieties. One trouble is that I have to listen to so many tales of suffering, misery and vice that my own heart gets weighed down beneath the load.' A year later, when their engagement had been arranged, Kelso again wrote of his wish to devote more time to his private life: 'Our most sensational paper had an article a short time ago saying that I was altogether too active in the moral reform line and that I should not worry so much about other people's children. I suppose there is a good deal of truth in this for when you are living in Toronto I shall be so anxious to hurry home I shall not want to do any work at all.'

Kelso's meeting with Irene Martin in Detroit took place in September. They became engaged, initially planning a wedding for the summer of 1900. However, circumstances made this impossible. The main problem was the strong opposition of Irene's mother, whose objections were partly that Toronto was so far away and, more importantly, that Kelso was not of sufficient social standing and means to marry her daughter. The Martins were a fairly well-to-do Southern family who had made their money in cotton. They were unimpressed with Kelso's position as a salaried official responsible for neglected children. Their strong opposition to the marriage was at first resisted by Kelso who was grieved by the Martins' attitude that he was not a suitable match for their daughter. In a letter to Irene in December 1899 he wrote: 'It hurts my sense of pride to have your relations look upon your engagement to me as a thing to be regretted and deplored. If I did not love you very dearly, I would not tolerate such a condition of things.' However, in April 1900 he reluctantly agreed to a year's postponement of the wedding. The letters he wrote to Irene afterwards made frequent mention of his distress that his income, position, and family background were considered inadequate by her family.

Kelso's intent to marry, and the snub he received from the Martins, led him in early 1900 to redouble his efforts to have his salary raised from $1500 to $2000. Kelso had been dissatisfied with his salary from the start of his public service career, but efforts to secure increases had been only slightly successful. He clearly considered the matter to be of utmost importance. Many times in letters to Irene he expressed his belief that the only possible drawback to their marriage was lack of money. Kelso was not especially hard pressed at this time. His salary was well above the average income of Torontonians. He owned two properties, the Long Branch cottage and a house on Beaconsfield Avenue. Nevertheless, he deeply wished to provide his fiancée with the comforts and luxuries to which she was accustomed and to better his own style of life.

Kelso's attempt to gain an increase in salary was, however, severely criticized, and brought the work of his office into some public disrepute. His application was supported by a deputation to Premier Ross, composed of Kelso's friends and colleagues. Some newspapers, such as the *Evening News*, supported Kelso's claims and complimented him on his work, but others such as the *World* expressed extreme criticism: 'Mr. Kelso's ambitious plans are well known ... his department should be raised to full dignity, independence and emolument with the other departments such as the Attorney-General's, the Provincial Secretary's and the rest. Mr. Kelso should then be taken into the Cabinet at a salary of $5,000. The title of the new minister might be the Hon. Provincial Kidnapper. His responsibilities would rapidly increase and his social influence would fast become enormous. It would be the duty of the Hon. Provincial Kidnapper to make the visible supply of children go round, and allow the women who won't follow the example of Mother Eve to get their babies ready-made from the Government. It is a grand outlook. It would break down the medieval superstition about parental rights. It would bring the era of socialism ever so much nearer and would make Ontario the pioneer in the glorious cause.'

The salary application, and its bearing on his marriage prospects, were uppermost in Kelso's mind during March and April 1900. In late March, still hoping to be married in the summer, Kelso communicated his anxieties to Irene: 'I have gone through a great deal of publicity in order to get a good increase and although nearly all the criticism was exceedingly flattering still it is not very nice to be too much in the public eye. I do not yet know how I will fare but I will not get as much as I want or deserve as it is too great a jump for the government. If I come off with an advance of $300, that is to $1,800, I will not do so badly. Anything less than that will be a great disappointment, but there is no use being too sanguine.' These doubts proved to be well-founded, for in late April Kelso received word that the government, apparently taking offence to the delegation, had refused to grant him any increase whatsoever. It was a crushing disappointment, and throughout the year he continued to worry about his financial affairs.

During the summer of 1900 a further sadness came into Kelso's life. His mother was ill. Kelso was thirty-six years old, and having lived with his mother all his life he felt a great loss when she died in October. During the winter of 1900–1 he lived alone, employing a housekeeper. This arrangement was only temporary. The Martins decided to accept the inevitable and agreed to their daughter's marriage. On 25 June 1901, with the consent if not the blessing of the Martin family, Kelso was married to Irene Maddin Martin at the home of the bride's parents. The Kelsos returned to Toronto and spent their first weeks of marriage in temporary quarters in a rooming house in Surrey Place, near the Parliament Buildings. After a short period they moved to a nearby house on St Vincent's Street. This was their winter home until 1907. In November of that year Kelso purchased half of a semi-detached house at 21 Prince Arthur Avenue, formerly the official residence of the chancellor of McMaster University. It was a large three-storey home with a spacious garden, only a ten-minute walk from the Parliament Buildings. The Kelsos enjoyed living in this house, remaining there until 1923.

The Kelsos' first child, Martin MacMurray, was born in Nashville on 29 March 1902. A daughter followed in September 1903 but after only eight months she incurred a fatal illness. In 1905 another daughter, Irene, was born. The marriage experienced early tensions. Mrs Kelso had considerable difficulty adjusting to her new surroundings in Toronto, and longed for the Southern way of life with which she was more familiar. During the first years of the marriage she made frequent and lengthy trips to Nashville. This was a sadness and a disappointment for Kelso. 'I admit I have miserably failed to make you happy,' he wrote to his wife while he was travelling in the United States in May 1906. 'I cannot yet convince myself that you wish to leave me or that your love for relatives is greater than it is for me.' This was a low point in the Kelsos' relationship but matters gradually improved.

Kelso's preoccupation with personal concerns did not distract him from reform pursuits. Now that the foundations of the Children's Aid Society work were established, there was a shift in the focus of his activities. Between 1899 and 1908 he concentrated his efforts on improving the treatment of children already in trouble with the law.

Kelso's responsibility for juvenile offenders under the 1893 act was limited, although this had not prevented him from taking an active role in the campaign for separate trial of juveniles. However, he did have formal responsibility for the inspection of industrial schools as well as institutions that aimed to reform children under fourteen who had been found guilty of petty crimes or who were considered to be potentially delinquent. The major advantage claimed for the industrial schools over other types of institutions for juvenile offenders was the 'cottage system.'[1] Under this system relatively small numbers of children resided in cottage homes under the care of a matron and guard, a married couple who acted as 'mother' and 'father' of the 'family.' Within each cottage the children were trained in trades or housekeeping tasks, attended day and Sunday school, and participated in drill and sports. Within a few years of the opening of the first industrial school in Toronto in 1887 the industrial school system was well established. When Kelso became superintendent in 1893 there were two industrial schools in Toronto with a combined population of approximately two hundred children. Amendments to the Criminal Code in 1890 gave magistrates the power to sentence children to the industrial schools for offences against dominion as well as provincial laws. By 1893 the Industrial School Association was actively encouraging judges, magistrates, and court attorneys to send juvenile offenders to the industrial schools.

Kelso's attitude to the industrial schools reflected several contradictory pressures. These schools arose from the same reform impulse as the Toronto Humane Society and the Toronto Children's Aid Society. Many of Kelso's colleagues in those organizations, including Beverley Jones, were leading figures in the Industrial School Association, and Kelso himself advocated the extension of these schools to the 1890 Royal Commission on Prisons and Reformatories. Central to the industrial school movement was the idea of providing a constructive environment for children on the point of drifting into crime. Kelso readily agreed with this notion. He viewed industrial schools as far superior institutions to the Penetanguishene Reformatory where many juvenile offenders were imprisoned. On the other hand, he strongly opposed institutional care for children, and was suspicious of industrial schools on this argument alone, despite the proclaimed merits of the cottage plan. Moreover, as the official responsible for the development of the Children's Aid Societies and the extension of foster care, his duties overlapped and to a degree conflicted with the administrators of the industrial schools. The 1893 act gave magistrates power to commit children guilty of minor offences or predisposed to a criminal career to a Children's Aid Society, an industrial school, or the reformatory. The Children's Aid Societies and the industrial schools were, in this respect, rival organizations.

Kelso's difficulty in reconciling these conflicting pressures was apparent in his first report as superintendent. He encouraged magistrates to commit boys to the industrial school rather than the reformatory: 'The industrial school with its kindly influences and home-like surroundings is particularly calculated to benefit and reform lads under fifteen, and can do all the work in this line that is necessary.' At the same time he emphasized the superiority of foster homes over both the industrial schools and the reformatory: 'There is a large demand in all sections of the province for the services of growing boys, and good homes are constantly offered where the lads would receive every kindness and consideration, with schooling half the year, or, in the case of older boys, moderate wages. It is a question whether many of the boys now in our industrial school and some in the reformatory would not do well in one of these homes, and be better prepared here for the real work of life than they could possibly be in the best reform school ever established.'

This ambivalence characterized Kelso's approach to the industrial schools throughout his career. In 1897 he instigated a major controversy by sharply criticizing the industrial schools in his annual report. The number of children in industrial schools had been declining. Kelso attributed this to the popularity of the Children's Aid movement and the simplicity and economy of its methods. His analysis may have been correct but he caused offence by the forcefulness of his remarks. He described the industrial schools as places 'where no permanent attachments can be formed, and where the highest incentives to nobility of life and conduct are lacking.' He asserted that the home-finding movement had been 'recognized on consideration to be the only true and correct principle in dealing with dependent youth.' There was a vocal and angry reaction by the advocates of industrial schools. Kelso was accused of inconsistency and immaturity, and the board of the Victoria Industrial School established a committee to refute Kelso's report. This dispute estranged Kelso from the leaders of the industrial schools. His relations with them from this time were strained and uneasy at best.

After this incident Kelso attempted to placate the Industrial School Boards by complimenting their work and suggesting that there was a place for industrial schools in the child-saving movement. In his 1898 report on these schools he wrote: 'The three industrial schools for the training and care of wayward or incorrigible children have been doing good work during the past year, and are filling a very necessary and important place in the general work of child-saving. There will always be children who have been neglected too long and for whom a course of training is necessary before they can be placed in family homes. There are, too, children who are guilty of repeated offences and as a punishment their temporary commitment is decided upon. Everything of a prison character or tendency is carefully avoided in these schools, and the children have been aided and encouraged in every possible way in the development of self respect and sterling character.' This praise was sustained in later reports, although Kelso continually stressed the importance of the personal rather than the institutional features of the schools. He objected to the grey and red uniforms worn by the boys at the Victoria Industrial School: 'However disguised it may be, the distinctive dress is a prison badge; the boys realize this, and it is a stumbling block to their reformation.' He emphasized the need for 'a high moral atmosphere' in the schools and the need to keep high ideals before the children: 'As the children are quick to discern character, and to copy the example of those over them, they should only be surrounded by instructors who are fully in touch with child life, and are actuated by motives of compassion and love. It is for this reason I believe that the schools are being efficiently conducted, for in my visits to these institutions I have been greatly impressed by the deep interest taken in their work by all the officers from the highest to the lowest.'

Although Kelso tolerated the existence of industrial schools, he continued to argue that only a limited number of children be committed to the schools. When their population rose sharply in 1901 he returned to the attack. 'The natural tendencies of all institutions is to increase both in size and number,' he wrote. 'There should be a constant effort put forth to decrease the number of those who have to be placed under restraint and discipline.' One of his main concerns was the long period of time children were being kept in the industrial schools. He gave his support to an amendment to the Industrial Schools Act in 1900 which provided that a child had to be given a chance outside the institution after a maximum of three years' confinement. However, he also supported a parallel amendment which introduced the indeterminate sentence for industrial school inmates. This provision established that Industrial School Boards had guardianship over all children committed to the schools until they were eighteen years old. Kelso considered it crucial for boards to be granted this power to avoid injudicious interference of parents: 'Many of the children who do well in the industrial and reform schools and who fall away afterwards, do so through being returned to their former wretched home and environment. This will always be a perplexing problem in child-saving work. One's natural desire is to seek to reunite the home and yield to the importunities of parents, and yet this yielding through kindly motives has often been the cause of children drifting into wrong-doing and becoming after a time confirmed and irreclaimable criminals and vagrants.' To facilitate the adjustment of children after they left the industrial school Kelso advocated better supervision, and he proposed that the schools take advantage of the province-wide system of supervision available through the Children's Aid Societies.

Although Kelso was ambivalent towards the industrial schools, he clearly considered them far preferable to the Penetanguishene Reformatory for Boys. The reformatory, located on the shores of Georgian Bay, was established in 1859 as an institution to reform delinquent boys. Prior to 1859 children convicted of offences were imprisoned in adult institutions. The founding of the reformatory was hailed as a major advance. For a number of years the reformatory enjoyed a reputation as an enlightened institution. However, in 1867 J.W. Langmuir was appointed inspector of prisons and reformatories for the newly formed Province of Ontario. For the first time the reformatory was subjected to close scrutiny by an external agent. Langmuir was unimpressed by what he saw. The reformatory was being operated as an adult prison, the boys were locked in cells most of the time when not working or eating. The major emphasis was on work: construction activities, road-building, quarrying, lumbering, farming, brick-making, tailoring, and cabinet-making. Very little time was devoted to education. The buildings, with their high stone walls and iron bars, were totally unsuited to the needs of a boys' reformatory. The water supply and sanitation systems were completely inadequate. Langmuir wrote: 'The appearance of the building is that of a prison; the interior construction is that of a prison; the discipline is that of a prison; the dress is that of convicts.'

At Langmuir's instigation the provincial government in 1880 introduced sweeping changes to the administration of the reformatory. A new superintendent was appointed, dormitories were built to replace individual cells, and adequate bathing and heating facilities were provided. Greater stress was placed on education. Officials were encouraged by Langmuir to 'exercise the greatest kindness, patience, forebearance and well-directed zeal in the performance of their duties.' For a few years these policies were implemented but in the late 1880s the momentum of reform slackened and criticism of the institution was renewed. The 1890 Royal Commission on the Prison and Reformatory System recommended sweeping reform, including removal of the institution to a more suitable location, reorganization into smaller cottages, and re-emphasis on educational objectives. These recommendations ushered in a period of great uncertainty for the reformatory's administrators. During the 1890s the advances of the industrial schools and Children's Aid Societies resulted in a steady decline in the number of committals to the reformatory. By the turn of the century its closure was under serious consideration by government ministers and officials.

As early as 1890, in evidence to the Royal Commission on the Prison and Reformatory System, Kelso recommended the closing of Penetanguishene Reformatory, describing it as a 'relic of a past age.' However, during his early months as superintendent he visited Penetanguishene and reported that the institution had been badly misrepresented. 'I am quite prepared to say that the school is in good condition and is doing good work. The reformatory is not intended for young boys under thirteen years, but for all youths which the industrial school cannot handle. It is as good a home and school as could well be designed having regard to safety and discipline. The boys who go there are, as a rule, pretty far advanced in crime, but notwithstanding this many of them do well on discharge.' The *Globe* quoted him: 'We have no hesitation in recommending the reformatory as a proper and desirable place for boys who are past the industrial school age, or have got beyond the control of primary institutions.'

Kelso's support for the reformatory at this time was surprising given his strong anti-institutional views, but his praise did not last long. Between 1893 and 1898 he paid little attention to Penetanguishene. However, as his general disapproval of institutional care of children hardened, his opposition to the reformatory grew. In 1898 he expressed this opposition in direct action. Together with the warden of the Central Prison in Toronto, he embarked on a scheme, almost certainly illegal, to intercept children before they were sent to the reformatory. The scheme was devised in response to the persistent practice of magistrates, particularly from country areas, of sentencing boys under thirteen years of age to the reformatory. This practice persisted largely as a result of the system of financing children's institutions. The upkeep of the reformatory was the responsibility of the provincial government only, whereas the municipalities, who appointed the magistrates, were required to pay two dollars per week for any child sent to an industrial school. In his annual report Kelso drew attention to the magistrates' continued violation of the law. However, the committals of underage boys continued. In 1898 an opportunity arose to intervene. Boys from the country who were sentenced to Penetanguishene were usually brought first to Toronto, where they spent some weeks in the Central Prison before being conveyed to the reformatory. The warden frequently contacted Kelso to come and see what he described as his 'kindergarten class.' The two officials reached an agreement to combine efforts to keep these young boys from the reformatory. In 1898 two boys, one nine and one eleven, sentenced to five years in the reformatory, were removed from the Central Prison by Kelso with the warden's approval, and placed in farmhouses under the care of a Children's Aid Society. Kelso recounted that he waited with great concern but no one showed the least interest or even inquired of the children. Over the next four years he intercepted over forty children in this way. By 1902 the matter had come to official attention, and the superintendent of Penetanguishene Reformatory asked the attorney-general to intervene. However, by this time it had been decided to close the reformatory, and the attorney-general, in Kelso's words, 'kindly consented to shut his eyes as to what was going on.'

The steady decline in the number of boys resident in Penetanguishene Reformatory, and the consequent increase in the per capita cost, resulted in a decision in 1900 to close the reformatory. At first the intention was to relocate it and funds were set aside for the construction of a new building on a site in Oxford County. However, concerns over the cost of a new building and arguments over its location led to delay. The ready availability of an alternative in the form of the industrial schools prompted consideration of entirely doing away with the reformatory. In 1903 this latter plan was adopted. In the parliamentary session of that year legislation was introduced empowering the provincial government to abolish the Reformatory for Boys and to transfer the inmates to either the Central Prison or the industrial schools. On 4 April 1904, by Order-In-Council, the Ontario reformatory officially passed out of existence.

Kelso supported the closing of the Penetanguishene reformatory but he was not directly involved in the decision. However, when the matter arose of disposition of the hundred or so boys still residing in the institution, the provincial government called on him for advice. Disposal of the boys presented a major short-term problem for provincial officials. The immediate addition of these boys to the industrial school population would have created serious problems of overcrowding, even with the extra allocation of $10,000 that the province provided the industrial schools for this purpose in the 1904 budget. For Kelso the situation presented an ideal opportunity to demonstrate the superiority of foster home placements over other methods of caring for neglected and delinquent children. He proposed that his office assume the guardianship of the boys at Penetanguishene and undertake to provide them with foster homes or jobs. After some hesitation, the government decided that this was the best alternative. In late 1903 the inspector of prisons, James Noxon, informed Kelso that his advice had been accepted and that the task of emptying the reformatory was his.

Kelso's first step was to gather as much information as he could on each of the boys in the reformatory. He wrote letters to constables and to parents and friends of the boys in their home towns. He visited Penetanguishene to review the situation and to discuss the likely prospects of each boy with reformatory officials. On the basis of the information gathered, he compiled special history forms on each boy. By February 1904 there were only eighty-seven boys left in the reformatory since those whose terms were nearing completion had been allowed to leave. In that month Kelso began regular visits to Penetanguishene to commence the process of releasing the remaining boys. He first interviewed the boys individually and privately with the aim, he explained later, 'of inspiring them with absolute confidence in the new policy and securing their loyalty in the plans that were about to be made for them.' He placed great importance on these interviews, which evidently were intense affairs. Describing his own involvement Kelso wrote: 'To win them over it was necessary to take them individually, and to concentrate every faculty of mind and heart on the great task of influencing, controlling and subjugating them to a will greater than their own. What this meant in personal suffering and sacrifice cannot well be explained for it could only be understood by those who have gone through the same experience of suffering for one whom they loved and sought to aid.' During the interviews Kelso stressed to each boy that his liberation was a matter of personal favour and responsibility. He emphasized that he would be fully trusted and helped and that he would always have a friend to whom he could turn. Kelso recounted: 'This promise and this appeal made a deep impression. In some cases tears flowed down their cheeks at the thought of somebody being willing to trust them and to give them an opportunity to show that they were not entirely lost to the sense of goodness and honour ... With all these boys, each with his own broken life and early misfortunes to contend against, it was impossible not to sympathize deeply, and these touching interviews gave an added incentive to help and befriend them.'

Each time Kelso visited Penetanguishene he conducted five or six of these interviews, beginning with those boys whose families or relatives indicated a willingness to have the boys return home. During February and March approximately twenty-five such boys were sent home. Attention was then directed towards boys who were acquainted with farm life and willing to accept situations in the country. These comprised the majority of the remaining boys. Next, a number of city boys were found suitable jobs and lodging in Toronto or elsewhere, and finally the most difficult cases were given special consideration. On 5 May Kelso wrote to the Hon. J.M. Gibson, now the attorney-general: 'I have now completed the task of emptying the reformatory at Penetanguishene and there is not a boy in that institution today ... So far the results have been highly satisfactory and I am keeping a close and careful supervision over the boys in order to be able to report in a year's time exactly how each one is doing. My aim was to thoroughly interest the boys in their own reclamation and rehabilitation in good society, first of all by showing them kindness and friendship, dressing them well, and drawing out their self-respect, letting them feel that someone was interested in them, and providing them with good surroundings and employment. Not one boy has, to my knowledge, got into the hands of the police for any offence up-to-date.'

Kelso's claim to be exercising close supervision over the released boys was not exaggerated. When each group of five or six boys was released they were first brought to Toronto by train, where they were met by Kelso, provided with a good supper, and shown around the city. Before being sent off to their homes or situations, the boys were provided with a valise, extra clothing, a Bible, and stamped envelopes so that they could write to Kelso of their progress. Kelso's logbook on the boys shows that he maintained contact with some of them up to six years later. Correspondence was also maintained with the boys' employers or foster parents for over twelve months after the closure. Almost invariably, according to Kelso, the reports of the boys' progress were favourable, and it was not until late November that any boy got into trouble with the police. Three years after the boys from Penetanguishene were placed in the community Kelso reported that only six had subsequently spent time in the industrial school and three in the Central Prison. This was a complete vindication of his belief in the superiority of his methods of dealing with delinquent children over other approaches. In the aftermath of the closure of Penetanguishene Reformatory his faith in the foster care method was unrestrained. In a detailed forty-page report on the closure written in 1905 he claimed: 'The closing was a great success – so great that one feels like exulting in the possibilities opened up for future efforts with so-called incorrigible boys. Clearly it has been demonstrated that lads, however degraded, can be reclaimed and restored to good citizenship if only the right methods are used; and if there is failure it is because of lack of faith, lack of thoroughness, and lack of sympathetic cooperation.' The experiment led Kelso to reaffirm his belief in the importance of a healthy environment and good example. He stressed the need to interest a boy in his own reform. Once this was accomplished, he asserted, the aim of the worker should be to 'get into friendly sympathetic relationship with the boy, learn his wishes and aspirations, at the right psychological moment place him amidst good surroundings, show that you trust and believe him, visit and encourage him from time to time.' According to Kelso, if a boy did not respond to such an approach, then he could be considered mentally deficient and should be sent to an asylum for the feeble-minded. The fundamental implication Kelso drew from the closure was that institutions for juvenile offenders were no longer needed. 'This unique movement and the undoubted success that attended it is worthy of the careful consideration of officials and philanthropists. It is simply a further demonstration of the fact that large and expensive institutions are not indispensable in dealing with homeless or delinquent youth. By proper organization and a helpful and sympathetic attitude on the part of good people, it is possible to readjust these unfortunate children to society in such a manner as to avoid long institutional confinement while at the same time ensuring for the children a happier and better environment.'

'Personally, I regard the part I have had in bringing about these results as the greatest pleasure in life,' Kelso wrote in December 1904 of his work in closing the reformatory. His involvement with the boys was close, and for years afterwards he delighted to hear of their progress and meet them again. A number of them called on Kelso for assistance during the years following their release, and he usually went out of his way to give help and encouragement. His close involvement became a severe drain on his financial, emotional, and physical resources. Many years later he wrote: 'Not only did I spend three or four hundred dollars out of a small salary in helping these lads to regain a place in society, covering a period of two years, but I gave up every other interest in life to make this experiment a success. For six months I lived in an atmosphere of prayer and consecration – literally taking the sins and shortcomings of these lads on my own shoulders. In pleading with and working for them I used up my own vitality to such an extent that although naturally healthy and strong I often found myself so weak that I staggered along, hardly able to walk.'

Kelso's involvement with the boys from the reformatory went well beyond his official duties as superintendent, and although he was not bothered by this, he was not loath to use his additional responsibilities as an excuse to reopen the issue of his salary. Since the failed attempt to improve his remuneration in 1900 Kelso had been given no increase in pay and by 1904 he felt he was long overdue for a raise. In March 1904 he wrote to the attorney-general requesting an extra $300 per annum to compensate for the extra work and anxiety entailed in placing the reformatory boys. To his disappointment he was offered only $100 which he grudgingly accepted. He wrote to Gibson on 23 April: 'I feel greatly disappointed and discouraged to think that my services are so lightly appreciated. My work in taking over the guardianship of seventy boys from the reformatory and providing for them in homes and situations ought surely to be worth more to the country than $100.' Gibson's reply two weeks later expressed extreme satisfaction with the job that had been done, and spoke of the results as being 'a matter of more than ordinary significance and importance.' He encouraged Kelso to take special pains to follow up the boys. But there was no word of additional remuneration.

Further support for Kelso's closure of the reformatory came from James Noxon, the inspector of prisons, whose approval was crucial when, in April 1904, a query was received from the acting under-secretary of state in the dominion government concerning the release of the inmates. As recently as November 1903 the Ottawa authorities had refused to grant pardons to several of the boys in the reformatory. They were now anxious to have the situation clarified. Noxon wrote a soothing, and not altogether frank reply, stating that subsequent to the closing of Penetanguishene Reformatory it had been decided 'to select a number of the best behaved youths for situations that were freely offered.' No further queries were received from Ottawa.

In contrast to Gibson and Noxon, the administrators of Penetanguishene, although they co-operated with Kelso, were skeptical of the wholesale release. The superintendent of the reformatory wrote Noxon on 11 March expressing his doubts: 'Of course the best possible has been and is being done for all the lads; yet I am not over hopeful that the majority of them will stay where placed. I will indeed be pleased should the future show that my fears have been groundless.' Kelso noted that nearly all his discouragements in the undertaking came from officials whose business it was to deal with criminals, a matter he attributed to their 'constant association with the derelicts of society which has evidently made them thoroughly pessimistic.'

Kelso's placement of the Penetanguishene boys in community situations was also criticized by the administrators of the industrial schools, further straining Kelso's relationship with them. In mid-April the superintendent of Victoria

Industrial School wrote an angry letter complaining that he had purchased extra furniture to the value of several hundred dollars on the understanding that at least twenty boys from Penetanguishene would be sent to the school. 'Personally, I was never anxious to have the management of the boys from Penetanguishene,' he wrote, 'but once it had been settled they should come here, and preparations for their accommodation having been made, then I think in all fairness to the school they should be sent here.' Kelso replied that 'when this subject was first being considered it was impossible to tell exactly how it would turn out and I suppose the government did not know then my capabilities in the direction of placing out boys.' He expressed no sympathy for the predicament of the industrial schools. This was hardly surprising given the effort he had expended in keeping the ex-reformatory boys away from the schools' control.

In January 1905 the Liberals, who had formed the government in Ontario throughout Kelso's career as superintendent, lost the provincial election and were replaced by the Conservatives under James Whitney. The new provincial secretary, W.J. Hanna, requested Kelso in May 1905 to empty the Mercer Industrial Refuge for Girls as he had the reformatory. The Mercer Refuge was established in Toronto in 1879 as an institution for young female offenders and young girls judged to be potential offenders. During the 1890s there were normally about seventy girls in the refuge, committed on account of parental neglect, vagrancy, immoral or disorderly conduct, or prostitution. After the passage of the 1893 Children's Protection Act, and the establishment of an Industrial School for Girls in 1891, the refuge became an institution for older and more incorrigible offenders. As the principal of the refuge explained in 1903: 'The girls are culled from the wayward and neglected girls of the province, the more promising and hopeful finding homes in respectable families under the supervision of the Children's Aid Societies.' The refuge was run on similar principles to those governing the operation of the industrial schools. In his 1902 report Inspector Noxon described the refuge as 'in no sense a place of punishment, but a school to train girls, to lead them into proper channels of thought, and to give them a correct standard of life.' The principal described the work of the refuge in more elaborate language: 'For those committed a long time under instruction is necessary to awaken the sluggish intellects, and an equally long time to foster the sentiment of kindness, friendship and womanliness; and cultivate habits of thrift and industry; and obliterate the influence of heredity and former environment that a higher type of citizen may be returned to the community. None of the elements that tend to ennoble is overlooked in our course of instruction – from the plodding and ever recurrent duties of the most menial of household arts to physical culture, literature, music, and moral and religious instruction. In each and every department she is treated as a friend and sister who needs the sympathy of a stronger and older one to guide rather than to lean on. How they have responded to those influences can be seen in their gentle demeanor and awakened intelligences.'

Despite these lofty aims, there was universal agreement that the refuge was severely handicapped in its work by its uncongenial environment. The buildings were cramped and close to factories and amusement grounds. 'It is difficult to conceive of a situation worse than it, in which to undertake the work of reformation of young girls just entering on womanhood,' wrote Noxon in 1902. Worst of all was the close proximity of the Mercer Reformatory for Women, the main female prison for the province. Although the reformatory and the refuge were administered separately, the two were associated in the public mind. Girls leaving the refuge carried the stigma of being known as former inmates of 'the Mercer.' It was recognition of these problems, and the desire to economize, that led the Whitney government to decide to close the refuge.

Kelso was pleased that the new government wished to continue the policy of deinstitutionalization. He agreed to be responsible for the placement of the girls, following similar methods to those employed at the Penetanguishene Reformatory. He first gathered as much information as he could on each of the girls, and then spoke with them individually, giving 'the assurance of every possible help, sympathy and encouragement, if only she on her part promised willingness to lead a respectable life.' At the next stage the girls were treated with somewhat more caution than were the reformatory boys. Rather than being sent directly to foster homes or situations, they were placed in a 'sheltering home' for a period of readjustment to the community. Great care was taken in selecting homes for the girls to ensure that they were at a considerable distance from old surroundings, so that nothing could hinder complete reformation and restoration to society. Although the success rate claimed by Kelso was not as spectacular as at Penetanguishene, only three of the girls failed in their new surroundings during the first year after their release. For Kelso this was further confirmation of his belief that institutional care for juvenile offenders was unnecessary.

But if the lesson of the Penetanguishene Reformatory and Mercer Refuge experiences was that even the most hardened juvenile offenders could be reformed by sympathetic understanding and well-chosen foster homes, what was the future of the industrial schools? The clear implication of Kelso's statements in the aftermath of Penetanguishene was that industrial schools should also be closed. However, he drew back from an outright call for their abolition. The reasons for his reticence were the same as those that had caused his ambivalence to the industrial schools earlier: his own role in the founding of the industrial schools and his personal ties with some members of the Industrial

Schools Association. Moreover, the industrial schools movement was now firmly established in the province, and the schools were far more formidable targets than the highly criticized reformatory and refuge. Rather than calling for the closure of industrial schools, Kelso adopted a reformist stance, stressing the need for the schools to adopt better methods of classification, to reduce the number of children in each classroom and cottage, and to increase the number of children placed in foster homes. This last point was particularly emphasized by Kelso, and his insistence met with moderate success. Between 1904 and 1910 approximately one-third of industrial school children were placed in foster homes under apprenticeship arrangements.

A test of Kelso's attitude to the industrial schools came in 1906 when the largest school, the Victoria Industrial School at Mimico, was destroyed by fire. This presented an excellent opportunity for him to recommend the gradual phasing out of industrial schools, as the govenment was extremely reluctant to pay the $50,000 requested by the Industrial School Board for restoration. The opportunity slipped by, however, as Kelso, after some hesitation, decided to support the rebuilding of the school. From this time Kelso's advocacy of total abolition of institutions waned and, despite his experiences in emptying Penetanguishene Reformatory and Mercer Refuge, he began to promote the use of reformatories as institutions of the last resort. He told a meeting of the Canadian Institute in April 1908 that the Penetanguishene Reformatory experiment did not suggest that reformatories could be done without, 'but that they should be resorted to only when other means fail.' This was a reversal of Kelso's stance three years earlier. It marked the end of his belief that institutions had no place in child welfare services.

The closure of Penetanguishene Reformatory ushered in a period of rapid expansion for Ontario's industrial schools. The legislation which abolished the reformatory also extended to sixteen the age at which a child could be committed to an industrial school, and despite Kelso's apparent success in placing juvenile offenders in foster homes, magistrates now began to commit to the industrial schools those children who formerly would have been sent to the reformatory. In the year after Penetanguishene Reformatory was closed the number of children in the industrial schools jumped from 267 to 320. The remainder of the decade saw a continuing steady increase in the industrial school population.

Although he now viewed industrial schools as necessary in certain circumstances, Kelso was dismayed by the growth of the schools and the accompanying problems of overcrowding and inadequate facilities. He spoke out strongly against the continuing practice of magistrates committing children as young as eight, nine, and ten to the industrial schools. He also strongly opposed the per capita method of funding, which he described as 'fundamentally wrong, ignoring as it does the policy of prevention, and putting a premium on the accumulation of inmates.' Although some extensions were made to the schools' buildings in the years after 1904, these lagged far behind the increasing number of inmates.

This concern with deteriorating conditions in the industrial schools led Kelso in 1913 to a position on institutional care of juvenile offenders directly contrary to his earlier stance. In his annual report for 1913 he advocated the establishment of a new reformatory for youths aged sixteen to twenty-one. His concern was that the presence of older, 'more hardened' boys in the industrial schools was making it impossible for the schools to meet the needs of the younger boys, particularly when some of the cottages were operating at twice the desirable capacity. 'In spite of various social preventative measures there will always be boys who escape observation and drift on in dissolute and criminal ways until at fifteen or sixteen these are in a fair way to become habitual idlers and criminals. They require a special institution, and a longer period of training to overcome and eradicate the neglect of years. Their case is not by any means hopeless, if special and adequate means are taken for their reclamation. Another school for delinquent boys is, then, one of the advance steps that should be considered in the near future.' The following year Kelso advocated the closing of the rebuilt Victoria Industrial School, and its replacement with a new institution with more adequate facilities and reflecting modern principles. 'Twenty-one years is long enough for a reform institution to remain unchanged,' he wrote. 'A Victoria Industrial School boy has come to mean an incorrigible boy ... The institution is in a rut, it is overcrowded, it is too close to the city.' Two years later, in 1916, he advocated the establishment of two or three new industrial schools. Rejuvenation and reform, rather than abolition of institutions for juvenile offenders, had now become his main theme.

Kelso's concern for the treatment of juvenile offenders was also expressed in the continuing campaign for a separate juvenile court. The passage of the 1894 amendment to the Criminal Code, making mandatory the separate and private trial of children under sixteen, proved an illusory victory. In some places in Ontario trials of youngsters after 1894 were held either in the magistrate's chambers or in the usual courtroom at a time when the police court was not in session. However, this practice was by no means universal. As late as 1903 the attorney-general of Ontario considered it necessary to send a circular to all police magistrates and crown attorneys reminding them of the obligation to try young offenders separately and privately. The circular also recommended that magistrates seek the advice of Children's Aid Societies in dealing with young offenders, as envisaged in the Children's Protection Act.

The campaign for separate and private hearings for juveniles was extended during the 1890s into what became known as the 'Children's Court Movement.'[2] Under the influence of experiments in the United States, most notably the establishment of a juvenile court in Illinois in 1899, many Canadians promoted the notion of a children's court completely distinct from the police courts. They advocated control by people whose primary interest was the reformation of juvenile offenders. These courts would have their own judges, their own detention homes (children's shelters), and probation officers to investigate the circumstances of each case and supervise children after sentencing. Kelso was a leading proponent of this system during the 1890s and early twentieth century. He developed a particular interest in the use of probation officers. Shortly after his appointment as superintendent he wrote an article published in the *Canadian Magazine*, proposing that first offenders be placed with a probation officer, 'who will help him to find employment, and in a general way act as his friend and counsellor, reporting to the court as to his general conduct and progress. It is a well-known fact that the first offence is due to special temptation, to uncongenial or defective home life, or to evil companionship, and that if these difficulties can be removed a second offence will rarely occur. Committed for the first time to prison, there is not only the disgrace, loss of self-respect and loss of employment, but there is the association with other offenders, that so often leads to hardness and indifference.'

Around 1900 Kelso's interest in the appointment of probation officers was heightened as a consequence of his moderating views on the need for separation of children from unsatisfactory parents. He still strongly urged complete and lasting separation in situations of gross neglect or cruelty, but was more willing than previously to attempt to work with children within their own homes if reformation seemed possible. The use of probation officers accorded with this new emphasis. In his 1901 annual report he recommended that 'every city or large town should have one or more probation officers whose constant duty would be to exercise supervision over wayward children, visiting them in their homes, seeing that they are in school, procuring employment for them, shielding them as much as possible from bad companionship, and thus effectively stopping them from getting into further trouble.' An act passed in Ontario in 1903 seemingly implemented this recommendation. Judges were given the option of placing children under sixteen, convicted of an offence, under the care of a probation officer, and the act specified that officials of the Children's Aid Societies and members of visiting committees were eligible for appointment as probation officers. However, the legislation did not specify who should appoint probation officers. As a result, the act was not implemented.

With the failure of the 1903 act Kelso stepped up his campaign. In March

1905 he wrote in the Toronto *Star*: 'Punishment as meted out by the Police Court never yet saved a young career, but love and sympathetic understanding, and friendly guidance, as exemplified in the work of the Children's Aid Societies, can and does turn away from evil ways. Instead of appointing twenty new constables, let the municipality but vote the means to employ two or three probation agents and it will not be long before the value of child-saving efforts will be rewarded.' This statement was strongly opposed by the Toronto Police Department. Inspector Archibald, who had been associated with Kelso in the Toronto Humane Society, accused Kelso in the *Globe* in April 1905 of 'foolish and childish sentimentality' and denounced the whole idea of probation officers as simply a means of pampering juvenile criminals and encroaching on the jurisdiction of police officers. Kelso replied with a long defence and explanation of the role of a probation officer. He reiterated his criticisms of the methods of the police force and police courts in dealing with juvenile offenders: 'The system is one that does not reclaim young fellows who have started on a career of crime. Over and over again those boys have told me that they hated the police, took delight in fighting them, and were only made worse by the Police Court trial and sentence. If this be true, as I believe it is in a large proportion of the cases of juvenile crime, then why not try some simpler method, such as appealing to the boy's sense of self-respect and manliness instead of driving him by punitive measures to the pentitentiary?' He then drew a contrasting picture of the work of a probation officer: 'The modern conception of a probation officer is not that he should exercise constabulary powers, but that he should be the friend of the parent equally with the child ... It is not his duty to seize a child and rush down the street with it to the shelter, but by friendly tactics to bring about the cordial cooperation of the parents in securing the child's best welfare and its continuance in the home, which is its birthright. Does any true friend of children think for a moment that taking a child from a parent is the best way to save it? ... Seeking to arrive at a sympathetic understanding of a child's nature and requirements, and to be patient and persistent in bringing about a youth's reformation by moral suasion, is not 'dandling and coddling,' and if it is 'foolish sentimentality' to save the child by love instead of by the lash then some of us are foolishly sentimental.'

Although Kelso was a leading advocate of probation officers and a juvenile court system, the final impetus which led to the establishment of juvenile courts throughout Canada came from elsewhere. In May 1906 W.L. Scott and J. Keane, officials of the Ottawa Children's Aid Society, attended the National Conference of Charities and Corrections in Philadelphia. During their visit they studied the probation system of that city and on their return proposed to their society the establishment of a similar probation service in Ottawa. The society agreed and in August appointed Canada's first two probation officers. After several months' work, these officers reported great success, hampered only by lack of legal powers. Scott and other members of the Ottawa society thus commenced a campaign for new dominion legislation to give probation officers formal powers within a new juvenile court system.

During this time the appointment of probation officers continued to be considered by the Ontario government. In June 1906 Kelso convened a meeting of senior officials to consider the role of the province in probation and parole. The meeting concluded that responsibility rested primarily with the dominion government, and it was agreed to send a delegation to Ottawa to pursue the matter. In December Kelso travelled to Ottawa as a member of this delegation. He established a close working relationship with Scott, and at a meeting of the Ottawa Children's Aid Society Kelso expressed his strong support for the society's campaign.

In 1907 the campaign gained momentum. Scott secured the assistance of his father, Senator R.W. Scott, who in the spring of 1907 introduced a Juvenile Delinquents bill into the Senate to encourage parliamentary and public discussion. The bill was passed unanimously by the Senate, prompting the dominion government to take interest in the measure. At the request of the minister of justice Senator Scott withdrew the bill, on the understanding that the government would give serious consideration to the establishment of juvenile courts. At this stage Kelso and W.L. Scott both began campaigns to ensure the introduction of a Juvenile Court bill in the next session of Parliament. Kelso and Scott spoke to numerous organizations including branches of the Women's Christian Temperance Union, Children's Aid Societies, Local Councils of Women, the boards of orphans' homes, and churches. Kelso also wrote extensively on the issue. His office issued a pamphlet which unreservedly extolled the virtues of the probation officer system: 'When one has had the experience of years in dealing with wayward youth, has studied the moral conditions, visited the wretched homes, comprehended the utter absence of real affection, the heart hunger, the longing for appreciation and sympathy, then they begin to recognize what is needed is not severity, not flogging, not jail or reformatory, but a true friend and an opportunity under clean auspices to develop worthy character.' Kelso also made the appointment of probation officers a central theme of his 1907 annual report.

The efforts of Scott, Kelso, and many others came to fruition the following year. On 8 July 1908 the House of Commons passed the Juvenile Delinquents Act which implemented most of the measures supported by Kelso since 1888. A new federal offence of delinquency was created, defined as an act performed by any child apparently under the age of sixteen in violation of any federal, provincial, or municipal law. Provinces and municipalities were given the right to establish juvenile courts with wide powers to deal with delinquency, provided they had first established detention homes. These juvenile courts could hear all cases of delinquency, no matter how serious. If a child was found guilty of delinquency, the court was to act in 'the child's own good and the best interests of the community.' The courts could fine the child up to ten dollars, commit him to the care of a probation officer, order him to be supervised by a probation officer while remaining in his own home, place him in a foster home or a suitable institution, or commit him to the care of a Children's Aid Society. Incarceration in any institution for adults was strictly prohibited. Juvenile court committees and probation officers were given powers to investigate cases and to advise juvenile court judges on how best to deal with a child. The philosophy of the act stated explicitly that each child was to be treated 'not as a criminal, but as a misdirected and misguided child, and one needing aid, encouragement, help and assistance.'

The establishment of juvenile courts was not mandatory for provinces and municipalities, and in Toronto the battle for a juvenile court continued for three years after the passage of the Juvenile Delinquents Act. Inspector Archibald of the Toronto Police Department continued to provide the main opposition. In a Report on Treatment of Neglected Children in Toronto published in 1907 Archibald warned against 'the superficial and sentimental faddists who seek to take advantage of the popularity of the child-saving propaganda to work upon the sympathies of philanthropic men and women for the purpose of introducing a jelly-fish and an abortive system of law enforcement, whereby the judge or magistrate is expected to come down to the level of the incorrigible street arab and assume an attitude absolutely repulsive to British subjects. The idea seems to be that by the profuse use of a slang phraseology he should place himself in a position to kiss and coddle a class of perverts and delinquents who require the most rigid disciplinary and corrective measures to ensure the possibility of their reformation.' Such extreme views received little support. Archibald succeeded only in delaying the implementation of the Juvenile Delinquents Act in Toronto. In November 1911 the Reverend J.E. Starr was appointed the first commissioner to hear children's cases in Toronto. Kelso's battle for a Toronto juvenile court, which had lasted almost a quarter of a century, was finally won.

During the first decade of the twentieth century Kelso's main concern was to transform the treatment of juvenile offenders. He perceived this task as central to his social reform strategy, stressing that proposed reforms would benefit both the individual offender and the broader community. He wrote in 1907: 'If the necessary legislation [for the juvenile court] is granted ... and the work is properly supported and carried out, thousands of children will undoubtedly be saved from a vagrant and criminal career. What this will mean to the Dominion of Canada in the reduction of prisons and refuges and the greater safety of its people from the constant menace of crime can readily be understood by any thoughtful person. And we owe it to the children. They have a right to the fatherly protection of the state, and when denied a fair and reasonable opportunity to grow up honestly and respectably it cannot be wondered at if in later years they become the enemies of society and enter upon a warfare of crime.' His reform policies and strategies reflected the prevailing orthodoxy. His faith in the therapeutic power of a loving family environment and 'kindly' influences was, at this time, unlimited. As a reformer, he experienced success. With the passage of the Juvenile Delinquents Act the planks in his early reform platform were implemented. His private life was less satisfactory and he remained deeply discontended with his salary as superintendent. But his public life had been rewarding and his achievements were not unnoticed. A well-known children's court judge, Ben Lindsay, in Denver, Colorado, praised Kelso unreservedly in a private 1908 letter: 'No man in America has done more for children than you have and all of us are indebted to you, as well as the children. I ... am delighted, pleased beyond measure ... with what you are doing. There is no better work anywhere in the world than that you are doing. Toronto and Ontario – all Canada – is to be congratulated in having such an able superintendent. I wish there were more like you in the world to go around. We need such men in every country.'

6

Social Reform

Not all Canadian social reformers at the turn of the century shared Kelso's interest in child welfare. Many considered the cities in which so many Canadian children lived to be the most strategic targets for their endeavours. Canada, between 1890 and 1920, was rapidly becoming an urbanized nation. The percentage of Canadians living in cities increased continually during this period, and by 1921 the rural and urban populations were nearly in balance. Every city was something of a 'boom town' as new settlers poured in. Toronto's population grew almost threefold from 181,215 in 1891 to 521,893 in 1921. Rapid and largely unplanned growth resulted in deteriorating living standards, particularly in the poorer areas of the cities. Poor housing, over-crowding, lack of proper sanitary conditions, and waste disposal problems became chronic in many areas of the larger cities. Alleviation of these conditions became the central concern of an active urban reform movement in these years.[1]

Like the child-saving movement, the urban reform movement received its major support from middle-class, anglophone Canadians in the larger cities, particularly Toronto and Montreal. The reform movement's themes were varied: the elimination of vice and crime, social justice, the creation of a healthy environment, the regulation of utility corporations, the beautification of the industrial city, town planning, better housing, tax reform, and the remodelling of municipal government.[2] The proposals of the urban reformers, like those of the child-savers, reflected their middle-class presumptions. Most of them accepted traditional standards of morality and existing patterns of social stratification: their hope was 'to convert the city into the bastion of bourgeois virtue, where all citizens would live an orderly, healthy, prosperous and moral existence.'[3]

In the period between 1900 and the outbreak of World War One in 1914 Kelso became closely associated with various strands of the urban reform movement.

Dependent and neglected children were still his chief concern and responsibility, but he was now more conscious of the limitations of this work as a strategy for fundamental social reform. 'We are curing the evil effects of poverty,' he told the Canadian Conference on Charities in 1899, 'but not reaching the causes.' He wrote in his notebook in 1908: 'Poverty, congestion, child labour, overwork, preventable disease and accidents, alcoholism, professional crime, and antiquated educational systems, exploitation of the poor in retail trade, in rents, in the conditions of labour, and by the profits of stimulated vice – all these are obnoxious and pauperising features of an imperfect environment which society can change by conscious social effort.' In common with many Canadians he believed the nation's social progress depended on a major assault on the cities' problems.

In his commitment to urban reform Kelso proposed abolition of the slums, provision of public playgrounds, better working conditions in industry, reorganization of social services, training of social welfare workers, and the establishment of settlement houses in poor neighbourhoods. His part in these campaigns ranged from support of other reformers to active leadership. He was often drawn into contact with the urban reformers through his duties as superintendent, and shared the background and aspirations of many of their leaders. His church connections also led him to urban reform. The social gospel movement was becoming firmly established in Canadian Protestantism at this time, and urban reform was one of its central themes.[4] Kelso was closely associated with the social gospel movement, and served as an executive member of the Board of Moral and Social Reform of the Presbyterian church between 1908 and 1910. This board was the main forum of the Presbyterian church on social problems, and Kelso was active in developing policies and programmes on urban and industrial issues.[5] He shared in the enthusiasm and optimism which characterized the urban reform and social gospel movements of this time. As he wrote in 1909: 'A new note is being sounded in public affairs – one that awakens hope in the breasts of many thousands, who on account perhaps of obscurity and lowly surroundings have not been entitled to more than a passing regard – it is that of SOCIAL WELFARE – the recognition of the rights of every human being no matter what the conditions of birth or material possessions.'

Perhaps the most important trigger of the urban reform movement was the development of overcrowded and unsanitary slums and ghettos in the centres, and sometimes on the outskirts, of most Canadian cities. Toronto had a number of such neighbourhoods. The most notorious was 'The Ward,' an area close to the centre of the city populated mainly by foreign immigrants.[6] These areas were studied repeatedly in the early 1900s by reporters, university researchers, and public officials, and their findings heightened the widespread feeling that

Canada was facing an urban crisis. Report after report drew attention to dilapidated houses and tenements, massive overcrowding, lack of sanitary and waste disposal facilities, and contaminated water supplies.[7] Concern over these physical and social problems was accompanied in the minds of most reformers by considerations of morality, public decency, and political stability. Overcrowding and lack of sanitary facilities were deplored because they deprived the individual of the privacy considered necessary to safeguard morality, as well as for their own sake. The growth of saloons, houses of prostitution, low theatres, and gambling dens in slum areas offended the sensibilities of the reformers, who saw the slums as the breeding grounds of plague, vice, crime, and political instability.[8]

Kelso joined in the widespread call for abolition of the slum neighbourhoods. He linked slum conditions to family breakdown, and in an address to the National Conference of Charities and Correction meeting in Buffalo in June 1909 he claimed that 'delinquent children are not caused so much by the home and by the family as by the landlord and the tenement house conditions.' In his observations on slum conditions he stressed the themes of moral decay and political instability. A booklet he issued in 1910 entitled 'Can Slums Be Abolished or Must We Continue to Pay the Penalty?' provided a clear statement of his views: 'The slums should be attacked and abolished because they are the great enemy of the home, which is the foundation stone of the State. Bad housing conditions inevitably tend to drunkenness in parents; to delinquency in children; to disorderly conduct; to wife and family desertion by men who get tired of it all; to immorality in the growing generation owing to lack of privacy and the consequent lack of modesty; to the spread of typhoid fever, diphtheria, scarlet fever, and the ravages of the great white plague.' In the booklet Kelso attempted to explain the development of slum conditions. He identified three factors: pressures of a rapidly growing urban working class, lack of regulation and supervision by the city, and the greed of landowners. He was particularly angered by this last factor: 'One could find in his heart some measure of sympathy and acquiescence if the hovels were built and owned by the poor themselves, but these places are owned by well-to-do citizens who sin against their city from avaricious motives, and live in luxury on the exorbitant rents imposed on the poor and comfortless occupants.'

Kelso's emphasis on family life and public morality in his attack on slum conditions was consistent with his earlier reform philosophy. He made no clear distinction between moral and social reform, and was in no way reluctant to impose his own moral standards on the rest of the community. His analysis of the development of urban decay also reflected earlier themes. He viewed the actions of absentee landlords as a breach of their responsibility as privileged members of society. But his analysis stressed the shortcomings of individual landlords and officials, and he left unquestioned existing patterns of social stratification.

The policies that Kelso proposed to abolish slum conditions were, for the most part, derived from other reform leaders. At various stages between 1908 and 1914 he advocated enforcement of health and building regulations, suburban planning, public housing for working men, and reform of municipal government. On these issues his was but one voice among many. One area in which he did play an important role, however, was in the establishment of public playgrounds in the poorer areas of Toronto. Kelso's first involvement in this issue was in 1889 when he unsuccessfully campaigned to interest the city authorities in the establishment of public playgrounds. He returned to this issue in 1906. The provision of adequate play areas had become an important strategy for urban reformers in many American cities in the early years of the twentieth century. It was widely believed that playgrounds could contribute to the preservation of the health and morale of young children, the strengthening of family life, and the reduction of juvenile delinquency. The Playground Association of America was formed in 1906 to promote the establishment of playgrounds across the United States.[9] Kelso was aware of these developments, and in 1906 he approached the Toronto city authorities with a request that schoolyards be opened for public use out of school hours. The matter was referred to the School Board, but no action resulted. He then commenced a major campaign. During 1907 and 1908 he gave over 125 addresses on the need for playgrounds, using picture slides obtained from the American association. Apart from the campaign for the Juvenile Delinquents Act, this became his major concern during this period. His vision was a network of children's playgrounds throughout the city such that no child need be more than five minutes' walk from a play area. The playgrounds should be well-equipped and, most importantly, supervised: 'If enthusiastic directors with the proper moral viewpoint are given charge of these playgrounds they can do a truly national work in the development of a sound physique and high character ... Play diverts from crime and low pursuits, creating contentment and cheerfulness and inspiring youth with noble ideals ... The best type of citizen can be evolved only from the healthy robust child, who has a free and well-rounded youth spent in cheerful and clean moral environs.'

Kelso's campaign was directed towards the municipal authorities and to the Board of Education. They were slow to respond and in May 1908 Kelso was instrumental, along with others, in calling a public meeting of interested citizens. A circular was sent to about four hundred prominent Toronto citizens, announcing a meeting to form a Toronto Playgrounds Association. The meeting was held on 2 June 1908 and an association was created with the stated aim: 'To arouse and develop an active interest in the general welfare of children and especially to show the supreme value of play as a means of developing children physically, intellectually, and morally, in order to convince municipal organizations and the public generally that one of their most important duties is to provide adequate opportunities for the children to play under conditions of physical safety and moral uplift.' The association received a good start with a donation of $25,000 from Sir Edmund Osler to establish a playground. Despite opposition from local residents, the first playground was opened in 1909 on Adelaide Street West, and another on Argyle Street in the following year. The City of Toronto, under the influence of reformist officials such as H.C. Hocken and James Simpson, was increasingly sympathetic to the playground movement, and agreed to take over and operate the association's facilities. After 1912, when Hocken was elected mayor, the city became strongly committed to the provision of recreational facilities, and expenditure on playground maintenance by the city in 1914 totalled $49,000, compared with only $1134 in 1909. By 1918 Toronto had twelve supervised playgrounds, which became the centres for many organized sports and other recreational activities. Kelso's contribution to the playground movement in Toronto must not be overstated. Other reformers such as James L. Hughes, C.A.B. Brown, and James Simpson also played key roles. In campaigns on issues outside his official jurisdiction, Kelso now frequently played a supporting and initiating role, with others taking the major responsibility for implementation of new policies.

Kelso supported playgrounds as places of moral uplift as well as physical enjoyment. Similar concerns with the moral surroundings of the young prompted his involvement in a campaign to improve the tone of theatres and amusement halls, especially those frequented by children. In 1905 he advocated a by-law prohibiting boys under sixteen attending theatres unless accompanied by their parents. He claimed that 'boys who attend these plays soon become confirmed cigarette smokers, use foul language, give up work, and develop criminal tendencies.' Two years later, in evidence given to a committee of the Ontario government investigating child labour, he listed the consequences of theatre-going as 'theft, idleness, nervous excitement and disinclination for regular work.' With the arrival of the moving picture theatre in Toronto Kelso stepped up his campaign. He particularly objected to the employment of children as entertainers in the 'five cent theatres.' In August 1910 he issued a circular to all Children's Aid Societies condemning such entertainment. The circular called for thorough enforcement of the law prohibiting children under ten from performing in places of public entertainment, and providing for the licensing of child entertainers under sixteen. He denounced the moving picture theatres in uncompromising language: 'Picture theatres are being turned into low-class vaudeville houses, with juvenile performers who outrage decency by immodest dancing and suggestive songs. They go much farther than adults in brazen effrontery and the influence is decidedly bad, both upon themselves and the audience ... In a recent visit to a number of shows, no less than ten children under sixteen were performing, and not an act could fairly be termed decent. In the interests of good morals they should be stopped and rigidly censored.' Kelso also received extensive support for his stand from the press and city aldermen, and closer compliance with the law by theatre operators resulted.

Kelso's role in the formation of the Toronto Playgrounds Association was his most important contribution to urban reform in the years 1906 to 1908. However, leadership of the association soon passed to others and Kelso diverted his attention to other issues. Most important of these was the settlement movement in Toronto, in which Kelso played a key role from 1908 until 1917.[10]

The settlement movement originated in British universities in the mid-1880s. A number of young students and clergymen, appalled by the living conditions in the slums of East London, decided to establish a university settlement in the worst slum area. The notion was that by living in a poor neighbourhood, university men could bridge the gulf that industrialism had created between rich and poor, and reduce the mutual suspicion and ignorance of one class for the other. It was envisaged that the settlement would offer educational and cultural programmes, and also be a focal point for the neighbourhood where workers and intellectuals could co-operate in promoting social reform. The first settlement house was opened in East London in 1884, and named Toynbee House after one of the pioneers of the movement.[11]

The settlement idea spread steadily in the late nineteenth and early twentieth centuries. By 1911 there were forty-six settlements in Great Britain. Transported to North America, the movement grew even more rapidly. A number of attempts to establish social settlements were made in various American cities in the late 1880s, and by 1891 there were six fully functioning settlements in the United States. The most well-known of these was Hull House, established by Jane Addams in Chicago in 1889. By 1910 there were over four hundred settlements in American cities, and they had achieved an established place in American social reform.

Kelso's first exposure to the settlement movement was in 1893 during his visit to Chicago shortly after becoming superintendent. On the invitation of Julia Lathrop, later head of the United States Children's Bureau, he spent a day at Hull House. He lunched with Jane Addams and met a fellow Canadian, William Lyon Mackenzie King, then a fellowship student at the University of Chicago. Kelso later recalled that he was 'greatly impressed with the value of a neighbourhood settlement house as a preventive and corrective social agency and also as an inspirational centre for the residents of the district. Here they might learn the better way of living and be encouraged to develop the latent possibilities that inhere in every life.' Several years after his visit to Hull House Kelso requested King, by then Canada's deputy minister of labour, to speak at a social welfare conference in Toronto on the desirability of establishing social settlements, but King indicated he felt this was premature. King did speak on 'Social Settlements in Crowded Centres' at the Fifth Canadian Conference of Charities and Corrections in 1902, but he concluded that the need for social settlements was not as yet as pronounced in Canada as in the United States.

The first settlement in Toronto was established in 1902 by two young women, Sara Libby Carson and Mary Bell. With the assistance of the Young Women's Christian Association, these women rented a building on Queen Street, east of the Don River, in a poor Anglo-Saxon working-class district, and there opened 'Evangelia,' the first Canadian settlement. The venture prospered, and with the backing of wealthy philanthropists moved in 1907 to new, well-equipped premises. In that same year a second settlement was begun by the Anglican Deaconess Training College in the old 'Cabbagetown' area of Toronto. Both settlements were active and growing at the end of the decade.

Neither of these settlements, however, catered for the large immigrant neighbourhoods of downtown Toronto in the west-central part of the city. Kelso had given consideration at various stages to the potential for a settlement house in this area, and in 1909 he conceived a plan. The House of Industry, the city's 'poor-house,' was located at the corner of Elm and Elizabeth streets in the centre of the notorious 'Ward' area. Kelso proposed that the poor-house be moved to a rural setting, and the buildings be used for a 'communal social centre' under university auspices. He outlined his plan to a Toronto *Star* reporter in March 1909: 'With a reasonable expenditure it could be fitted up with gymnasiums, swimming pool, bath and toilet rooms for both sexes, reading and smoking rooms, kindergartens and cooking classes, an assembly hall for popular lectures and concerts, and as the headquarters for philanthropic social workers. If requested to do so, I have no doubt the university students would undertake its management, establish a social laboratory, and bring in an influence that would bridge over the chasm between rich and poor, the learned and illiterate, and especially help to Canadianize the thousands of foreigners who swarm that neighbourhood.'

The proposal that university students undertake the management of the social centre was related to another of Kelso's campaigns. For several years he had been attempting to persuade the University of Toronto to commence a course of studies in philanthropy. A number of schools of practical sociology and philanthropy, with university affiliations, were already established in the United States, and Kelso envisaged the development of similar courses in Canada. He had been frustrated for many years by the lack of suitable people to provide leadership in child welfare work. He voiced this concern publicly at the 1905 Canadian Conference of Charities. 'Instead of spasmodic volunteer work and the appointment of agents who could not command public respect, there should be trained, efficient and well-paid officials seeking the improvement of social conditions,' he told the delegates. He elaborated on this theme in both his 1907 and 1908 annual reports. In October 1908 he raised the matter with Robert Falconer, the recently appointed president of the University of Toronto. Kelso had met Falconer in 1905 during his visit to Nova Scotia, where Falconer was principal of Pine Hill Presbyterian College. They were fellow elders of St James Square Presbyterian Church, and Kelso was hopeful that Falconer would be sympathetic to the establishment of a School of Philanthropy at the university. He broached the subject with Falconer in 1908, stressing that many Toronto students were leaving for New York and Chicago where such schools had been established. However, the president's initial reaction was that social work did not come within the purview of a university, and that while a course of training should be encouraged, it should be undertaken under some other auspice.

In Kelso's mind social settlements and university training for social work went hand in hand, and he saw the establishment of university settlements as a means of involving the University of Toronto in social work training. Only a few weeks after Falconer's arrival in Toronto in 1907 Kelso sent him information on settlement houses, and Falconer indicated that he was familiar with and supported the movement. When the newspaper report of Kelso's proposal for a 'communal social centre' appeared, he sent Falconer a clipping. He wrote: 'I believe, from a conversation we once had, that you recognize the importance of having an outlet for the social activities of your young men and women and no opportunity could be better. There would, of course, be a capable head worker appointed, and a number of students who felt specially called to that class of work could take up residence there and study social conditions by actual contact with the poor.' Falconer replied with cautious enthusiasm. However, the proposal did not proceed further as the House of Industry did not move from its premises.

Impetus for the establishment of a university-based settlement house was provided by a group of University of Toronto students. In the summer of 1909, as an offshoot of a series of evangelical meetings, students from Victoria College conducted a survey of social conditions in downtown Toronto. They visited thousands of people in their homes, and collected a mass of information concerning housing and sanitary conditions. The survey led to the formation of a new society at Victoria College, the Students' Christian Social Union, with the twin aims of studying social problems and finding means of involving students in social service. Kelso came into contact with these students when he was invited by them to speak on the subject of preparation for a career in social work. In his address he stressed the potential role of university settlements. At the students' request, he prepared a paper outlining in detail his views on social welfare issues, including the concept of social settlements. He wrote:

... the idea of a social settlement first originated among university men who realized that potency of education and culture in solving some of the intricate social problems that affected the daily life of the poor. There was, first of all, the influence of example: a little group of educated workers of high vision and purpose might, by taking up their residence with the poor, raise the standard of living and inspire even the lowliest to an effort at self-improvement. Then there was the power of initiative. The poor need leaders to secure and maintain their rights. Civic rules of health and cleanliness that are scrupulously observed in aristocratic neighbourhoods are scandalously abused and ignored in poor districts. With leadership and effort, good lighting may be obtained – more prompt and efficient scavenger service, less crowding and better sanitary conveniences, a limitation of the saloon evil, etc. Then, too, there is the great opportunity to create a social atmosphere. The Social Settlement becomes the centre of attraction for young and old, because the varying needs of all are catered to in a spirit of comradeship and goodwill, and with an entire absence of the charity or patronizing spirit. In these days of eagerness for social service there should be a well-equipped social settlement in every poor district, for no other agency is so well calculated to touch fundamentally and yet acceptably the problem of congestion, poverty and social distress. There is a great work here for cultured men and women. It is well to bear in mind also that the social settlement is not a dispenser of charity. Worthy cases may be referred to the proper authority, but emphasis must always be laid on the neighbourly spirit.

During his visits to the university to address the students Kelso made the acquaintance of James M. Shaver, a theology student who had taken a leading part in the 1909 social survey. Shaver was associated with the university YMCA, which since 1908 had contemplated the formation of a settlement house. Early in 1910 the university YMCA gained access to funds to commence settlement work in Toronto, and Shaver was appointed to begin operations later in the year. Knowing Kelso's interest in settlements, Shaver called on him for advice and consultation. Together they discussed the issue with Falconer, and obtained his agreement to start the settlement work as a university-based project. Several conferences were held during March and April 1910, and agreement was reached with the university YMCA that a settlement affiliated directly with the university was most appropriate. 'All agreed,' Kelso wrote, 'that as an aid to the study of social conditions a settlement under the auspices of the University and as a clinic for socially-minded students would be desirable.' In May 1910 Falconer publicly announced the decision to commence a university settlement, 'to afford an opportunity to members of the University to understand better the social conditions of a portion of the city, and by personal intercourse with the people to introduce them to the ideals of life for which the University should stand.' He expressed his belief that 'it was to the educated university student actuated by the great Christian dynamic that the world must look for effective reform.'

Kelso was invited to serve on the organization committee of the University Settlement, which was appointed in June 1910. He was a member of a small sub-committee established to develop a constitution and plans for the permanent organization of the settlement. When the first Board of Directors was appointed, with Falconer as chairman, Kelso was chosen as a member. He remained active on the board until 1914 or 1915. Kelso's role in the establishment of University Settlement was, in his own words, primarily one of 'instigator and consultant.' He played a more central role in the establishment of Toronto's next settlement, Central Neighbourhood House.

While he supported the establishment of the University Settlement in central Toronto, Kelso continued to promote the further need for a settlement in 'The Ward,' Toronto's worst immigrant slum area. He was approached in 1910 by two theology students, Arthur Burnett and George P. Bryce, 'to discuss social methods and to enquire what line of activity they could take up.' Burnett had played a leading role in the students' social survey in 1909. Bryce had just returned from a year's study at the New York School of Philanthropy and had been active on the City Missions Committee of the University of Toronto YMCA. Kelso was confident of their abilities and suggested to them that they start a Neighbourhood House in 'The Ward.' This was a daunting proposal, but Burnett and Bryce, with promises of support from Kelso, accepted the challenge. They began their work by starting a Boy Scout troop at a local school. By spring 1911 they felt ready to organize a settlement project. Kelso called a preliminary planning meeting for 13 April 1911 in the Opposition Lobby of the Parliament Buildings. In the letter publicizing the meeting Bryce wrote: 'A proposal has been made to begin work on the lines of a social settlement in "The Ward." The idea is to proceed on broad and non-sectarian lines, and to meet the people of the vicinity, Jews, Italians, and others, as far as possible on common ground. Clubs, classes and other means would be utilized, and the ultimate aim would be the promotion of the best Canadian citizenship, and a contribution towards solving the problems of the modern city.' Kelso chaired the meeting. It was decided to seek the co-operation of the Toronto Playgrounds Association and call a further meeting to which representative people could be invited. A small committee, which included Kelso, Bryce, and Burnett, was appointed to make arrangements for the meeting, and to draw up a statement of aims and objectives.

The formal organization meeting for the new settlement was held in the City Hall on 1 May 1911. Kelso chaired the meeting and began by outlining the proposed aims. He stressed that the settlement would be run on non-sectarian lines, unlike the various religious missions operating in 'The Ward': 'workers will emphasize matters of common agreement instead of making prominent the points of greatest difference.' The proposed settlement was described as a meeting place, a social centre, a headquarters for social research, 'a centre where various methods of social service could be tested and developed,' and 'a kind of power-house where data properly interpreted and methods sufficiently tested could be used for promoting definite movements for social reform.' After discussion of these points, and further speeches, the meeting resolved to start a settlement, and an organizing committee with broad representation of religious leaders and businessmen was appointed.

Central Neighbourhood House, as the new settlement was named, commenced operation in a narrow, three-storey brick house at 84 Gerrard Street West in the fall of 1911. Miss Elizabeth B. Neufeld, a young Jewish settlement worker from Baltimore and a graduate of the New York School of Philanthropy, was chosen as the salaried head worker. Bryce and Burnett were the first residents, but like all the other volunteers at the settlement they worked without pay. The house was an immediate success. Within two weeks of opening over four hundred residents of the area had participated in Neighbourhood House activities. Most of those who attended regularly were the children of immigrants, and training in Canadian citizenship was a central theme of the settlement. Activities included a kindergarten, held for an hour or so each day for the small children, and an after-school programme for young girls where they could cook, sew, dance folk dances, play folk games, and make paper flowers and scrapbooks. Classes were held in the evenings in English, providing instruction for matriculation subjects and for various technical skills. A library was established, and monthly concerts were organized. Legal advice and medical attention were also provided on occasions. The settlement became involved in a number of civic reform campaigns on issues such as housing conditions, lighting, and garbage collection. During her four-year term Miss Neufeld participated in planning for improved urban housing for working men, joined with the Toronto Local Council of Women to persuade the mayor to appoint a commission to study moral conditions in the city, played a leading role in the

movement to gain increased use of school premises as community social centres, and led a deputation of neighbourhood boys to City Hall to request
increased playground facilities.

Kelso was elected as the first chairman of the Board of Central Neighbourhood House. The settlement experienced financial difficulties in its initial
months, and Kelso spent much time seeking financial support. He experienced
reasonable success; by the end of its first year the settlement had an impressive
list of subscribers. However, the continuing growth of the settlement's activities meant continuing financial problems, and in October 1912 Kelso stepped
aside as chairman in favour of W.A. Firstbrook, a businessman who it was
hoped would strengthen the settlement's ties with the business community.
Kelso became vice-president, a position he held until 1916. In that capacity he
continued to exert leadership, as Mr Firstbrook, for business and health reasons,
became an increasingly inactive board member. Kelso played an important role
in 1915 in defending Central Neighbourhood House from allegations that it was
an anti-religious organization. He denied this charge, but stressed that the
settlement was non-sectarian and non-evangelical in its aims: 'We do not
profess to be an evangelistic organization or mission, and religious doctrines are
not taught. Workers connected with the House are, however, actuated by deep
religious conviction, and are believers in creeds broad enough to include Protestant and Catholic, Jew and Gentile. Surely we can all unite on the command-
ment, "Thou shalt love thy neighbour as thyself." The Neighbourhood House
believes in cultivating and exercising a friendly, kindly feeling for all human-
kind, giving to the neighbourhood of our best and gaining in return a richer
experience of friendship and goodwill. It is a co-partnership, a peaceable,
righteous and loving living and working together for the improvement of social
relations and the upbuilding of our civic life.'

Kelso resigned from the board of Central Neighbourhood House in July 1917,
bringing to an end a decade of leadership of the settlement movement in Toronto.
As in so many previous ventures his role was to act as a catalyst in the local
community for a new idea derived from elsewhere. The concept of social
settlements held particular appeal for Kelso. It fitted with his strong belief that
those in privileged positions had a responsibility to aid the less fortunate, and
with his belief in the power of moral suasion. As he wrote in his paper for the
university students in 1909: 'In all work for human beings, whether of a
preventive or reclamatory character, the thought should run through all our
efforts, like a golden thread, that it is not law, or systems or institutions that
save, but only the personal influence of good men and women, thoroughly
imbued with the spirit of love and compassion.'

One major by-product of the establishment of social settlements in Toronto was the decision by the University of Toronto in 1914 to commence a new social service course. Kelso had publicized the need for such a course, and it was a central point in his 1909 paper, written for the university students, on current social welfare issues. He had stressed the need for moral commitment as well as intellectual ability in intending social workers, whom he felt should 'feel the call to social service as imperative as to the ministry or the mission field – all heart and no head has characterized many failures heretofore; to substitute all head and no heart would be the greater calamity.' Kelso was instrumental in persuading Mrs H.D. Warren, a wealthy woman in Toronto society, to provide the initial salary for a director for the proposed new department. Her offer was made to the university in the autumn of 1913, and the following year the social service course commenced. All members of the teaching staff were people who had been closely involved in the initial stages of the settlement movement in Toronto. Kelso's expectation that the establishment of a university settlement would raise interest in a social work course was fulfilled.

The playground movement and the establishment of social settlements were Kelso's main commitments, outside of his duties as superintendent, in the decade before World War One. But his range of interests was wide. In 1909 he was appointed to a new committee on industrial problems, established by the Board of Moral and Social Reform of the Presbyterian church. This appointment led Kelso to give serious consideration to the employment conditions and opportunities of Canadian working men. In 1909 he issued a pamphlet urging the creation of labour exchanges to help the unemployed find jobs, and he continued to press for this policy until the establishment of labour bureaus by the Ontario government in 1917. He gave his support to the campaigns for workmen's compensation, better wages and factory conditions, shorter hours of labour, health insurance schemes, and old-age pensions. In his writings and speeches Kelso emphasized the rights of working men to a fair share of the profits of industry. 'The workers create wealth and often give their health and their lives in doing so,' he wrote in 1913. 'They should have a greater share in the profits of their labour – at least to the extent of decent and comfortable quarters to work in.' In testimony to the federal parliament's Special Committee on Old Age Pensions in March 1912 he repeated this theme: 'I believe that the Old Age Pension is desirable because it would remove to some extent that fear which oppresses people in their declining years. It would be a recognition of a long life of service to the country and it would bring about a better division of wealth and it would give these people some little taste of the comforts of life before they die.'

Kelso stressed the advantages which would accrue for Canadian families and children from the passage of progressive industrial legislation. This was the theme of his address to the Social Service Congress which met in Ottawa in March 1914. It was the first national Canadian congress on social problems and Kelso shared in the enthusiasm and optimism of other delegates, claiming that 'the world is entering upon an era of social justice ... before the advancing wave of an enlightened public opinion.'[12] Kelso's topic was 'The Importance of Child Welfare,' but his speech focussed on the implications of industrial conditions for children rather than more traditional child welfare issues. He supported workmen's compensation as it would ensure that children were not destitute if their father met with an accident. He advocated sunny and clean factories so that fathers' lives might be prolonged for the sake of their dependent children. Higher wages would give fathers more money to spend on their children, and shorter hours of labour should be introduced so that fathers had time to become better acquainted with their children. 'There is no social question that does not either directly or indirectly bear upon the welfare of the child ... If we deal justly with The Child of today undoubtedly Canada will rise among the nations to be a great and lasting blessing and example to the world.'

The same themes were pursued by Kelso in his advocacy in this period of other social measures to support family life including widows' pensions, legal aid for poor families, and homemaker services. He did not, however, encourage the use of day care, which he considered destructive of family life: 'society's apology for compelling poor mothers to go out working by the day to support their children.' 'It is fundamentally wrong to take a mother away from the little family circle that depends so much on her guidance and inspiration ... An absentee mother means untrained and delinquent children. Ask any juvenile court judge or reform school superintendent if this is not correct. The Creche is merely a compromise and while it may be necessary as a temporary expedient social workers should not give it too much prominence, but continue to plead for the rights of the children and the struggling mothers.'

Another issue which preoccupied Kelso in the early twentieth century was the system of granting unemployment relief. During the first two decades of the century the fear of unemployment was ever present for a large proportion of Toronto workers. In the course of a normal year some 10 per cent of the work force was unemployed during the winter months. During periods of depression, such as those of 1907–8 and 1913–15, unemployment reached massive proportions and destitution was widespread.[13] The system of unemployment relief in the city was hopelessly inadequate and disorganized. The province assigned responsibility for relief to the municipality, but the municipality was continually reluctant to accept this task, arguing that the destitute should be provided for by private charities. There was no shortage of private charitable organizations in Toronto at this time. One contemporary estimate was that in 1909 there were

244 churches and fifty-five institutions and organizations of a charitable character.[14] However, when faced with a major crisis the resources of the private charities proved totally inadequate. In 1908 the city was forced to make special grants to the House of Industry and the Salvation Army to enable them to continue their relief work. This was only a temporary measure and it was clear that some more fundamental action was needed.

The lack of co-ordination and integration of the private agencies was viewed as a central problem of Toronto's relief system. As early as the 1890s an attempt had been made to remedy this situation by the establishment of a Board of Associated Charities. This board was formed to implement the principles of the charity organization movement, which was influential in many North American communities at the turn of the century.[15] The movement began in London, England, in 1869 with the formation of the London Charity Organization Society. The London society, and similar organizations which were formed in other cities, had two main objectives. Firstly, they aimed to provide a forum where agencies could discuss common problems and co-ordinate their efforts. Secondly, they sought to promote careful investigation of appeals for help and a city-wide registration of applicants. Charity organization principles were hailed by many reformers as an application of scientific methods to the problem of destitution. This movement had considerable influence in Britain in the late nineteenth century.

The charity organization movement was first introduced into North America in 1877 in Buffalo, and it was taken up even more eagerly in the United States than in England. By 1909 225 American cities had established a charity organization society. Canadians first came under the influence of charity organization principles at the 1897 meetings of the National Conference of Charities and Correction, which were held in Toronto. The Toronto Board of Associated Charities was established shortly thereafter, and similar associations were formed in Montreal, Ottawa, Winnipeg, Calgary, and Vancouver.

From its inception the Toronto board experienced extreme difficulty in co-ordinating relief activities. Although it received some support from the City Council, which encouraged agencies to co-ordinate their efforts through the board, it never played an effective role. This was a source of disappointment to Kelso, who had been a strong advocate of charity organization principles since the 1890s. In his 1908 annual report he drew attention to the spirit of rivalry amongst charitable agencies, denouncing what he described as the 'unspoken desire on the part of each charitable association to make his or her particular charity larger and more independent than the others ... It should be borne in mind that the true mission of every charitable society should be to seek its own elimination.' Kelso's concern was not simply that too many charities led to inefficiency and uneconomic administration. More serious in his view was that competition among charities resulted in excessive preoccupation with relief-giving. Granting charitable relief to the poor Kelso considered pointless and misguided: 'It is absolutely useless to give families temporary relief when there are certain conditions that keep them down and make it impossible for them to become self-supporting. Improved laws, clean, healthy and remunerative employment, decent and sanitary homes, moral instruction and play facilities for their children, are what the poor need far more than alms.' Opposition to indiscriminate relief-giving became one of Kelso's most oft-repeated themes in the years prior to World War One, and the issue continued to be a major concern for the rest of his life. He based his opposition on his belief that charitable relief resulted in 'professional pauperism.' 'To give money without expecting any return is simply holding out an inducement to people to rely upon charity instead of upon their own exertions,' he wrote in his 1910 annual report. Kelso's opposition towards those who exploited charity was intense, and although he stressed that most poor families were self-respecting and worthy to receive the assistance of social welfare workers, he advocated drastic measures to stamp out the 'pauperist spirit':

The average poor family should not be confounded with that wretched class of people who seek to live by charity and who have long since lost all pride, self-respect or decency of conduct. We should pity rather than despise this class, for experience goes to show that they have been in nearly every instance reduced to helpless beggary by misfortune, oppression and unwise giving. The aim should be to restore them to self-respect by steadfastly withholding charitable aid and adopting drastic measures to force them to self-exertion and support ... For pauperism is hereditary. Children are quick to learn that it is easier to beg than to work and they grow up to continue the same vicious life as their parents. Charity breeds paupers, fosters and pampers them and inflicts upon the community a long and ever-increasing succession of degenerates to fill the brothel, the poor-house and the prison. It is truly a deadly disease that can only be cured by extermination.

These views, expressed so forcibly by Kelso, were widespread in Canadian society, and were a faithful reproduction of charity organization principles. In place of spasmodic and overlapping relief efforts he proposed co-ordinated social services run by trained workers: 'What is needed is personal service, the complete organization of charitable forces, harmony of action, and the appointment of trained and experienced workers instead of isolated action, rivalry and jealousy, and spasmodic and amateur administration. Only then can we hope to adequately relieve genuine distress and at the same time prevent the evils of pauperism taking root in this young and rapidly expanding country.' To implement this programme Kelso placed his faith in reform of the Toronto Board of Associated Charities. He argued that this body could successfully undertake the rational organization of all relief agencies and proposed that it undertake research into social needs, ensure that relief work was allocated to agencies in a reasonable manner, maintain a library and information bureau for social workers and societies, and generally be the clearing house for all charitable and social effort. He also suggested that, in accordance with charity organization principles, the board maintain a register of all those who, after receiving charitable aid twice, continued to apply for help. He dismissed the objections of those who viewed this as undue interference into the private lives of families, and described it as simply a reasonable business precaution. He claimed that registration and investigation of poor families was only undertaken in the best interest of the individuals concerned: 'Organized charity asks questions, but only in order that it may give intelligent assistance. It is not like the policeman who approaches you in a spirit of suspicion and asks questions that he may convict, but rather like the physician who must thoroughly understand your ailment if he is to effect a cure.' It is difficult, however, to reconcile this analogy with many of Kelso's other statements concerning the central register. Discussing the idea with a *Globe* reporter, he claimed: 'It is safe to say that the great bulk of those who appeal for relief would have avoided any necessity for such appeals had they been reasonably temperate, frugal and thrifty. There has grown up a class in this city who regard public charity as a right and spend their money freely in the summer in the expectation that their families will be taken care of when the cold weather sets in. These persons should be carefully sifted out and made to work for all that they receive.' The analogy with the police officer's spirit of suspicion seems appropriate to this statement, despite Kelso's contrary claims.

In addition to a reformed Board of Associated Charities, Kelso advocated the establishment in every municipality of a Department of Charities and Corrections. The department 'would be strong enough to gather together the scattered forces and encourage and inspire all existing agencies.' Its functions should include inspecting and regulating municipal charitable institutions; organizing labour depots; studying slum conditions and encouraging the building of decent homes for the poor; assimilating the foreign population; co-operating with the health department in conserving public health; superintending public comfort stations, bath houses, social centres, playgrounds, and arranging for free entertainments and lectures of an instructive character; publishing a monthly magazine as a vehicle of information to social workers; and, generally, bringing expert knowledge and action to bear in all matters affecting the social welfare of the community. Neither this proposal, nor that of a reformed, effective Associated Charities, were implemented in Toronto in the early twentieth century. In 1912 the city created a Social Service Commission, which was envisaged as a central bureau to co-ordinate charitable activity. But its powers were primarily advisory, and it never played a major role. To some extent the Neighbourhood Workers' Association performed the tasks Kelso proposed for the Associated Charities. This association was founded in 1912 as a family casework agency, and during the depression of 1913–15 it assumed a major role in relief programmes. During the war and immediately afterwards it spearheaded a campaign to organize a new Federation of Charities, and in 1917 the city's Social Service Commission backed the Neighbourhood Workers' Association's bid to have all relief centralized in its hands. The Board of Associated Charities gradually faded out of existence.

Kelso continued to support charity organization principles of relief-giving throughout his career. One issue which illustrates the strength of his opposition to indiscriminate relief was the problem of children arriving at school in the winter months poorly clad and unfed. A charitable organization undertook to provide such children with a breakfast of bread and jam, and a pair of shoes. Kelso wrote to the *Globe* protesting that this action was based on entirely wrong principles, which if generally adopted 'would be subversive of all good government and self-respecting citizenship.' He claimed that experience had shown that such alms-giving was inevitably abused, and that the correct approach was to attack the social conditions which resulted in poorly clothed, underfed children, so as to 'conserve for the children their natural birthright to food, clothing, education and moral training in their own home under the direction of their own parents.' In reply, the president of the charity concerned accused Kelso of theorizing and ignoring the immediate needs of children. 'Do all possible to make the parents accept their responsibilities,' the president argued, 'but do not let the child's foot go bare and the child's stomach go empty in the meantime.' Kelso did not respond, but his statements suggested that he considered temporarily hungry and cold children to be the necessary price to be paid if pauperism was to be abolished.

The recurring theme throughout Kelso's activities in this period was the need for moral reform. This is reflected in his call for abolition of the slums, his advocacy of playgrounds and settlement houses, his opposition to picture theatres and indiscriminate charitable giving. All these campaigns were centred on the need for moral uplift among the poor and working classes. Kelso's reform proposals also stressed the moral responsibilities of the more privileged members of society. As playground supervisors, settlement workers, or discriminating contributors to charity, middle-class men and women could and should exercise a potent and salutary influence on the recipients of their endeavours. As in his child welfare work, Kelso took for granted the suitability and desirability of his own moral standards and showed no reluctance to impose these on all members of the community. The provision of public playgrounds and the establishment of social settlements, Kelso's main ventures in this period, were designed to improve living conditions in Toronto's slums. Kelso did not look to the social and economic structure of Canadian society to explain poverty and the resulting problems. Instead, he wished to pour Ontario into a mould of middle-class standards through moral suasion, education, and social reform.

7

From Reformer to Administrator

Although Kelso was involved in a wide range of causes in the pre-World War One period, his official duties as superintendent of neglected and dependent children required considerable time and effort. He remained convinced of the value and importance of child welfare work. In speeches and articles he continued to praise the Children's Aid Societies in glowing, even grandiose, terms. In August 1911 he wrote in the *Presbyterian Record*: 'Every criminal and every tramp was once a bright winsome little fellow with high hopes and a clean untainted mind. That they subsequently became outcasts and wanderers was due to somebody's neglect ... If our Children's Aid Societies were better supported and people everywhere realized the importance of prompt and practical aid so that every young life might be hedged around with saving influences, this Canada of ours would prosper, not only agriculturally and commercially, but also morally, and the prophesied millennium would soon arrive.' Kelso's faith in the efficacy of child-saving work was undiminished. He still used his lantern slides, showing the miraculous transformation in young lives through the intervention of the Children's Aid Society. He wrote of the work of the Children's Shelter in 1906:

The Children's Shelter is often the means of saving a home from being broken up. When a child enters the shelter the first place visited after the history particulars have been recorded is the bathroom. Here the ill-smelling rags are speedily taken off, the dirt that has encrusted itself on little legs and arms is removed with a plentiful supply of hot water and soap; the hair is anxiously inspected and combed; clean garments are brought in from the storeroom. By these means the child's self-respect develops at once. He feels that he amounts to something, that he is among friends, and that swear words and lies would be entirely out of place. Mothers who come to the shelter after a debauch or a term in jail almost fail to recognize their own offspring, so clean and neat and happy do they look under the kindly regime of the children's love-centre. Maternal pride is awakened, the father is sent for, new promises are made, the home is cleaned up, and the superintendent hands over the children with a parting word of praise and encouragement. In this way hundreds of homes are converted into fit places to live in through the Children's Shelter acting as a friend.

Kelso most enjoyed the promotional aspects of his work as superintendent during these years. He took every opportunity to address meetings, speak to reporters, and organize new campaigns, rather than involving himself in routine administrative work. This meant that he spent a considerable time away from his office. In the decade preceding World War One he regularly spent a total of two or three months each year travelling outside of Toronto. He crossed the province many times attempting to complete the network of Children's Aid Societies. His efforts were not fruitless. Between 1904 and 1910 the number of societies in Ontario jumped from thirty-six to seventy-five. The main difficulty was sustaining the interest among residents of some small outlying areas. The British Poor Law Commission, which devoted several pages to the Ontario child welfare system, commented on Kelso's difficulties: 'The system has too much the character of a "one-man" affair. The local aid societies are in reality an uncertain quantity; one or two drop out of existence every year though fresh ones are constantly being formed and one of the greatest difficulties which the Superintendent's reports disclose is the necessity of constant stimulus to local effort.'

Kelso's travelling was not restricted to Ontario. In 1905 he was invited to Halifax by the National Council of Women to deliver a series of lectures on child protection legislation. Nova Scotia was still without strong child protection laws, and the fifteen public meetings at which he spoke were well attended and caused considerable interest. At the final meeting, held on 27 November, a committee was appointed to organize a Halifax Children's Aid Society and to press for new legislation. In the following year the Nova Scotia Legislature passed an Act for the Protection and Reformation of Neglected Children, closely modelled on the Ontario Act of 1893.

Kelso made a similar visit to Saskatchewan in February 1909, at the invitation of the provincial attorney-general. The purpose was to gain Kelso's assistance in drafting a Child Protection Act, and while in Regina Kelso consulted with government ministers and officials. He also spoke to eight public gatherings about child welfare work and social reform. He travelled extensively in Saskatchewan, advocating the establishment of Children's Aid Societies at meetings in Moose Jaw, Indian Head, Saskatoon, and Prince Albert. Shortly after his visit the Saskatchewan legislature passed a Children's Protection Act. Kelso travelled to the west coast and enjoyed revisiting the scenes and renewing acquaintances made in his 1898 visit, and reviewing the progress of child welfare work. He also spent time in Calgary, and consulted with the provincial attorney-general concerning the Children's Protection bill about to be introduced into the Alberta legislature. The trip took two months, but when he returned to Toronto he had the satisfaction of knowing child protection legislation on the Ontario model now covered all Western Canada.

Kelso made a further trip to Western Canada three years later. Early in 1912 he was elected an elder of St James Square Presbyterian Church, and subsequently was named a commissioner to the Presbyterian National General Assembly meeting in Edmonton in June. When the news of his visit spread, he received numerous requests to speak to Children's Aid Societies and other child welfare organizations in Western Canada. The trip became a whirlwind speaking tour, in which he delivered seventy-two addresses in Alberta and British Columbia, including an address to the delegates of the General Assembly.

The only province of Canada yet to adopt comprehensive child protection legislation was New Brunswick. In February 1913 Kelso accepted an invitation from the Canadian Club to visit St John to promote child welfare work. A Children's Protection Act was passed in the province the following year. This completed the network of children's protection legislation across Canada. Apart from Quebec, where the child welfare system reflected the strong influence of the Roman Catholic church, all provinces passed legislation modelled on the Ontario Children's Protection Act of 1893, establishing Children's Aid Societies as the key organizations for the protection of children. The spread of the Ontario system was stimulated by Kelso's promotional trips between 1898 and 1913, and he justly claimed to have been influential in the development of the child welfare system throughout English-Canadian society.

Besides these trips to various parts of Canada, Kelso frequently attended conferences in the United States, usually several times each year. In 1905 and again in 1913, the Kelso family visited the Martins in Nashville, and on these holidays Kelso combined work with recreation, investigating child care methods in the areas through which he travelled and addressing meetings in various Southern cities.

A memorable event in Kelso's career occurred in January 1909 when President Theodore Roosevelt invited him, along with other leaders in child welfare work in North America, to attend the White House Conference on Dependent Children. The conference was a landmark in federal government involvement in children's services in the United States and a forerunner to the establishment of the Federal Children's Bureau in 1912. Kelso attended the banquet at which the president outlined his child welfare policies, and was introduced to

Roosevelt. The conference provided Kelso with an opportunity to renew his acquaintance with child welfare leaders from across America, and he missed no opportunity to promote Ontario's child welfare system. Largely as a result of his efforts, Ontario had a good reputation in the United States for child welfare work. A representative of the newly formed Russell Sage Foundation, visiting Toronto in August 1909, expressed the view that the work being done for children in Ontario was sixteen years ahead of that in the United States.

Despite this favourable image, Kelso's office and the Children's Aid Societies were experiencing political difficulties. The major problem was financing. The expansion in the number of societies, and the emphasis placed by Kelso on supervision of children and strong leadership of the societies, resulted in a need for more provincial government funding. This was slow to come. By 1912 the annual provincial expenditure on neglected and dependent children was still less than $15,000, exclusive of Kelso's salary and office expenses. Most of this expenditure was on salaries and travelling expenses for a provincial inspector, two full-time agents, and about twenty agents employed on a part-time basis. The agents had the task of helping in the organization of local societies, propagating the work in local communities, and assisting the central office to supervise the system. None of the expenses of the Children's Aid Societies were met by the provincial government at this time. They had to rely completely on the municipalities and charitable donations.

Kelso had an ambivalent attitude to provincial funding of child welfare. He strongly believed that voluntary funding of children's work was the preferable method. 'The inevitable tendency of large government grants is to limit the personal activities of good people and thus destroy what we regard as the triumphant feature of the work,' he wrote in his 1909 annual report. At the same time he chafed under the restrictions of inadequate funding, and continually complained that lack of funds was hindering his work. This was a regular theme of his reports to the government. In 1912, for example, he argued: 'There is just one drawback to the general success that has characterized the year's work, and that is the insufficiency of the appropriation. While the work has been making tremendous progress, the funds necessary for pioneer work and to link up the organization on a basis of thorough efficiency have been inadequate. Few experiences can be more painful than to be confronted daily with pressing needs, to recognize the weak points in the system of child protection, to have the willingness and the ability to remove the defects, and yet be quite unable through lack of funds to take any forward step.' Kelso's response to the problem was to urge wealthy individuals and corporations to make bequests or donations to the societies, but his successes as a fund raiser were only moderate.

The shortage of funds was a constant irritation to Kelso, even apart from its deleterious effect on child protection work. His ingrained dislike of administrative work made him impatient of the requirements to submit estimates for his branch well ahead of expenditure and to account for every dollar spent. He frequently found himself refused reimbursement for expenditures which were not permitted, according to the strict interpretation of the Children's Protection Act by the provincial auditor and others. Often he was obliged to write to his field workers concerning trifles such as receipts for meals and railway fares, and, far more often than he wished, to inform them that the auditor had refused authorization of their expenses. These matters Kelso found irksome and a great waste of time.

To assist Kelso with these administrative duties, which the provincial auditor considered he performed most unsatisfactorily, the government provided him with a trained accountant in 1910 as a full-time administrative assistant. At first Kelso welcomed the appointment of Mr J.A. Blakey to this position. 'I consider myself fortunate in having secured so efficient and willing an assistant,' he told Blakey at Christmas 1910. However, the following year the two men began to disagree sharply over office administration. Blakey found Kelso slipshod in his business practices. He was appalled by what he considered inadequate record-keeping, lax control over staff, poor financial control, inefficient office layout, and failure to interpret strictly the Children's Protection Act. Kelso, on the other hand, was irritated by Blakey's constant criticism and preoccupation with bureaucratic detail. Prior to Blakey's arrival the office was an easygoing, informal working place, but the clashing administrative styles of Blakey and Kelso disrupted the relatively relaxed and harmonious atmosphere that had prevailed.

In 1911 the financial problems reached a crisis point. Without an increased provincial appropriation, supervision of many foster children and the development of new societies would have ceased. Many of the established societies now accepted the value of trained, full-time leadership, and there was a widespread feeling that the province should extend its staff of agents to assist in their work. The outcome was a delegation of representatives from thirty Children's Aid Societies, which met government officials and ministers at the Parliament Buildings on 26 January 1912. The delegation requested that the grant for child protection work be increased from $15,000 to $40,000 per year, citing in support the large sums voluntarily donated to the work and the enormous savings of preventive child welfare work for the community. W.H. Hanna, the provincial secretary, promised serious consideration of the request. The main outcome of the deputation, however, was the formation of an Association of Children's Aid Societies to represent their interests at the provincial level. An organizing committee was appointed, and the inaugural meeting of the association held in Toronto on 8–9 April 1912. The first president was W.L. Scott, the man who had led the campaign for the Juvenile Delinquents Act and who was in 1912 the president of the Ottawa Children's Aid Society. At its first meeting the association passed resolutions on a range of issues, including the need for stricter laws concerning wife desertion and the payment of widows' allowances. The conference also called on the provincial government to provide funds for the salary of at least one Children's Aid officer in each municipality or district. The association met on a regular annual basis from this time, and was to play an important part in strengthening child welfare legislation and administration.

The agitation for increased funding of children's protection work led Provincial Secretary Hanna to request Blakey to prepare a confidential report on the administration and financing of Kelso's office. This report, written without Kelso's knowledge, denied the need for increased funding and was highly critical of his administration. Blakey stated that with better accounting, a reduction in the frequency of foster home visits, and a cessation of attempts to extend the work, the existing appropriation would be adequate. He expressed the need for complete reform of the record-keeping system, the preparation of guidelines and job descriptions for societies and agents, and an improved filing system. He made no attempt to disguise his view that Kelso displayed a 'remarkable lack of ordinary business instinct,' and cited examples of Kelso's failure to abide by the most basic office principles and regulations. He particularly objected to Kelso's numerous outside interests, and his use of the resources of the office in these ventures. Kelso's frequent statements to the press, and his agitation for causes not directly related to his official duties, particularly annoyed Blakey: 'His greatest drawback is his weakness for personal publicity. "J.J. Kelso" in print fascinates him. He has thus far failed to realize that the work is greater than the man and that efficiency is the watchword of today. As a private philanthropist he would be a success, but he finds it difficult to comprehend his own status and responsibility as a governmental official.' Blakey concluded his report with these allegations: 'The cause of the chaos is to be found in Mr. Kelso's absolute lack of method and his wilfully ignoring the most ordinary business rules. He is constitutionally unsystematic. His sympathies and large heartedness lead him into actions and situations which a careful and methodical person would avoid. *Any* regulations or limitations are irritating and distasteful to him, and if he can evade restrictions he will do so. This is his chief idiosyncrasy. He was never intended by nature to be anything but a philanthropic free-lance bound by no regulation but that of doing good to fellow mortals in distress.'

The irony of Blakey's criticisms is that Kelso, had he seen the report, would probably have agreed with much of it and considered it complimentary. By Blakey's bureaucratic criteria Kelso undoubtedly was a poor administrator – but to be a good bureaucrat was never his ambition. It was unfortunate that Blakey and Kelso could not work together in a complementary fashion, Kelso propagandizing, encouraging, and leading, and Blakey sympathetically introducing system and order. But neither man respected what the other represented, and their relationship continued to be one of animosity and fruitless bickering.

Opposition from within his office was but one of several matters troubling Kelso during 1912 and 1913. At this time the practice of the central office directly placing children in foster homes was discontinued, and although the number of children being placed this way had been steadily decreasing for some years, Kelso now felt even more cut off from direct child-saving work than ever. The bureaucratic demands of the job were becoming steadily greater. There had been no positive response to the Association of Children's Aid Societies' request for increased funding, and Kelso felt keenly that child protection work was undervalued and poorly treated by his political superiors. There was, moreover, a sense in which he felt that there was but little new ground left to conquer. The major legislative enactments concerning neglected children which he advocated as a young man had been achieved, and while he felt many more reforms were still needed, these mainly concerned matters not strictly within his jurisdiction.

One incident in particular upset Kelso, and brought to the surface all his anxieties and frustrations. In 1911 he compiled from his personal papers a volume of reminiscences of his early child protection work which he entitled *Protection of Children*. It was highly personal in style, and emphasized Kelso's role in pioneering Ontario's child welfare system. He claimed that the book was 'for the information and encouragement of fellow workers, and for the preservation of records that, with passing years, would be increasingly hard to collect together.' On this basis he published the book as an official government publication, using government funds. The provincial secretary was willing to authorize the $300 involved, but the provincial auditor refused, on the grounds that the book was essentially autobiographical and could not be properly considered a government publication. Consequently, Kelso was ordered to pay the printing costs of the book from his own pocket. The wrangle continued until March 1914, when the government finally agreed to pay the bill. But the dispute further soured Kelso's feelings towards government service.

In the early spring of 1914 Kelso, tired and depressed with his work, handed in his resignation to the provincial secretary. Hanna refused to accept it, proposing that he take a leave of absence to travel at government expense to Great Britain to study child care methods. The leave was ostensibly a reward for twenty-one years of continuous government service. Kelso decided to accept the invitation, and set sail for England on 19 May 1914 on the liner *Royal Edward*, accompanied by his family and a niece from Nashville.

The sea voyage was not without interest, as the ship was stalled in thick fog for two days and hit an iceberg before slowly limping its way across the Atlantic. In England the Kelsos settled into a relaxed routine of sightseeing, visiting children's homes and institutions, and travelling around the country. They spent three months in London, and then travelled in the north of England and Scotland before returning to London. Kelso spoke at many gatherings of child welfare workers, and was received with hospitality and friendliness. An address on the subject of juvenile emigration to Canada in which he referred to the British waifs being sent overseas as 'the scum of the streets' was widely reported in the British press, but otherwise the trip was not controversial, a welcome change from the Ontario scene. Unfortunately the outbreak of war curtailed the visit, and a planned trip to Europe was cancelled. The Kelsos arrived back in North America in mid-November via New York, and spent several restful days with friends on a farm in Connecticut. By the time Kelso returned to Toronto he had reversed his earlier decision to leave the superintendency, and settled back into the position that he was to hold for the remainder of his working life.

Although Kelso was refreshed by his visit to Britain, on his return to Toronto he was beset by similar problems and concerns as those which had prompted him to tender his resignation. 'Owing to discouragement, etc., not so active in the social propaganda since my return,' he noted in his diary several months after resuming his duties. In his annual report written in April 1915 he nostalgically compared the enterprising early days of child protection work with the more routine nature of his current responsibilities: 'During the formative stages of this work it was necessary that the spirit and purpose of the Act should be liberally interpreted and a great deal of pioneer work done in order that public interest might be aroused and a settled policy arrived at along the lines of modern social progress ... Recently, [however] instructions have been issued that the Act must be literally interpreted and followed, and in consequence any work or procedure not specifically provided for in the Act will in future be discontinued.' From this time until his retirement from government service, Kelso's public life was dominated by prescribed and formal duties and his zeal for reform and innovation underwent a gradual and steady decline.

A major irritation for Kelso was the deterioration of his already unhappy relationship with Mr Blakey, which resulted in a strained and tense working environment. Blakey was in charge of the office while Kelso was overseas, and he was discontented to revert to a subordinate position on Kelso's return. His criticisms were expressed in letters and memoranda to Kelso, complaining about office procedure, the work of other members of staff, and lax compliance with regulations. Kelso normally replied to Blakey's typewritten, formal, and often extensive communications with brief jottings written on small scraps of paper, but by June 1915 he tired of the dispute and asked Blakey to stop writing these letters of criticism and disapproval. Kelso appears to have made a genuine effort at this time to bring about a reconciliation, but Blakey did not respond and he continued to oppose Kelso for the next ten years.

Of particular concern to Kelso was the effect of Blakey's opposition on other members of his office staff. By this time the staff had grown to include two inspectors and seven stenographers, besides Kelso and Blakey. Kelso's warm personality and easy-going administrative style enabled him to attract great loyalty from most of the office workers. He was friendly, slow to criticize, and generous on such matters as hours of attendance and leave. In these respects he was a complete contrast to Blakey, whose belief in punctuality, hierarchy, formalism, and efficiency won him few friends, either within the office or among Children's Aid Society members. The outcome was open hostility towards Blakey from the secretarial staff, and continual disharmony and friction in the day-to-day work. Kelso's many absences from the office meant that Blakey was often left in charge, and his interpretations of the Children's Protection Act and the instructions he gave to agents frequently differed from Kelso's established policies. Kelso's control over the office was thus jeopardized, and his efforts to reassert his leadership within the organization were not completely effective. Indeed, Kelso now tended to shy away from bureaucratic conflicts, which were a source of great anxiety for him. For the first time in his career he began to absent himself from the office on grounds of minor illness; often these absences followed disputes either with Blakey or the provincial auditor.

The provincial auditor's office had been an irritant to Kelso ever since his first days as a civil servant, and the ever-present need to justify each small item of expenditure was a task to which he was never reconciled. The continual lack of funds continued, and was exacerbated by the advent of World War One. 'Neglected children need, deserve, and should receive, the best professional care that love and money can devise,' Kelso wrote in his 1915 report, 'and yet one has almost daily to make the excuse that those things cannot be done because of lack of means.' In the same report, however, Kelso showed that he was still clinging to a belief that the work could best be financed through voluntary giving: 'When the Children's Protection Act was first being considered it was decided to make it a voluntary and benevolent movement as far as possible, with the hope and expectation that wealthy people who love children would provide all the funds necessary for the proper establishment and equipment of the work. This hope has not been realized to any great extent. The fact that the work was partly under Government control has led many people to believe that it was either being financed entirely by the Government or that it should be, and an excellent excuse was found here for not doing anything practical.'

Kelso's continuing belief in the necessity for a predominantly privately financed child welfare system gave a certain half-heartedness to his campaigns for increased government funding. This partly explains his lack of success. He never reconciled his advocacy of trained, well-paid professional child welfare workers with his suspicions of the damaging effects of paying these workers from the public purse. The growth in the number of children's agents and paid secretaries of societies, and the decline of large private funding sources, made Kelso's faith in voluntary giving increasingly unrealistic.

The public issues in which Kelso became involved after 1914 were mainly related to the building up of child protection work. In most cases, too, he was reacting to circumstances and situations created by others, rather than, as in his younger days, initiating reforms. One such issue, which received widespread attention in the newspapers, concerned the work of the Toronto Children's Aid Society and the conditions in the Children's Shelter operated by the society. For several years there was growing concern in social work circles in Toronto over the Children's Aid Society. It had retreated from its early role as a reforming organization working on behalf of neglected children in the city, and was simply performing its minimum obligations under the act. Kelso watched the decline and stagnation of the organization he had founded with considerable regret, and was finally stirred to take action. In February 1916 he received a letter from the Social Service Commission of Toronto, the body established to co-ordinate the social welfare activities of the City of Toronto, raising critical questions concerning the operation of the society. The commission wanted information on the length of time children should be kept in the shelter, and the type of children who should be detained there. Kelso was invited to make a statement on the policy of the Toronto society on these matters, and to make any suggestions for improved efficiency.

Kelso was more than willing to comply with this request. Although he was friendly towards the married couple who administered the Children's Shelter, he was antagonistic towards the board of the society and particularly towards its president, J.K. MacDonald, whom he considered responsible for the decline. After consulting with the provincial secretary, Kelso drafted a letter outlining his criticisms which was sent to the mayor of Toronto on 19 March 1916. Copies were also sent to the press, and were published the following day. The vigorous and unrestrained tone of the letter was reminiscent of Kelso's earlier crusades. He claimed that conditions in the Children's Shelter were scandalous and worse than those found in common jails. The boys, he said, were locked in a basement room for a week or longer without being permitted to enjoy open air. Boys from ages eight to sixteen were mixed indiscriminately in this room, some of them for truancy and other trivial offences, and without constructive occupation. He claimed they slept on beds without mattresses and pillows, with only a rough blanket, and that the whole shelter was overrun with insects. In Kelso's opinion, because of the large number of children unduly detained in the shelter, it had practically developed into an orphanage, and another shelter was now needed to do the work originally contemplated. Kelso went on to criticize the work of the Toronto society in more general terms. He asserted that it was behind the times in its child welfare work, citing the administration of the shelter as a prime example. He drew attention to the fact that only eighty-one children had been placed in homes by the society during the previous year, far fewer than might be expected given the number of neglected and delinquent children in its charge. He stated that the society's system of dealing with the boys sent on remand by the Juvenile Court was inadequate and disgraceful: 'It has not employed the right type of men nor provided the proper facilities for improving the moral and physical condition of those unfortunate lads.'

There was a sharp reaction to Kelso's public letter. The superintendent of the shelter admitted that conditions were far from perfect, but claimed that Kelso's letter exaggerated the seriousness of the situation. He attributed the verminous state of the shelter to the condition of many of the children when they arrived, and explained that mattresses were not provided due to the difficulty of keeping them clean. These statements merely strengthened Kelso's case. The City Council's representative on the Board of the Children's Aid Society supported Kelso's charges and the Toronto chapter of the National Council of Women called for a full investigation. The case was brought before the city's Board of Control in July 1916. MacDonald, defending the society, claimed that Kelso's letter was a deliberate misrepresentation, that he had not inspected or even visited the shelter for at least five years. He stated there was only one child in the care of the society at that time who should have been in a foster home. He managed to convince the Board of Control that Kelso had not presented sufficient evidence to prove his allegations, and the outcome of the hearing was that the Toronto City Council passed a motion expressing its confidence in the Toronto Children's Aid Society. It was, on the surface, a defeat for Kelso. However, later in the year the society did appoint a committee to recommend improvement to the shelter, and in December a $2000 programme was commenced to improve physical conditions there. This was the beginning of a complete re-examination of the work of the Toronto society, which was eventually undertaken under the direction of Mr R.E. Mills, a researcher with the

Toronto Department of Health, who was appointed director of the society in the early 1920s. Under Mills the society regained its position as a highly respected child welfare agency.

The dispute with the Toronto society caused Kelso considerable anxiety, and it had an important influence on his future career. Although the eventual outcome of his action was the reform of the shelter, at the time he was criticized by many of his associates in the Children's Aid Societies for taking such an uncompromising stand. Even prior to this incident his standing with the workers in the Children's Aid Societies was declining, and this incident strained the relationship further. Although many workers respected him as the pioneer of child welfare work in Ontario, his views were now sharply questioned. Looking back in retrospect on the altercation with the Toronto society, Kelso recognized the damage it had done to his standing in the movement and to his relationship with old colleagues, but he felt that his action was unavoidable. 'This whole affair was one of the sorrows of my life,' he wrote. 'But looking back I cannot see that I could have done otherwise since I owed a supreme duty to the children of Toronto and to the social movement for which I was to a large extent responsible.'

During the First World War and the post-war period Kelso was called on many times to arbitrate in disputes within Children's Aid Societies and to act as government spokesman on child welfare issues. These incidents regularly brought him into conflict with others working in the child welfare system. Although it was not new for Kelso to be in conflict with others, his criticisms were now most often in defence of an established system, whereas earlier in his life he had criticized in order to implement reform. The change of stance did not suit him temperamentally, even though his belief in the system he was defending was genuine and strong. The issues in which he became involved were varied. Towards the end of the war he spoke out forcefully against proposals to establish new institutions for the care of the children of soldiers killed in the fighting. He also opposed a scheme of the Salvation Army to bring 5000 widows of British soldiers and their children to settle in Canada, claiming that this would detract from Ontario's responsibility towards its own war widows. In the post-war years he resumed his criticisms of the industrial schools system, and advocated, not for the first time, the closure of the Victoria Industrial School and its replacement by a system of farms for delinquent boys. He attacked conditions in children's shelters in various cities and criticized municipalities for their slowness in establishing juvenile courts. He also spoke out against sectarianism in child welfare work. One such issue which was widely publicized concerned a dispute between the Catholic and Protestant members of the Sudbury Children's Aid Society. Kelso supported the rights of the Catholic members to have a majority on the board of the society in a predominantly Catholic area, and for this he was severely criticized by the Protestant churches.

Although Kelso was preoccupied with these relatively trivial issues, he was aware of the agitation for broader social reform taking place in Canada in the aftermath of the war. 'Many radical reforms are in process of enactment as a result of the awakening caused by the war,' he told the readers of the *Globe* in October 1918. 'Evidently there is before us a great period of reconstruction that will, to a large extent, transform the world.' However, Kelso himself partici- pated only marginally in the movements for new legislation in the fields of health, housing, employment, urban planning, and special services for returned soldiers. He was briefly involved with the Civic Improvement League, and was quoted in the *Canadian Municipal Journal* as advocating health insurance in November 1917. Apart from this, he observed rather than participated in post-war social reform activities.

Kelso's discouragement and consequent lack of involvement were closely related to a strong concern that his earlier efforts were now unrecognized and unappreciated. He confided this to a clergyman friend in December 1915: 'I must say that occasionally I have felt greatly discouraged through lack of friendly appreciation. As you know I have since early youth given up my life to this work and have suffered a good deal financially and otherwise in conse- quence. As I grow older I am glad to find myself caring less about earthly reward, nevertheless an occasional pat on the back is sure to be acceptable to most of us.' He received one such gesture of appreciation on 11 June, 1918, when he was guest of honour, together with Sir John Gibson, at a meeting sponsored by the Ontario Association of Children's Aid Societies to celebrate the twenty-fifth anniversary of the passage of the Children's Protection Act. Kelso was pre- sented with a cheque in recognition of his services. The premier of Ontario, Sir William Hearst, presided, and speeches praising the work of Gibson and Kelso were made by the premier, the leader of the opposition, and leading officials of Children's Aid Societies. Kelso's speech to the gathering focussed on familiar themes. He spoke of the difficulty of combining the philanthropic spirit with the red tape of government service and, perhaps uncharitably, given the occasion, of the financial difficulties he had experienced since becoming superintendent. He stressed the non-material returns of the work: 'I have been amply rewarded – rewarded in the consciousness of discharging my duty, and also rewarded in the fact that I was surrounded at all times by people of warm hearts, people of sympathy who loved children and who were glad to do something for them.' He contrasted the pioneering days of the work with his present routine responsibil- ities: 'Today we have the work so well organized that my chief business is in guiding the movement. At first it was necessary to do a great deal to get things going, and now it is almost necessary to do as much to keep things back ... it is necessary to hold back the (misdirected) enthusiasm of other people while retaining some enthusiasm yourself.' He concluded by expressing his delight with the appreciation which had been shown him. 'It will be an encouragement and an inspiration to me to work harder and better than I have ever done before for the children of this province.'

The Toronto newspapers covered the anniversary celebration, and several of them carried editorials praising Kelso for his achievements. The *Globe*, a consistent supporter throughout his career, eulogized his human qualities: 'Things institutional have never with him replaced things human. He is not a patron; he is a friend. He is not an official; he is a chum. His work among the children has been fruitful because they knew him as their friend.' The *Star* also stressed that Kelso was not a man who believed in institutions: 'His zeal has not been abated by officialdom ... Mr. Kelso is the very opposite of a bureaucrat. With him, the child is greater than the institution, and he continually emphasizes the superiority of the home to institutional training and environment. He does not belong to the class of philanthropists who pat the children on the head, and tell them how thankful they should be for all the good things the State and the Societies have done for them.' The Canadian Press news agency also picked up the story, and Kelso's achievements of twenty-five years were publicized in newspapers throughout the country.

Although government ministers honoured Kelso at the anniversary celebration, his relationship with the Conservative government in power was by no means amicable. The new provincial secretary, W.B. MacPherson, made it clear that the freedom Kelso had previously enjoyed to advocate reforms and promote causes in which he believed would not be continued. Kelso was refused permission to speak at several conferences of social welfare workers. He was told to restrict himself in his annual reports to summarizing briefly the activities of the superintendency rather than, as previously, commenting in a discursive and personal style on a wide range of matters relating to child welfare. The most galling restriction of all occurred in 1918 when MacPherson directed Kelso to cease his involvement in the campaign for mothers' allowance legislation. This was the only major social reform not falling within his responsibilities as superintendent in which Kelso was involved during the war and post-war years. The instruction to divorce himself from this movement left him bitter and resentful.

Kelso first advocated mothers' allowances in the mid-1890s. As superintendent he frequently came across widowed mothers who were forced to work in order to support their families. He was often asked by these women to place their children in foster homes, as they could no longer provide for them. Kelso was reluctant to accept children in these circumstances, and in 1895 he proposed assistance for such families: 'Widows applying for release from parental responsibility through poverty, should be assisted to keep the home together rather than encouraged to part with their offspring. The aim of the Society through all its work should be to elevate home life and strengthen and ennoble family ties.' In his annual report for 1896 he repeated this message, emphasizing again the overriding importance of family life: 'There are poor but respectable mothers who require temporary help, but this should be given to them in their own homes ... so that the home may not be broken up. It is no real charity or help to a poor mother to close up her home and send her children, one to this institution and one to that, thus robbing both of the ties and influences that are, after all, the only things worth living for.'

Kelso continued to advocate widows' allowances in his speeches and reports, and extended the group of mothers to whom he would give financial support to include those deserted by their husbands. He claimed that in families where the mother worked the children frequently became juvenile delinquents and that therefore it would in the long run be an economy to assist deserving mothers to stay at home and devote their full time and attention to the training of children. In 1902 Kelso was elected a vice-president of the National Conference of Charities and Correction and in speeches in several American cities he advocated mothers' allowances as his central theme. During those years he proposed that municipalities and churches take primary responsibility for needy mothers, but in 1906 he suggested for the first time that this was a matter for the provincial government. This was the theme of his address to the annual convention of the National Council of Women in Hamilton in 1906, and from this time he persistently advocated provincial action in this field.

The Toronto branch of the National Council of Women provided the initial impetus that led to serious consideration of mothers' allowances by the Ontario government. In March 1914 the branch received approval from the Social Service Commission to approach the public to raise $10,000 for an experimental project to give pensions to a number of widows in the Toronto area. Although the project involved only a small number of mothers, the council was delighted with the progress made by the families over a two-year period. Almost all the homes receiving an allowance remained intact, the children staying in their mothers' care. The passage of mothers' allowance legislation in Manitoba in 1916 and in Saskatchewan the following year gave further impetus to the movement, as did the increase in the number of widows and deserted wives in the population caused by the casualties and social disruption of the war. In 1918, in co-operation with the Social Service Commission and labour and church organizations, the Council of Women sponsored a special committee to press the Ontario government to introduce mothers' allowance legislation. In view of his long association with the campaign for mothers' allowances, Kelso was named as chairman of the committee.

In this capacity Kelso acted as spokesman for the movement for several weeks during 1918. He wrote articles for the press criticizing the Ontario government for its tardiness in not introducing the measure, and for allowing other provinces to take the lead. In an article written for the *Star* in June he linked the provision of mothers' allowances to workmen's compensation, introduced in Ontario a few years earlier: 'The Workmen's Compensation Act has conclusively proved that by a fair levy upon the industry concerned all who are bereaved of husband or father by accident can be protected against hardship and injustice. And this being true, does it not pave the way for a widow's or mother's allowance law that will recognize the claim of fatherless children to support and education – not as charity, but as an act of justice and self-interest on the part of the State?'

Kelso's public identification with a group pressuring the government to take action, and his open criticism of their delay, were unacceptable to Sir William Hearst's government and to Provincial Secretary MacPherson. The expectations governing the behaviour of civil servants had changed since Kelso was first appointed superintendent, and it was no longer acceptable for government officials to dissent publicly from official policy. Kelso was aware of this change, but throughout his career he had never been bound by such regulations. MacPherson's refusal to permit him to remain as chairman of the mothers' allowance committee while holding the office of superintendent signalled the end of his dual career as reformer and official. He reluctantly and bitterly accepted the government's decision, resigned as committee chairman, and withdrew from active participation in the mothers' allowance movement. This was the last time he took a leading role in any reform movement.

The campaign for mothers' allowances continued without Kelso's involvement. The chairmanship of the committee was taken over by the Reverend Peter Bryce, a Methodist clergyman. The Hearst government continued to hesitate over the issue, and in January 1919 appointed Dr W.A. Riddell, deputy minister of labour, as chairman of a committee to prepare a report for the government's consideration. The report was still unfinished in October 1919, when the government was replaced in office by the United Farmers of Ontario, headed by E.C. Drury. Riddell presented his report in January 1920. His recommendation that Ontario proceed with mothers' allowance legislation was backed by a large delegation comprising representatives of the churches, the Toronto Trades and Labour Council, the Great War Veterans' Association, the National Council of Women, and philanthropic and educational bodies. In a reversal of roles, which underlined his changed situation, Kelso sat with Premier Drury to receive the delegation. The United Farmers' government was receptive to Riddell's recommendations, and Toronto's leading newspapers endorsed mothers' allowance legislation. On 12 May, 1920 the minister of labour, the Hon. Walter Rollo, introduced a Mothers' Allowance bill in the provincial Legislature.

The bill followed closely the recommendations of the Riddell report. A Mothers' Pension Board was proposed at the provincial level to supervise the new scheme. Detailed administration was to be the responsibility of local commissions appointed by municipalities. The cost of the scheme was to be shared by the provincial government and the municipalities. Beneficiaries were to include widows, wives of inmates of hospitals for the insane, and wives of men who were permanently disabled and thus unable to contribute to the support of their families. Only mothers of at least two children were eligible for benefits, and only a mother who was, in the eyes of the local commissioners, 'a fit and proper person to have the custody of her children' was to receive assistance. A maximum and minimum level of allowance payments was to be set by the Mothers' Pension Board, and the local commissions were given discretionary powers within these limits. Amendments proposed during the second reading of the bill to extend the scheme to deserted wives and unmarried mothers were opposed by government ministers and voted down. Apart from their desire to keep down the costs of the scheme, the ministers expressed the concern that if deserted wives were included it would make desertion too easy. The premier also explained that in most cases of desertion both parties were at fault, and that there was a danger of supporting mothers who were not fit persons to be in charge of their children. 'Let us take one step at a time,' he told the legislature, 'and not three steps and fall down.' The bill was passed without major amendments and came into effect on 1 July 1920. The Reverend Peter Bryce was appointed as first chairman of the Mothers' Pension Board.

Although Kelso preferred an act with broader coverage, he was pleased to see the enactment of a measure which he had supported for a quarter of a century. He was, however, deeply disappointed not to have participated in the final campaign for the act, and he felt strongly that his role in the mothers' allowance movement was not sufficiently acknowledged. In later life he blamed the government's refusal to allow him to participate in the campaign for his subsequent decline in influence, claiming that it 'caused me to be ignored, slighted and hindered in my general work for the children.' The whole episode was saddening for Kelso, making him even more aware of his diminishing role in social reform in the province.

The Drury government passed several important pieces of social legislation during its term in office between 1919 and 1923. Two of these, the Adoption Act and the Children of Unmarried Parents Act, had a major influence on the later years of Kelso's career. Both acts provided for the appointment of a provincial officer to be responsible for their administration, and in both cases Kelso was named by the government as this officer. He was given these tasks in addition to his responsibilities as superintendent of neglected and dependent children. The demands of these new positions were such that Kelso came to devote most of his time and energy to meeting these new official responsibilities. This became his main contribution to child welfare work during the 1920s.

Of the two pieces of legislation, both passed in 1921, the Children of Unmarried Parents Act drew the most public attention. The question of how to deal with illegitimate children and their parents was widely discussed in Ontario in the early twentieth century. Kelso was prominent in the debate. His viewpoint, first expressed in 1901 and essentially unaltered thereafter, was that an unmarried mother should nurse and care for her child during its first year, after which it should be placed in a foster home: 'The experience of ages has proved conclusively that no unmarried mother can successfully bring up her child and save it from disgrace and obloquy, whereas the child, if adopted young by respectable, childless people, will grow up creditably, and without any painful reminder of its origin.' In the context of the times, Kelso showed sympathy for the plight of the unmarried mother. 'Some better method must be found of dealing with young unmarried mothers,' he wrote in his notebook in 1906. 'Turned adrift from the hospital with a babe in their arms, cut off by relatives, no money or friends – despair naturally seizes hold of them.' Nevertheless, his prime concern was clearly with the child. He called attention to the advertisements for infants which frequently appeared in the newspapers, and advocated the banning of this practice without investigation of the suitability of the prospective parents. He also spoke out against the maternity boarding homes, or 'baby farms' as they were often called. The conditions in these institutions were notorious, but despite high death rates government regulation was lax or frequently nonexistent.

To deal with the problem, Kelso called for stricter registration of illegitimate births in the province, supervision of all illegitimate infants during their first year, and laws compelling unmarried mothers personally to look after their children for at least twelve months. His views were strongly coloured by his opinion of the character of the typical unmarried mother. He told an annual conference of the Association of Children's Aid Societies: 'I have rarely found that these young mothers are well-balanced women, able to make their own way in the world. Strong physically and all that, and yet not mentally or morally strong, nor able to fight life's struggle alone.' He told the Toronto

News that unmarried mothers were 'mostly of the soft, easily-led type, with a great deal of the animal instinct in them. They are ignorant of what to do with their child, and thus they make up their mind to get rid of what is a disgrace to them, and often loathsome to remember.' Because he believed unmarried mothers were usually weak-minded, Kelso proposed that Children's Aid Societies should come to the mother's rescue and be willing to place the child under the society's guardianship, 'telling the mother that they will see that it grows up to be a respectable citizen.' He stepped up his campaign for more vigorous home-finding for illegitimate children after thirty-five infants died in an epidemic which broke out in the Toronto Infants' Home in December 1912. There were other reasons, apart from this tragedy, for Kelso's opposition to the establishment of institutions to care for unmarried mothers and their children. He wrote in his 1915 annual report: 'It is not desirable to encourage the growth of charitable institutions as they often prevent true social progress ... The experience elsewhere has been that when an institution for unmarried mothers and their infants is established it encourages rather than checks evil, as men recognize that the community makes provision for just such cases. I can tell you also that the association together with these unmarried mothers is very disastrous to character, as girls who have gone to such places have often told me that they received more harm than good through the evil acquaintanceships formed. I would strongly urge ... when emergency arises, board the girl and her child with some family, locating the man responsible and making him pay expenses ... It is most important also that parents and relatives be induced to help and befriend young women who get into trouble, instead of turning them adrift.'

A large increase in the number of illegitimate children born in the province towards the end of the war led to renewed public concern. In response, Kelso in April 1917 circulated a questionnaire to social workers asking for their views on the policies that should be implemented towards unmarried mothers and their children. The response led him to write to the provincial secretary in February 1918, formally proposing more stringent regulations for the care of illegitimate children. By this time the problem was reaching crisis proportions, as the infants' homes in Toronto were filled to capacity, and stories of abandoned babies were appearing regularly in the newspapers. In March 1918 an emergency meeting convened by the Toronto Children's Aid Society passed a resolution calling for the establishment of a bureau for the registration and supervision of all illegitimate children. In October the City of Toronto responded by authorizing the Social Service Commission to establish a register of illegitimate births. However, action by the provincial government was still not forthcoming.

In May 1919 a scandal concerning a child missing from an unauthorized maternity boarding home refocussed the attention of the provincial government on the problem of unmarried parents. Mr Robert Martin, who had been appointed an inspector under Kelso by Provincial Secretary MacPherson, gained considerable publicity by proposing the establishment of a maternity refuge in every county of the province under government supervision. This proposal was, of course, strongly opposed by Kelso, but it evidently had the support of MacPherson. Fortunately, from Kelso's point of view, the government lost office before the plan could be implemented, and Martin lost his official position.

The Drury government showed no interest in the establishment of maternity refuges, but it was responsive to the proposals of the social work community. The act of 1921 provided for close supervision of the children of unmarried parents by a provincial officer, who was given the responsibility of obtaining all information possible about children born out of wedlock and of taking whatever action seemed advisable to him in the interests of the child. The provincial officer was required to respond to all requests for advice and protection from unmarried mothers. In particular, he was charged with securing support from the father for the child, and procedures were established for taking action against the alleged father. This task of obtaining financial support from putative fathers became Kelso's most arduous and time-consuming duty in his remaining years as a civil servant.

Kelso was appointed as the administrator of the Children of Unmarried Parents Act by Order-in-Council in June 1921. Although he was not consulted prior to being given the job, nor offered any increase in salary for the extra work involved, he was at first keen to take on the new task. It was a new challenge, and Kelso viewed the act, together with the Adoption Act, as the final component to the modern system of child welfare inaugurated in 1893. Replying to criticism of the Unmarried Parents Act by the Brantford Council of Women, Kelso stated: 'The Act ... is one of the most advanced steps in social legislation that has been taken by any country. Having been confronted daily for thirty years with the suffering, abandonment and premature death of children belonging to this class, I can appreciate more than most people the need that exists, and the splendid opportunity for service. This legislation is extremely difficult to enforce, but it is worth testing out to the fullest possible extent, and I feel a deep sense of responsibility in being appointed the Provincial Officer to superintend its administration.'

The sense of responsibility remained, but Kelso's enthusiasm soon flagged. At first the problem was that the government failed to allocate any additional finances to Kelso's office to enable it to carry out the new duties. 'Mr. Kelso has had to worry along with his existing staff, which necessarily means only partial and inefficient enforcement,' the *Star* complained in February 1922. During the first two years the administration of the act left much to be desired. From the start attention was focussed on efforts to obtain financial support from the putative father. This involved Kelso in time-consuming investigative work and in increasingly complicated financial accounting, as all monies paid to the mothers and children were channelled through his office. This led Kelso into further disputes with the provincial auditor. A report prepared by the auditor on the accounts of the Neglected and Dependent Children's Branch in September 1923 uncovered a whole range of irregularities including discrepancies concerning cash on hand, poor reporting procedures, and uncertainties over the financial status of some fathers. The report claimed that total payments by putative fathers were over $30,000 in arrears, and it observed that 'there is need for stronger pressure at times as many of these men must be dealt with firmly.' Two years later the situation had not improved. In a report prepared in December 1925 the auditor expressed doubt as to the value of the whole scheme: 'The Act is but in its infancy and if it shows after four years of operation that over 90% of the accounts are in arrears, it proves that in this regard it has failed in its purpose of providing maintenance and education for the children it assumes the responsibility for.' Soon afterwards there was some improvement, largely resulting from an increase in staff. In 1922 a 'clerk investigator' was added, followed one year later by a 'junior inspector.' In 1924 these were joined by two permanent clerical workers and fourteen temporary workers. By 1928 these were all permanent workers, and the cost of running the branch had jumped from $17,000 in 1919 to $60,500. This facilitated the collection of paternity payments, but the expansion of his staff and budget involved Kelso even more deeply in the bureaucratic routine which he disliked so much. His vastly increased administrative work tied him to his desk. By the mid-1920s his visits of inspection and encouragement to Children's Aid Societies around the province had all but ceased. Nor was there any time left over to give sustained attention to co-ordination and planning of child protection work, and Kelso began to lose his influence in matters pertaining to neglected and dependent children. His new responsibility, which at first seemed to present a new challenge, had become instead an encumbrance.

Kelso's duties as the administrator of the Children of Unmarried Parents Act also placed further strains on his relationship with the Children's Aid Societies. He had to rely on the societies for much of the investigative work involved in tracing the putative father and ensuring payments were being made, tasks which the societies were loath to perform. They were given no additional funding or staffing for this work, and felt its legal and financial nature meant that it should have been handled by some other organization. The societies were given little or no discretion in this work, all final decisions concerning the disposition of a case having to be referred to the provincial officer. Not only did this increase Kelso's workload, but it also led many societies to resent his control over their work and to identify him as the official chiefly responsible for this unpopular policy. The Toronto Children's Aid Society refused to participate in the implementation of the Children of Unmarried Parents Act unless they received a grant for that purpose. As a result Kelso's office had to undertake investigations and collections in the Toronto area. This imposed extra demands on him, and strained his relationship with the Toronto society still further.

Despite these problems, Kelso's office investigated 13,848 cases involving unmarried parents during the first decade of the act. Of these, approximately a quarter resulted in a settlement being made to the mother and child. In half the cases no settlement could be reached owing to lack of evidence against the alleged father or failure to trace the father, and in the remaining cases no action was desired by the parties concerned. Although many of the children were legally adopted or placed in foster homes, many more were raised by their natural mothers or left to the care of infants' homes.

Even though Kelso did not enjoy his work as provincial officer, he continued to believe in its importance. He told a reporter from the Toronto *Sunday World* in June 1924 that the act was 'an earnest effort to improve conditions and secure some measure of justice to children who are innocent sufferers, and its provisions make it no longer possible that ostensibly respectable men will be fathers of illegitimate children and have the offspring supported by the public.' He also expressed sympathy for the mothers concerned: 'In the main the girls in the cases have lived decent lives aside from the one big mistake, and when the law steps in to assist them in establishing the rights of the offspring they are as a rule truthful, penitent and humiliated ...' As the decade progressed, however, Kelso's sympathy for the unmarried mother declined. He expressed regret that the act did not give him the power forcibly to remove a child from an 'incompetent and penniless' unmarried mother, and he advocated closer investigation by the courts into the character and conduct of a woman filing a paternity suit: 'The mere fact that there is an infant to provide for is not sufficient to justify court action. If the girl's character has been notoriously bad and she has been known to go with several men, then she forfeits the right to consideration under this Act.' He also urged caution against the initiation of court action when the evidence of paternity was somewhat doubtful, claiming that this often did more harm than good: 'The result of such court proceedings, whether established or not, can entirely destroy the happiness of a family and possibly break up the home.' Nevertheless, Kelso went to great pains to persuade unmarried mothers to divulge the identity of the father of her child, even when she was most reluctant to do so.

Kelso's increasingly unsympathetic attitude to the unmarried mother reflected in part his belief that in all cases involving children born out of wedlock, the interests of the infant should be paramount. His concern for the well-being of unmarried parents was tempered by his strong disapproval of their conduct, and the misery he felt they had almost inevitably brought upon their offspring. He expressed his feelings concerning the fate of these children in a poem written in the late 1920s, entitled simply 'The Child of the Unmarried Mother':

> Oh, lot most sad! When these sweet opening buds,
> Fresh garnered from the fair, celestial fields,
> No welcome here when first they touched earth-shore!
> When tender untried feet must learn alone,
> Without a loving guide, Life's thorny path
> To tread! With jostle rude they're hurried on,
> E'en driven to the path of sin and crime,
> And no kind hand points to a better way,
> Down, down they go! 'Tis not as it should be,
> And God, our just and good, will not of them
> Require full talents ten.

The Adoption Act, although passed during the same session as the Children of Unmarried Parents Act, was a quite separate piece of legislation intended to enable foster parents to confer on their foster children all the legal rights of natural children. No provision for this arrangement was included in the Children's Protection Act, and for many years Children's Aid Societies had drawn attention to the need for formal adoption procedures. Many anomalous situations arose in which children were unable to inherit from their foster parents, or to take on their name. The need to provide a means by which children could be fully and permanently integrated into their new families was widely supported by child welfare workers, and the passage of the Adoption Act in 1921 was considered long overdue. The act gave county judges the authority to grant adoption orders, after obtaining the consent of the parties involved. The role of the provincial officer was to certify that the child had lived with the applicant for at least two years and that during that period the conduct of the applicant and the conditions under which the child lived were satisfactory. The provincial officer could also recommend that the two-year period be waived, if he considered the applicants to be fit and proper persons to have the care and custody of the child. He was to be assisted in the work of assessing prospective adoptive parents by the Children's Aid Societies.

Kelso's appointment as provincial officer to administer the Adoption Act proved more enjoyable than his responsibilities under the Children of Unmarried Parents Act. Most of the applications for adoption, particularly in the early years, came from foster parents who already had guardianship of a child, and it was a simple matter of substituting the more formalized legal adoption procedures for the earlier written agreements. Kelso gained great satisfaction in establishing permanent links between parents and children, and he followed the progress of many of the adopted children with interest. He expressed great pleasure if an adopted child came into an inheritance, which he viewed as an indication of the act's success.

Towards the late 1920s an increasing number of unmarried mothers began to give up their children for adoption. Previously the children had either been given to another family through the maternity boarding homes, left to the care of an infants' home, or brought up by the mother herself. Kelso became active in finding homes for the children of unwed mothers given up for adoption. He frequently inserted photographs of these children in the Toronto newspapers, and many children were placed in this way. He also frequently wrote articles for the newspapers, and women's and church magazines, discussing the issues involved in adoption of children and giving advice on the raising of adopted children. His advice to those thinking of adopting an infant was to 'see the child for yourself, and instinct will quickly tell you whether or not you can love it as your own. A clear skin and good strong eyes are two of the qualities to be desired.' He cautioned against publicizing the fact that a child had been adopted, and felt that it was not particularly important for a child to be told that it was adopted: 'When you take the baby home don't call in the neighbours to show them your treasure. Publicity of that kind is hurtful to the child's future. Do not even allow your closest relatives to refer to the adoption. If promptly discouraged they will soon cease to think much about it. It is not necessary to tell a child he has been adopted until he asks the question himself. A child will always yield a quicker obedience and respect when he considers himself an integral part of the family.' Kelso's advice received wide circulation in magazines and newspapers, and influenced the policies and practices of Children's Aid Societies and adoptive parents throughout the province.

In statistical terms the Adoption Act was a success during Kelso's term as administrator. In the early 1920s a large number of foster parents took advantage of the act, and towards the end of the decade the increasing number of children of unmarried mothers given up for adoption produced a steady supply of infants to meet the demand from childless couples. Kelso boasted in his annual report for 1930 that 'the fact that in nine years of operation [of the Act] nearly six thousand adoption orders have been completed indicates that the public are alive to the advantages it offers.' He was particularly proud that in not one instance had a legal adoption order been upset on appeal to the courts. He attributed much of the success of the act to the goodness and kindliness of those families that were willing to adopt a child. 'We must bear tribute to the depth of affection that springs up in the hearts of foster parents for children bereft of other earthly ties. Often we have thanked God for the marvellous winning power He has given to little women – if it were not for this the world would indeed be a cold and dreary place.'

By the mid-twenties Kelso's transition from social reformer to public administrator was virtually complete. His day-to-day activities differed little from those of most other middle-to-senior rank government officials. His attitude to reform underwent a parallel transformation. No longer did the imperfections of Canadian society prompt him to advocate legislative changes, and he was more and more content to rest on his laurels. He summed up his views on the tasks remaining for child welfare workers in his annual report for 1924: 'There is little left to strive for in the way of new child welfare legislation. The child protection laws now on the statute books, with workable improvements from time to time, should suffice for years to come, for progress has been so rapid we have more legislation on our statute books than can be digested. A few years could profitably be spent in assimilating these laws, getting them understood by the people, developing the machinery for efficient administration, and coordinating all the many activities that have been called into existence through popular demand.'

8

Declining Influence

Despite the Drury government's legislative achievements in child welfare matters, its defeat in the general election of 25 June 1923 caused Kelso no regret. He was discouraged by its failure to provide adequate funds for the implementation of the Children of Unmarried Parents Act, and by its failure to increase his salary. 'The end of a Government that did nothing for me,' he commented in his notebook shortly after the election. Drury was replaced by Conservative premier Howard Ferguson. This result did not particularly please Kelso, as his political sympathies lay generally with the Liberal party, but the change of government did provide him with an opportunity to attempt to extricate himself from his burdensome administrative duties.

Just prior to the election Kelso proposed to the annual conference of the Association of Children's Aid Societies that the administration of social welfare in Ontario should be completely restructured. His concern was the proliferation of departments dealing with social welfare matters: 'We have children's aid work under the Provincial Secretary, Juvenile Court work under the Attorney-General, health work in the Department of Labour, school attendance under the Minister of Education, and child labour under another department. All these various units dealing with aspects of the same problem are working independently of each other, and in many cases without one knowing what the others are doing. There is large expenditure and not the coordination there should be.' To remedy this situation, Kelso proposed the establishment of a Social Welfare Department encompassing all these activities, with child welfare being given the status of a 'very important sub-department.' This was not an original idea as social workers for some time had been aware of the inadequacy of the existing administrative structure. However, Kelso's public support of administrative change and the election of a new government gave the issue new prominence, and a number of leading social service organizations advocated consolidation of the province's social welfare activities during late 1923 and into 1924.

Kelso supported the establishment of a Department of Social Welfare for two reasons. Firstly, he strongly believed that such a consolidation would enable social work to be undertaken more efficiently, effectively, and economically. He felt that the prestige of a separate department devoted entirely to social welfare would result in this work being given a higher priority by the provincial government. Secondly, Kelso saw in the reorganization proposal a chance to gain the freedom from bureaucratic routine which he so earnestly desired. It was this latter factor which prompted him in May 1924 to write to Premier Ferguson raising again the need for a Department of Social Welfare. In his letter Kelso reiterated the usual arguments in support of this change, but also raised the question of his own role in the proposed department. He made it clear that he was not interested in becoming the head of the new organization. That job, he proposed, should be given to a capable businessman, not older than middle-age, with a woman social worker as assistant. 'Regarding myself, the ... numerous pieces of social legislation passed ... have been largely brought about through the educational work I have been doing for the past thirty-five years and I recognize that in the interests of the work it is better for me to stand aside and allow entirely new people to take charge of the situation. I might continue in the capacity of Social Advisor to the government without any special duties and generally give the Province the benefit of a lifetime's experience.' A position as adviser without administrative duties would have ideally suited Kelso at this stage of his career, but once again he was disappointed. Although the Ferguson government gave serious consideration to an amalgamation, strong opposition from within the civil service resulted in the scheme being dropped late in 1924. The idea gained prominence again in the late 1920s, but by that time it was too late to have a major influence on Kelso's prospects and he continued to carry a heavy administrative load.

Kelso's involvement in administrative tasks, and his declining energies, resulted in others taking over the leadership of the child welfare movement during the mid-1920s. The government increasingly looked to other social workers for advice on child welfare policy, and particularly to Robert Mills, the director of the Toronto Children's Aid Society. Mills sympathized with the problems of shortage of staff and funds which were hindering Kelso in his work, but nevertheless critized him for lack of leadership and out-of-date methods. In a confidential memorandum written in January 1924 to the Hon. Lincoln Goldie, provincial secretary in Ferguson's cabinet, Mills claimed that Kelso was to blame for many of the shortcomings of the child welfare system: 'It is only fair to the Government to say that Mr. Kelso has not of late years given the leadership ... required. His standards of social work have not always been up to the level recognized by social workers and his general "laisser faire" attitude has lost for him the confidence of progressive people in social work.' Mills' specific complaints about Kelso's leadership included lack of supervision of Children's Aid Societies, failure to enforce high standards in methods of child care, bias against professional social workers, and failure to resolve the continuing financial problems of child welfare work in the province. He claimed that inspection of the Children's Aid Societies by Kelso's office had all but ceased by the early 1920s, and he was critical of the child placement methods in adoption and fostering work. Mills claimed that adoptions were being approved by Kelso with only a minimum of investigation, as speed in making the placement was the main consideration. He believed that each case should be intensively investigated before an adoption was approved. He applied the same principle to foster home placements, and questioned Kelso's policy that all foster care should be undertaken on a voluntary basis and his belief that love of children was the only essential quality for foster parents. Mills was not himself a trained social worker, but he held a Masters Degree in Political Economy from the University of Toronto and strongly favoured the employment of professional university-trained workers by child welfare agencies. Kelso was by no means opposed to this in principle, but in the eyes of Mills and others he did not fully appreciate the contribution which professional social workers could make, and did not press strongly enough for their employment by Children's Aid Societies.

The major disagreement between Mills and Kelso, however, concerned the method by which child welfare service should be financed. Mills shared none of Kelso's reluctance regarding government funding, and he held Kelso largely responsible for the failure of the municipalities and the province to provide adequate funds for children's services. The Children's Protection Act had been amended in 1919 to compel the municipalities to pay a minimum of fifty cents a day for each child from that municipality committed to the care of a society. Kelso was wary about enforcing this provision, as he feared this would lead to increasing political control of the Children's Aid Societies by the municipalities and a decline in voluntary giving. It was left to Mills to press the municipalities into compliance, to work out a formula to determine the liability of the municipalities, and to propose further amendments to the legislation to ensure that the societies received all the monies to which they were entitled. Kelso's neglect of these matters lowered his popularity and standing with the younger generation of social workers still further. By the mid-1920s he was seen by many younger workers as the standard bearer of an old guard of child welfare workers whose day had passed.

By this time, moreover, Kelso's interest in child welfare work was waning, and he began to devote more attention to other aspects of his life. He now spent most of his evenings in the company of family and friends. The Kelsos did more entertaining and dining out together than had been possible in the earlier, busier days of their marriage. Kelso's close friends were few, but many evenings were spent in the company of his small circle of intimates, particularly Dr Robert J. Reade, a dental surgeon whom Kelso had known since school days, and Mr Nicolson, a fellow official in the provincial secretary's department. Kelso frequently lunched with his wife in the city, and they also regularly attended the theatre together. Weekends were often spent gardening, or going for motor car rides with their son, Martin. All this was a pleasant change from the hectic pace of the previous forty years.

Kelso's family life was a source of great pleasure to him during these years. He celebrated his twenty-fifth wedding anniversary on 25 June 1926, and he and Mrs Kelso were sent congratulatory messages from the executive of the Association of Children's Aid Societies and many other associates. Although Mrs Kelso suffered from frequent illness and still missed her southern home, the marriage had settled into a pleasant and quite happy routine. Mrs Kelso was active in the Women's Art Association and the Big Sisters Association, and took part in the social activities associated with Kelso's work. Martin, the Kelsos' eldest child, graduated from Osgoode Hall Law School in June 1927, and their daughter Irene was attending an art college. Both children still lived at home, and their achievements and interests were a major source of enjoyment to Kelso during these years.

The Kelsos were of sufficient means to employ a servant, dine out frequently, take summer holidays, and invest in stocks and real estate, yet Kelso's long-standing habit of fretting over his financial affairs remained. Financial concerns were the main topic in his diary during the mid and late 1920s, and the entries show his preoccupation with the value of his shares, the returns from his real estate, and the state of his almost perpetual salary negotiations with the provincial government. He received a salary increase from $3150 to $3600 in September 1925, and two years later this was raised to $4,000. However, until his retirement, he continually complained that he was underpaid, and missed no opportunity to press for an increase.

Despite his absorption in financial concerns, Kelso's judgment in these matters was often poor. He made his worst blunder in 1923 when he sold the family home on Prince Arthur Avenue for what he considered to be a good price, without checking market prices with sufficient care. The result was that he could not afford to purchase a replacement home of equal quality and convenience. Finally, in some desperation, the family purchased the upper two floors of a single family house at 96 Albany Avenue, which had been converted into a duplex. It was conveniently located, near the Parliament Buildings, but it was not nearly as fine a dwelling, and the move was regretted by the whole family. Kelso resided at the Albany Avenue house for the remainder of his life.

Kelso's gradual withdrawal from reform activities also enabled him to devote more attention to church work. He became superintendent of the Sunday school at St James Square Presbyterian Church in 1919 and held that position until the church closed in 1929. Mr and Mrs Kelso regularly attended the St James Square Church throughout their married life, and Kelso was a keen student of the Bible, frequently quoting texts and passages in his speeches and reports. In 1929 the Kelsos transferred their membership to the Bloor Street United Church, where Kelso was elected an elder in January 1931.

Kelso also stepped up his involvement in the Toronto Humane Society. He had regularly attended the meetings of the society since its founding in 1887, and had continued as a member of the Board of Directors. However, in 1918 he became the society's treasurer, a position he held until 1935. The job presented a considerable challenge. The society was several thousand dollars in debt during the early 1920s, and Kelso had the main responsibility for getting the organization back on a sound financial footing. Showing some of the flair of his younger days, Kelso successfully led a fund-raising campaign which not only wiped out the debt but also provided enough income for the society to build a new headquarters which was opened by Premier Ferguson in November 1928. Kelso was the only charter member of the Humane Society in attendance at the opening of the new building, and it was a memorable occasion for him. 'The culmination of my hopes and expectations for the Humane Society,' he wrote in his diary. Another event which had a special significance for him took place in October 1924 when, largely through his efforts, the American Humane Association held its 48th annual conference in Toronto. Kelso chaired the session on child protection, and reminded delegates of the previous occasion in 1888 when the conference was held in Toronto and of the important role which the local Humane Society had played at that time in promoting child welfare reform.

Although Kelso's influence and active involvement in child welfare matters was declining, he continued to make frequent public statements on current issues, and was often asked to state his opinions on various matters by the press. Occasionally in these statements he advocated new programmes and policies. He proposed, for example, the establishment of supervised family playgrounds in residential blocks to reduce the number of children killed on the roads. He also suggested the formation of a Mothers' Help Association to provide over-burdened mothers with a voluntary home help service. Most often, however, he spoke in public to oppose developments in public policy, particularly those which he viewed as attacks on family life and proper child-rearing. He strongly opposed the establishment of divorce courts to ease the process of obtaining a divorce, claiming that 'the evils of divorce are ten times greater than the hardships imposed by a strict and unbreakable marriage law.' He claimed that 60 per cent of the children in juvenile institutions were from divorced parents. 'The sacredness of the marriage relationship is the foundation on which the home rests and thoughtful people should insist on its inviolability.' He also spoke out against the establishment of birth control clinics, drawing attention to the dangerous effect they might have on public morality. During the campaign prior to the plebiscite for repeal of the Ontario Temperance Act Kelso came out strongly for prohibition, once again stressing the overriding importance of satisfactory home life: 'The passage of the Ontario Temperance Act brought an immense change in the treatment of children, and an equally marked change in the whole social work of the province. Homes that were being broken up by drunkenness were straightened up, and there was great improvement in the feeding and clothing of the children. In the early days we used to be deluged with letters describing the suffering of children whose parents were the victims of drink, but after the Act was passed that ceased almost entirely. In the light of these facts I would regard the repeal of the Act as a backward step of grave importance.'

Kelso also opposed, even more strongly than earlier in his life, all forms of charitable donations to the poor. His strong views on this subject led him to the extreme position of advocating 'judicious starving' in order to discourage the poor from becoming paupers: 'Those who look for charity and accept it un-blushingly have already lost their self-respect and have fallen to the lowest depths of degredation ... They should be made to suffer a little and to realize that "if they will not work neither should they eat."' The range of programmes which Kelso now defined as charitable relief was extensive. Not only did he continue to oppose giving hungry children free meals at school but he also spoke out against allowances to deserted wives and expressed doubts about old-age pensions. Both of these were policies which Kelso had supported as a younger man. The policy which he opposed most strongly, however, was the granting of relief payments to unemployed men. Even the mass unemployment of the early 1930s did not weaken his belief that public relief was without benefit to society, and that the only return was 'confirmed idleness and pauperism, loss of the fine spirit of thrift and independence, and an ever increasing social burden.' The remedies he proposed at various times for mass unemployment included shorter working hours for the working classes, an expansion of public works programmes, and more friendly concern on the part of good citizens. He also proposed a reduction in the number of women in the work force: 'Women have supplanted men in many occupations and they neglect the tasks that nature intended them to do. The natural desire to be with men prompts them to go to university and to mannish employments. All this should be checked and more women kept at social and domestic duties.'

Kelso's views on charity reflected the strict paternalism which increasingly dominated his approach to social questions in the late 1920s and early 1930s. He had no qualms about proposing drastic policies affecting the lives of the least fortunate members of the community if he felt such policies were in the interests of society as a whole. The wishes and aspirations of the poor were given only scant consideration. This approach was particularly evident in his attitude towards criminals and the mentally deficient. He argued that criminals should be treated as sick persons, who were mentally and morally diseased and in need of therapy from respectable members of society: 'To restore criminals to a normal condition their physical health should be improved and then the mental attitude should be brought into harmony with what is worth uplifting.' He advocated giving many criminals indeterminate sentences, early release depending entirely upon 'the patient's responses to kindly influences.' He also proposed, contrary to his earlier beliefs, that juveniles guilty of minor offences who showed no signs of penitence should be whipped in the hope that this would awaken them to the errors of their ways. Kelso's answer to the problem of mental deficiency was even more severe. He believed that the feeble-minded constituted a major threat to Canadian society and advocated the establishment of separate colonies or villages for the care of this class and compulsory sterilization. He expressed his concern on this issue in dramatic terms: 'Is there not the danger, with the great and admirable advance in humane sentiment, of perpetuating and increasing the unfit of our own race – spending our time and money in the preservation of human derelicts that can never be other than a burden and expense to us and to themselves? No radical attempt has yet been made to limit the propagation of the insane, the feeble-minded, the diseased, the congenital and incurable criminal, and in this helpless and irresolute position, are we not in grave peril, as a race, of ultimate and certain destruction at the hands of a worthless and unregenerate horde, now being tenderly cared for through a wrong conception of Christian duty?'

In many of these statements concerning the treatment of criminals and the feeble-minded Kelso was simply echoing the common wisdom of the day. On no issue was he any longer to be found among those advocating major changes in social policy. On the contrary, he was now usually in the company of those defending existing policies and established institutions. Not that many listened to him any more; but those who did noticed but few traces of the enthusiasm for new ideas which characterized much of his earlier public life.

Kelso's declining enthusiasm for his work was related in part to his health.

His hearing began to fail in the early 1920s and as he got older it became difficult for him to take part in group conversations. He tired easily, and throughout the twenties he frequently took afternoons off or arrived at the office late in the mornings. In 1928 he slipped on the ice near the Parliament Buildings and injured the ligaments in his right shoulder. This kept him away from work for several weeks. In November 1930 he began to experience severe stomach pains.

His illness was diagnosed as cancer of the liver in December. He commenced regular visits to a clinic for x-ray treatment, and from this time only appeared at his office for a few hours each day. His condition was stable for almost two years, but in the summer of 1932 he became weak and listless and his physician recommended surgery. He was operated on in September 1932, and spent the remainder of the year recuperating. On Christmas Day he dined with the family for the first time in many months, and on 3 January 1933 he returned to the office after an absence of almost four months. He received a warm welcome from his staff, and was exceedingly pleased to be back: 'Bright! Cheerful! Happy!' he exclaimed in his diary on 10 January. However, he was still very weak and from this time on he only went into work in the afternoons.

Kelso's ill health led to others taking over his authority in child welfare matters. In September 1929 the Ontario government had appointed a Royal Commission on Public Welfare, headed by P.D. Ross, an Ottawa newspaper publisher. The commission's report, presented in August 1930, recommended the establishment of a Department of Public Welfare, including a Child Welfare Branch responsible for supervision of Children's Aid Societies, orphanages, infants' homes, adoptions, and the work with unmarried parents. This was almost identical to the recommendation Kelso had made six years earlier. With unusual speed the government moved to adopt the commission's major proposal, and in September 1930 the new ministry was formed, with the Hon. W.C. Martin as the first minister. Kelso was retained as head of the Child Welfare Branch, but from this time he was virtually in retirement.

The Royal Commission made a number of recommendations concerning the Child Welfare Branch. It proposed increased financial support to the Children's Aid Societies, employment of trained workers in child protection work, reorganization of the superintendent's office, and greater control and direction of child welfare work by the province. Between 1930 and 1935 a number of amendments to the Children's Protection Act were passed to implement these recommendations. The provincial government for the first time was given power to make regulations governing the mode of incorporation, type of constitution, and by-laws of the societies, and the appointment of superintendents of local societies was made subject to the approval of the Department of Public Welfare. Greater stress was placed on the employment of trained staff and the maintenance of accurate records. Kelso was not involved in implementing these changes, many of which he opposed on the grounds that they amounted to excessive government interference in the work of the voluntary societies. He was not asked for his opinion, however, and most of the work of the Child Welfare Branch at this time was directed by M.A. Sorsoleil, the deputy minister of welfare. This was an unsatisfactory arrangement for the government, and Kelso's inability to provide leadership was beginning to present major difficulties. Public inquiries into allegations of maladministration in the Windsor and York Children's Aid Societies were required in late 1933 and early 1934, and the government was inclined to blame Kelso for allowing the situation in both societies to get out of hand. Government ministers and senior officials began to plan for the appointment of a successor to Kelso, who, according to government regulations, was due to retire on his seventieth birthday, 31 March 1934.

Kelso was first informed of his impending superannuation by an official letter from the Public Service Superannuation Board in December 1933. The notification was not unexpected, but it was most unwelcome. Kelso's income had fallen sharply during the 1930s, partly due to the failure of several of his investments and partly as a result of the reduction in civil servants' salaries in Ontario in March 1933. He was eligible for a pension of some $2000, but this meant a further substantial drop in his income, and he had hoped that the government would decide to maintain his appointment even if most of his responsibilities were transferred to others. With this possibility in mind, Kelso circulated the notice of his superannuation to Children's Aid Societies around the province, and let it be known to his friends among the older workers in the societies that he wished his appointment to be continued. He also raised the matter directly with the minister. On 19 March 1934, less than two weeks before the day he was due to retire, Kelso was personally informed by the minister that the government wished him to stay at his post.

It was a victory for Kelso, and the farewell dinner sponsored by the Department of Public Welfare on 22 March turned into a celebration. Kelso was presented by the minister with a suitcase and a book, and many old friends and colleagues were present to offer their congratulations. 'One of the happiest evenings of my life,' Kelso wrote in his notebook the next day, and he was also pleased by the newspaper reaction to the government's decision to retain his services. The Mail devoted several columns to a review of his achievements, and asserted that it would have been folly for the government to have superannuated Kelso when there was nobody else so well qualified to supervise child welfare work: 'We have not seen Mr. Kelso for a long time, but we understand that he is in good health and as full of enthusiasm and the milk of human kindness as ever he was. Therefore, we congratulate the Government upon its decision to request him to remain as honorary Superintendent. In whatever capacity he is retained his advice ought to be invaluable.'

Kelso's pleasure in being retained was short-lived. In early April he went on holiday, and when he returned he was requested by the deputy minister to move out of his office to make way for Mr. B. W. Heise, a young social worker of extensive experience in child welfare who had been appointed as field supervisor of Children's Aid Societies the previous month. Heise was clearly being groomed as Kelso's successor, and his presence in the branch brought home to Kelso the fact that his own career had come to an end. 'Sad, sad day!' he wrote in his diary for 16 April. 'Nothing to do. Office at 10:30. B. W. Heise there – in my room! Spent an hour packing up – no place for me now.' For the next two months Kelso continued to go into the office for a few hours each day, but he spent most of his time putting his papers together and writing to friends and colleagues. His contribution to child welfare administration had come to an end.

On 19 June 1934 Ontario went to the polls and the government changed hands, the Liberals under the Hon. Mitchell Hepburn coming into office. On 9 July the deputy minister called Kelso into his office and informed him that, as an economy measure, the new government had decided to cancel his extension of service and that his salary would terminate at the end of the month. 'Rather shabby treatment after so many years of devoted service,' Kelso commented in his notebook, but he was now aware that there was nothing left for him to do and he reluctantly accepted the decision. He spent most of the remaining days of July gardening at his home, and in his absence his books and papers were removed from his office in the branch and piled up on the floor of a cellar. His career was finished.

News of Kelso's retirement brought in a flood of letters from friends, colleagues, and associates congratulating him and conveying best wishes for his retirement. Mackenzie King, leader of the opposition at the time, wrote expressing his appreciation of Kelso's contribution: 'Your career has been of so great service to your fellowmen that you can afford to sit back and view it with pride, and feel that your day's work has been well done. What delight you must experience in the countless numbers of dependent and neglected little people whose lives you have helped to make self-supporting and full of hope. I remember quite distinctly the time of your first appointment under the Ontario Government. What a pioneer you have been in the all important work instituted at that time.' Miss Charlotte Whitton, the director of the Canadian Welfare Council, reviewed Kelso's contribution in the March 1934 issue of *Canadian Child Welfare*: '... Systems and methods have changed, old procedures passed and new principles come to the fore and yet, in charge of the program in Ontario, there remains the same official who, as a young man, left his newspaper desk to demonstrate the depths of his precepts. Later years and events have brought other figures onto the stage; the younger warriors have perhaps obscured the real importance of the role which Mr. Kelso has played in the development of child protection in Canada. The extent of his contribution, however, is unquestioned and will come into greater perception as social work itself develops and extracts its history from the general mass of records of recent years.' These and other tributes flattered Kelso, but he was gratified most of all by the award of the Silver Jubilee Medal in July 1935, in recognition of his services to child welfare and the humane treatment of animals. It was fitting that this presentation was recommended to the king by the Toronto Humane Society, the organization with which Kelso commenced his activities as a social reformer more than forty-nine years before.

Kelso's transition to retirement had been gradual, and apart from not being obliged any longer to attend his office for a few hours each day, his life continued much as before. Both his children were married in 1932, and his first grandchild was born in May 1935. He spent considerable time with his family, and took his holidays in 1934 with his daughter and son-in-law. He regularly attended church and meetings of the Humane Society, and in May 1935 he presided and spoke at the annual convention of the Ontario Society for the Prevention of Cruelty to Animals. Many of his friends and former colleagues passed away in the early 1930s, and he often attended the funeral services. He also attended a number of reunions and dinners, including a gathering of old members of St James Square Presbyterian Church and a final dinner to mark the closing in December 1934 of the Victoria Industrial School. Ex-colleagues kept him up-to-date on developments in the Child Welfare Branch, and he wrote a number of articles for the *Journal* of the Ontario Humane Society and other publications. He also spent time going through his papers, putting them in order and reflecting on his life and career.

Kelso was an inveterate collector of papers relating to his career, and by the 1930s he had many boxes full of scrapbooks, correspondence, diaries and notebooks, jottings, reports, and other memorabilia. He planned for many years to write his memoirs, and during his last few years in government service he dictated accounts of various incidents and projects in which he had been involved. He also set down his views on child welfare methods, and recounted his personal feelings on his life's work. Although Kelso never managed to compile an orderly draft of these memoirs, they do provide a valuable picture of his retrospective evaluation of his activities and contributions.

In the discussion of child welfare methods contained in the memoirs Kelso reasserted the themes which had dominated his thinking throughout his life, and attacked the views of some of the younger social workers. He stressed that the child should be the focus of all social reform efforts: 'In concentrating philanthropic effort upon the children we have the simplest, the surest, and the most economic method of advancing the general happiness and welfare of our country.' He emphasized, as he had throughout his career, that child-saving was not charity but sound economics: 'Every child developed in mind and body and trained in habits of industry is of great potential value to the community. Child-saving is an investment yielding big returns.' Kelso wrote extensively concerning the crucial role played in child-raising by the family which he described as 'the bulwark of the State, the foundation pillar on which our entire social superstructure is built.' The support of family life, he therefore reasoned, should be the first priority in child welfare work. He displayed an intolerance of neglectful parents which was stronger than ever before, and advocated strictness and severity in dealing with those who were not raising their children in the correct manner.

Kelso wrote at length on the role of modern social workers, and his views reflected his concern with the rapid professionalization of child welfare which was taking place towards the end of his career. He restated his support for the training of social workers, but proposed that the personality and attitude of the worker was still the crucial factor in his or her effectiveness: 'A loving and sympathetic attitude towards the poor and distressed is the first essential. Sometimes we meet workers who can talk very learnedly about cases of distress, and yet feel instinctively that they have but little real understanding of the human being, with sad and troubled heart, who is behind the problem. They speak officially or as an expert diagnosing the case instead of as a friend anxious to bring relief and consolation.' He also asserted, even more strongly than earlier in his life, the importance of religion in social welfare work, and he wrote that all who engage in social service should be motivated by the Gospel of Christ. He recommended religious belief for the underprivileged as well: 'The Gospel message imparts an inward joy that makes poverty endurable, and sets at work those spiritual forces that can surely overcome temporary adverse conditions.'

Kelso's assessment of his life's work reflected the heightened religiosity of his old age. He described his efforts as 'the fulfilling of a divine purpose,' and stated that his life had been dominated by the conviction that God was working in and through him. This did not, however, lead him to downplay his own role or contribution. He attributed the success of the Children's Aid Societies not to the provisions of the 1893 legislation, but to the fact that 'provision was made for an interested official to put life and enthusiasm into the movement.' He repeatedly stressed the pioneering nature of his contribution, which he contrasted with the lesser tasks of consolidation and review which were the lot of those that came after him. He stressed that the most difficult phase of child welfare work had been completed and that there was little left to do, other than to implement the structures and procedures which had been established and to strive for greater efficiency. Looking back on his efforts and accomplishments gave Kelso great satisfaction, and he had no doubt that his life had brought much good into the world. 'It is only now in my retirement,' he wrote, 'that I am able to grasp the full significance of early endeavours to advance the comfort and happiness of the people.'

Kelso expressed greatest satisfaction of all, however, with his achievements in securing good homes for thousands of neglected and dependent children. He claimed that in the course of his career he had personally placed four thousand unwanted or neglected children in homes, and described this as a 'great and abiding joy.' He maintained contact with many of these children after they grew up, and among the most satisfying experiences of his last years of life were the invitations he received to dine or to meet with former wards who had established themselves in society. Kelso's concern for children had always been rooted in his warm and sympathetic personality, and in retrospect he felt that his friendships with the children he had helped were the most rewarding experiences of his long career.

Although Kelso expressed his sense of achievement and satisfaction in his accomplishments, the predominant tone of his memoirs was one of regret. He expressed concern that he had never had the time to enjoy recreation and leisure activities, and recommended to others that they 'don't put off reasonable enjoyment till some later day for alas as the years go by you lose the capacity for enjoyment. Be happy now or never.' He ruefully wrote in the margin that 'the advisor did not follow his own advice.' He also stressed the importance of friendships, and his disappointments on this score: 'The greatest loss: the sacrifice of friendship. Thought I could not afford the time to cultivate the friendship of companions. My work gained but oh! what a loss to me personally, especially now when my work is done and when most needed the friends of youth and strangers! My advice therefore to young people is to maintain the intimacy of association with congenial spirits. Few ambitions or occupations are worth the sacrifice of friends.'

The most important mistake Kelso felt he had made in his life was his decision to enter government service. He explained that his intention had been to be the connecting link between philanthropic work and the government, 'combining the interest and sympathy of the former with the official and authoritative attitude of the latter.' This aim, he felt, he had failed to achieve, and he stated that his career could have been far more successful had he confined himself to philanthropy:

Philanthropic and social work of all kinds is better in the hands of private organizations than under Government control. The fact that I was for forty years a government official might prove that my work was properly governmental, but that would be hardly correct, since nearly everything that I did was more philanthropic than official. All those years I was in the wrong place. My hope, desire and aim was to carry on great Christian rescue work, somewhat similar to that of Dr. Barnardo in England, and had I only got started right there is no doubt I could have raised hundreds of thousands of dollars for such a worthy cause. No one would give money to a government enterprise and the Government was not interested enough to vote the funds necessary to ensure efficiency ... Had I my life to live over again it would certainly not be as a government official. For had my original purpose been realized the Children's Protection work would now have been a great national movement, well organized, well endowed, and well thought of by all classes of the community. I say this as a carefully considered belief and not at all in a boastful spirit and all I ask is that in any appraisal of my work the handicaps be remembered. I laboured in confined space, with hands tied, lips sealed, and with only such supplies and tools as I could manage to secure by the most strenuous effort.

Two other consequences which Kelso attributed in large part to a life spent in government service were lack of appreciation and inadequate financial compensation. 'Sometimes in these latter days of retirement one is apt to cultivate a gloomy outlook and to conclude past efforts quite forgotten,' he wrote in his diary in January 1935, and the same theme cropped up repeatedly in his memoirs, mixed with strong feelings of resentment towards his successors. He expressed his feelings in a metaphor concerning a new machine: 'A youth sets out to invent and design an intricate piece of machinery. Not understanding the object in view, no one bothered him much so that he succeeded in creating a valuable and much-needed machine. When it was all ready to do its work men came forward and claimed they could run it better than he could. They succeeded in setting him aside but not having built it they could not get the best results. In addition to slow speed it was constantly being "repaired" when all it needed was a capable engineer – such as the inventor. The application of this illustration is to the social reformer who receives but little attention until his work becomes familiar and popular when others immediately seek to claim the credit. After enduring the heat and burden of the day he is pushed aside by unscrupulous people who arrive at the last moment.'

Finally, Kelso in his memoirs returned to a complaint which he had expressed many times throughout his life – lack of financial reward. He described this as his 'greatest handicap and embarrassment' in life, claiming that he was 'always in debt; always compelled to stint and economize both in personal expenditure and in general activities.' Kelso aspired throughout his life to the image of the wealthy benefactor who, having achieved worldly success, was motivated by kindliness and sensitivity to aid his less fortunate fellow humans. The life of a moderately paid government official working steadily for social improvements he considered a poor second best.

Kelso's failure to complete his memoirs was the result of the recurrence of his illness in mid-summer 1935. His health steadily declined. He received many letters wishing him a speedy recovery, but by September he knew that he was dying. On 25 September he wrote a farewell letter to his wife. Five days later, at 3:00 AM on 30 September 1935, he passed away.

Newspapers throughout the province carried editorials praising his contribution to child welfare work. The *Globe* described him as one of Canada's greatest social reformers: '... all his actions, public and private, were governed by kindness and consideration for others.' A private funeral service was held by the family on Thursday, 3 October, followed later in the afternoon by a public service at Bloor Street United Church. Among the many who sent flowers were a number of Kelso's former wards, expressing their thanks for the last time to the man who had befriended them and worked for the protection of children in similar circumstances for the whole of his adult life.

9

In Retrospect

Kelso was an innovator who advocated or introduced social measures many years ahead of others. He was among the first Canadians to promote such policies as foster care for neglected children, juvenile courts, public playgrounds, mothers' allowances, and social settlements. However, none of these reform proposals was novel. His contribution was not as an original thinker on social issues but rather as a popularizer and promoter within Ontario of policies and programmes already developed elsewhere. Kelso read widely and regularly attended conferences of social reformers in the United States. He was sensitive to public opinion, and showed great determination and perseverance in pursuit of his chosen policies. As a young man he had a remarkable gift for inspiring and encouraging others to join and work for his causes. In retrospect, his major contribution to the cause of neglected and dependent children was to mobilize into effective reform movements those Canadians whose conceptions of children and child-rearing underwent radical change in the late nineteenth century.

Kelso was at his best as the instigator of a new reform organization. His usual tactic in initiating a movement was to call a meeting or speak individually with a small group of selected citizens. Those he first approached included leaders of community organizations and those with a known interest in the topic. If his proposals were well received, he would then call a public meeting. The purpose of this gathering was not to encourage debate, but to initiate action in response to the problem or concern. The format of the meeting varied somewhat, depending on the locale and the issue. However, two features were constant. Well-known citizens would be invited to speak in support of the principles of the proposed action, and Kelso himself would make a speech outlining in more detail what needed to be done. He was an inspiring speaker, and often used lantern slides to heighten the impact of his presentation. The climax of these meetings was usually a motion, proposed by a prominent member of the audience, that an organization be formed to take appropriate action, and that a committee and office-bearers (already informally agreed upon) be elected. These motions were usually accepted unanimously, and a social reform organization was created to carry on the work.

These organizations played the key role in Kelso's reform movements. Typically, he became an officer of the organization, most often honorary secretary. From this position he controlled and guided the organization, simultaneously acting as fund-raiser, public relations officer, theoretician, and record-keeper. When his control of an organization was threatened, as happened in the Toronto Humane Society and the Toronto Children's Aid Society, he was not averse to resigning and finding or forming a new means by which to achieve his goals and exert his influence. Kelso's attitude to the organizations with which he was involved was that they were first and foremost instruments for his own reform objectives. Although he believed in the importance of the participation of respectable citizens in social welfare activities, citizen involvement as such was not his primary aim. His over-riding concern was the effectiveness of his organization as a reform agency, and all else was subjected to this aim.

Having formed and gained control of an organization, Kelso used it as the base from which to engage in pressure-group politics. In the name of the organization, he led deputations, organized conferences, wrote submissions, addressed meetings, raised funds, and wrote letters and articles to the newspapers. When he became superintendent he simply transferred his reform tactics to the public sector. He did not consider that as a government official he would necessarily exert more influence. Rather, he viewed the superintendency as a base from which to organize social reform. His annual reports, for example, were clarion calls to reform activity rather than simply administrative accounts. For many years Kelso found the superintendency a most strategic position, giving him both added prominence and statutory powers and responsibilities. His discontent in later life was in large part due to his failure to recognize that the role of civil servants had changed, and that the superintendency was no longer a viable base for reform activities. The notion of working quietly and discreetly within the bureaucracy to influence new and on-going policies was never seriously considered by Kelso as a social reform strategy.

Kelso's reform tactics reflected his views about the causes of social problems and his notions of social change. He believed that societal improvement resulted primarily from concerted action by committed private individuals who were motivated by concern for the public welfare. He thought that there were no conflicts in society that could not be solved by appeals to man's better nature. All Kelso's social reform activity was predicated on the assumption that reform could be successfully implemented if politicians, parents, officials, employers, and the general public could be persuaded to act in a more humane and moral manner.

In Kelso's view there were four sectors of society with a crucial and distinctive role to play in social reform. Firstly, he saw the social and economic élite of the community as indispensable elements in any successful reform movement. These were the people whose support Kelso sought when forming the Toronto Humane Society and the Toronto Children's Aid Society, and his ability to involve leading businessmen, churchmen, professional men, and politicians in his organizations was one of the major factors in his success. One of the key roles of this group, in his view, was to provide funding for social welfare, through bequests, large donations to specific causes or projects, and regular financial support of reform organizations. Kelso believed that voluntary private giving was preferable to public funding of social welfare activities. Even late in his life, when government funding of Children's Aid Society work was an established principle and an obvious economic necessity, he maintained his belief that public funding was inimical to child protection work. Besides providing funds, élite support provided influence and access for Kelso's reform movements. As members of the boards of reform societies prominent businessmen and politicians could ensure access to government leaders, and the receptiveness of provincial ministers to Kelso's solicitations and requests during the early years of his career was largely due to his prestigious backing. Kelso was a far more influential figure as the spokesman for organizations comprised of members of Toronto's social and business élite than he was in later life as a senior civil servant.

The second group on whom Kelso relied for the implementation of his reform strategy was the Canadian middle class. Professionals, small businessmen, civil servants, clergy, students, and the wives and daughters of these men comprised the rank and file of the reform organizations with which Kelso was associated. To a certain extent this group, like the élite, contributed money and influence. They paid annual membership fees to the reform organizations, donated relatively small sums of money, and attended public meetings. In smaller communities, in particular, they provided the financial and political backing for the work of the Children's Aid Societies. The most important contribution of the middle class, however, was to provide the manpower for reform organizations. The work of the Children's Aid Societies in the early years was performed principally by volunteers, as also in the Humane Society, the Fresh Air Fund, and the visiting committees. In later years such organizations as Central Neighbourhood House and the Toronto Playgrounds Association, and the movement for mothers' allowances, were also supported predominantly by the middle class. Another major, although somewhat less tangible role played by the middle class was to provide the example, the model, for child-rearing and proper moral behaviour generally. The ethical code and standards of conduct espoused by the middle class were, in Kelso's view, the ideals towards which less privileged members of society should strive. The middle class had a responsibility to live up to its ideals and thus be an illustration of proper living for others to follow. This attitude was most clearly expressed in the settlement movement, but it underlay all Kelso's efforts in the child welfare field.

The middle class also provided the recruits for the emerging profession of social work, the third group in Kelso's strategy for social reform. By the turn of the century Kelso had come to realize that complete reliance on volunteers in social welfare work was not feasible. He gave his support to the training of social workers and their employment by social agencies. However, he did not favour the substitution of skills and techniques for the benevolence of the voluntary worker. In his view the most important quality for a trained social worker was compassion, and only secondly knowledge and erudition. His growing belief that social work was becoming little more than book learning prompted Kelso's distrust of social workers towards the end of his career.

The fourth and final agency of reform in Kelso's strategy was the government. He saw several roles for governments to play in social reform. Governments could provide voluntary societies and agencies with the statutory authority necessary to achieve their goals. The prime example of this was the 1893 Children's Protection Act, which gave the Children's Aid Societies wide powers to remove children from families in certain circumstances. Secondly, governments had a regulatory or supervisory role with respect to social agencies, ensuring certain standards of service and the economical and efficient provision of services. This Kelso saw as part of his own task as superintendent of neglected and dependent children. Governments also had a major role in prescribing and regulating standards of moral behaviour in the community. Finally, Kelso saw government as having a role in the financing of social welfare. Although he felt voluntary contributions should finance most social services, he believed government financing had a place, such as in the provision of mothers' allowances and in the employment of paid agents to supervise child protection work. Throughout his life, however, Kelso opposed extensive governmental involvement in the direct provision of services, believing that reliance on governmental initiatives sapped the voluntary spirit. For him the only completely acceptable role for the government was to encourage and co-ordinate organizations of private citizens in their work for social welfare.

Energetic, respectable, middle-class voluntary workers, assisted by trained professionals, backed by the wealth and prestige of the social and economic élite, and armed with statutory powers – these were the forces Kelso primarily relied on to reform Canadian society. In his overall strategy there was, however, no place for the participation of the poor. Kelso viewed the poor in an essentially patronizing manner. Although he recognized the difficulties arising from the social conditions in which poor families were forced to live, he believed that poverty was primarily a result of individual weakness or shortcoming, and that the poor needed to be assisted by those better equipped for social action. He did not envisage the poor taking political action in their own interests; this was the task of the charitable members of the middle and upper classes, with their greater experience and more responsible attitude towards political activity.

Kelso could certainly claim some responsibility for many accomplishments. The most significant achievement of his career was the design and establishment of Ontario's child welfare system. He was the leading figure in the establishment of the Toronto Children's Aid Society, the prototype for the Children's Aid Societies which became the key child protection agencies after 1893. Together with his colleagues, Kelso successfully persuaded the Ontario government to grant these new societies broad powers to intervene in family situations in which neglect or cruelty was suspected. As superintendent, he played the key role in providing leadership and direction in the new system. He was personally responsible for the establishment of Children's Aid Societies throughout the province, and was instrumental in the development of similar child welfare systems in the rest of English Canada. Through his annual reports and personal contact with child welfare workers he prescribed the policies and procedures to be followed by the Children's Aid Societies, and the interpretations he gave the Children's Protection Act had a critical influence on the development of child welfare services. Of major significance was his stress on supervised foster care as the preferred method of substitute child care. Kelso's insistence on the superiority of foster homes over all forms of institutional care for children, and his determined and successful struggle to introduce a system of supervised foster homes throughout the province were achievements of lasting consequence.

Against these successes must be weighed Kelso's failures and shortcomings as child welfare administrator. The more specific features of the child welfare system that he advocated were not realized. His fight against institutionalization of neglected, dependent, and delinquent children was ultimately only partially successful. Industrial schools continued to play a role in the care and education of young and potential offenders. Kelso became reconciled to their continued existence.

The Children's Visiting Committees were a complete failure, causing Kelso to modify his beliefs about the superiority of voluntary over paid welfare work. He subsequently promoted the use of paid officials to supervise foster home placements and assist the work of the Children's Aid Societies. But he did not anticipate or support the dominant role of full-time, salaried agents and social workers in the societies that developed towards the end of his superintendency. Kelso's faith in volunteerism and his equivocal views on the appropriateness of government support for private welfare agencies resulted in his failure to provide support to the funding of Children's Aid Societies at a crucial stage in their development. He experienced difficulties in maintaining effective control over the societies. He was also unsuccessful in getting the municipalities to fulfil their responsibilities under the Children's Protection Act, especially in establishing children's shelters.

It might be argued that most of Kelso's failures were due largely to circumstances beyond his control. He was never given adequate resources to perform his responsibilities and there were many obstacles and opponents to be overcome. Working under such constraints, Kelso's achievements as superintendent were considerable. However, there were personal factors that compounded these difficulties. Throughout his career Kelso displayed considerable lack of tact in his dealing with other officials and child welfare workers. He had difficulty, particularly as a young man, establishing effective working relationships with associates in reform organizations, often causing offence by publicly criticizing the work of others. Kelso was unsystematic and ill-suited to routine administrative tasks. This became a major handicap in the later years of the superintendency, when his main responsibility was the orderly supervision of an established system. His greatest achievements as superintendent were in the early years when promotional and inspirational qualities were needed. His chief strengths were his talents as public speaker and journalist, his self-confidence, energy, and enthusiasm, his ability to gain the support of subordinates, and his facility in relating to children. These latter qualities also account for Kelso's success in areas beyond his official jurisdiction. He played a major role in the establishment of the Toronto Humane Society, the campaign for juvenile courts, the playground movement, the development of social settlements in Toronto, and the fight for mothers' allowances. He was also involved to a lesser extent in a score of other issues. He enjoyed public life most of all when he was campaigning for the adoption of a new policy or programme, or establishing a new organization. He considered himself a crusader and an innovator, and was relatively disinterested in details of implementation. In his fifties, however, he lost his enthusiasm for pioneering work. Expanding administrative responsibilities and tighter restrictions on his political activities by the provincial government made it difficult for him to maintain the role of social reformer. His contribution to movements for social change in the post-World War One period was minimal, and much of his dissatisfaction in his later years stemmed from the necessity to undertake work for which he was temperamentally ill-suited.

Many terms have been used to describe J.J. Kelso – social reformer, philanthropist, child-saver, social worker, and humanitarian. All of these labels are to some extent appropriate. However, better insight into Kelso's career comes from an understanding of the major concerns that dominated his social thought, exercising a pervasive influence on his work and writings. The theme of moral uplift runs consistently throughout his writings and speeches. He strongly supported legislation enforcing moral standards in child-rearing, and the penalizing of drunkenness and sexual licence, especially when these impinged on dependent children. He considered the ideal foster home to be one where 'morality, temperance and industry' prevailed, and the qualities he required of foster parents included sobriety and religious belief. At times he seemed as concerned with the bad language, rude behaviour, poor dress, and lack of cleanliness of poor children as with their neglect or abuse. He was prepared to tolerate institutional care of children only if the institution was characterized by a 'high moral atmosphere.' Kelso was dogmatic in his approach to moral issues, and unhesitatingly advocated public enforcement of his own moral standards. In his view social reform was inseparable from moral betterment, and the reformer should strive to create a society of individuals who subscribed to his own moral values.

A second theme which ran through Kelso's career was humanitarianism. Throughout his career his perspective on social welfare was dominated by his feelings of benevolence and compassion for the poor, especially for the children of the poor. It was this humane impulse which first led him to give up his journalism career to embark on a life of service to neglected and ill-treated children. Kindliness, friendliness, and generosity were the hallmarks of all his dealings with neglected children. His close personal association with poverty, as a member of a near destitute immigrant family and then as a police reporter, heightened his awareness of the plight of poor children, and coloured his activities with a passion and urgency not common among his more prosperous fellow reformers. He was highly sensitive to the inhumane treatment received by animals, children, and other defenseless or powerless groups at the hands of the police, government officials, parents, employers, and others in powerful positions. Kelso was angered by the parents who neglected or abused their children, the judges who insensitively tried children charged with petty offences according to the same procedures as hardened criminals, the slum landlord who exploited his tenants, and the employer who overworked and underpaid his employees. For Kelso there was nothing systematic about such behaviour, in the sense that it was based in the structure or ideology of Canadian society. On the contrary, he saw exploitation as essentially the result of unsympathetic or unkind behaviour by a thoughtless or, in some cases, vicious minority. The task of the social reformer, therefore, was to encourage these individuals to see the error of their ways. If this was not possible, then the reformer should press for laws penalizing or prohibiting their behaviour. His aim was to humanize, rather than to transform, Canadian society. Kelso's humanitarianism was practised within certain ideological boundaries. His belief in the dangers of pauperizing by indiscriminate or excessive charitable giving led him, later in life, to advocate 'judicious starving' of children, an attitude difficult to reconcile with the humane impulse. His humanitarianism conflicted at times with his reluctance to permit parents to abdicate their responsibilities and his desire to maintain the spirit of self-help. In short, his moral standards greatly influenced his humanitarianism.

A third dominant theme in his brand of reformism was the importance of social stability. There were several strands to this central theme. Kelso consistently expressed concern over the incidence of crime, especially among the urban poor. His concern for neglected children was not only that they were being physically harmed or denied happy and enjoyable childhood experiences, but also that they were potential offenders. Child-saving, for Kelso, meant not only saving children from cruelty but also saving them from a life of crime. His opposition to reformatories, industrial schools, and other institutions for children was based on his belief that these were ineffective means of diverting neglected children from criminal careers. He advocated juvenile courts to avoid the 'systematic manufacture of criminals' which resulted in 'swelling the criminal classes.' His concern was partly that property and safety were seriously threatened by urban crime. But the themes which dominated his discussions of juvenile delinquency were the loss to the child of its opportunity for a life of honest, useful, and industrious citizenship, and the corresponding loss to the nation of a valued citizen.

Closely related to his desire to combat criminality was Kelso's dislike of disorder and social disorganization. He attacked slum conditions because they did not conform to his vision of an orderly, healthy society. For this reason he recognized there was a need to improve the standard of living among the working class.

Another theme was the importance of efficiency and economy as a rationale for solving social problems. His concern over poverty and neglect was based to a large extent on his belief that these conditions inevitably led to unnecessary expense for society in maintaining police forces, prisons, and various forms of institutional care. The formation of the Toronto Children's Aid Society and the passage of the 1893 Children's Protection Act, two of the most decisive events in Kelso's career, were both strongly influenced by the belief that it was 'less expensive to save Children than to punish Criminals' (as the motto of the Toronto Society proclaimed), and the theme recurred frequently in Kelso's later writings and speeches.

Kelso's stress on social stability reflected his basic satisfaction with the society in which he lived. He eschewed doctrines or philosophies based on notions of conflict among interest groups or social classes. Nowhere in his writings does he raise questions, or even express doubts, concerning the structure and ideology of Canadian capitalist society. He admired those who were successful in the world of business, generally accepted the existence of economic inequality in society, and espoused the merits of hard work and individual effort. It was a deep disappointment to him that despite his energy and exertions he never attained the material rewards he believed were due successful entrepreneurs in all fields of endeavour. His limited aims as a reformer are highlighted by his judgment, in the mid-1920s, that there was little left to accomplish in the child welfare field. Kelso worked, not to bring about fundamental changes in Canadian society, but to promote morality, humanity, orderliness, and stability within that society.

Kelso threaded these strands of his social criticism together by placing children at the centre of his social reform strategy. His involvement in social reform was first motivated by his compassion towards young children. However, it was not long before the child became not merely the object of his pity, but rather the pivot around which his whole reform strategy turned. This focus reflected the upsurge of interest in childhood and child-rearing which developed in late nineteenth-century English Canada, and Kelso became a prominent spokesman of those advocating new attitudes and policies towards children. He became a firm believer in the malleability of a child's character and the overriding importance of environmental influences on a child's development. Although he referred from time to time to the transference of criminal proclivities through heredity – 'the inherited seeds of vice' as he called it – his main stress was on the possibility of reform among even the most 'degraded' children, provided the right methods were used. He described the mind of a child as 'the tenderest and holiest thing on earth,' and his prescription for the reform and rehabilitation of neglected children was simply to expose them to 'kindly influences and home-like surroundings.' He stressed that all those working with neglected or delinquent children should be motivated by kindly and benevolent feelings, and that the example of right living provided by the worker was a most potent force in reforming children. He believed that those working with children should appeal to the child's better nature, and that almost all children would respond positively to a display of love and affection. He opposed institutional care of children on the grounds that children were likely to be exposed to the detrimental influence of more hardened or incorrigible offenders. Central to his work with neglected and dependent children was his emphasis on the importance of the family. He considered the family the major influence, for good or ill, on the development of young children. A child raised in a devout and loving family was, in his view, almost certain to grow up a valued citizen. For Kelso, such a family was the repository for all those values which he saw as the mainstays of social well-being – industry, honesty, thrift, modest behaviour, cleanliness, religious conviction, respect for the law, and a benevolent attitude towards fellow beings. Kelso's advocacy of foster home care was based on this faith in the restoring influence of a good home. Although later in life he reluctantly accepted the need for some form of institutional care for some juvenile offenders, his concern was always that institutional care should be structured to resemble family life.

Kelso's views on the central issue in child welfare – of when to separate a child from allegedly neglectful parents – were modified in the course of his career. In the 1880s and late 1890s he advocated removal of children and placement in a wide range of circumstances. This was reflected in his practices during his early years as superintendent. Around the turn of the century his emphasis changed. He began to stress the value of providing support to families and keeping children with their natural parents if at all possible. Late in life he returned to his earlier stance that separation was desirable in all cases in which there was doubt as to the suitability of the upbringing a child was receiving. Despite these changes, Kelso remained committed throughout his career to certain basic principles in his child welfare work. He consistently advocated placing the interests of the child above those of its parents. He was unwavering in his support of extensive discretionary powers for child welfare workers. He remained firm in his belief that separation of a child from its parents, if undertaken, should be decisive and absolute, the natural parents completely forfeiting their rights to the child.

Kelso's thinking on child welfare methods and social reform dominated the child welfare system in Ontario during the 1890s and early years of the twentieth century. However, during the post-war period other, apparently more sophisticated, approaches came into vogue. Kelso's focus on child welfare as the basis for reform of Canadian society, and his belief in love and compassion as the basis for social work practice, seemed somewhat naïve to a younger generation of social workers trained in psychology, social casework, and research methods. Kelso, who made little effort to adapt to the newer trends, acquired a reputation as an old-fashioned thinker, whose views reflected the approach of an earlier, and now surpassed era. This was of little or no concern to him. He believed the younger social workers to be misguided in their approach to child welfare, and he did not find their views challenging. What concerned him far more was that his contribution to social action was undervalued and unrecognized by his younger colleagues, and this theme recurred frequently in his writing and speeches in his declining years.

A strong desire to receive public recognition for his efforts characterized Kelso's whole career. As a young man he felt a keen sense of shame as a result of his family's misfortunes, and he was deeply motivated to strive to restore his social standing and position. One unpleasant manifestation of his ambition was his continuing preoccupation with financial matters. He was a generous man, but his frequent requests for a higher salary gave an impression of avarice. His failure to accumulate a personal fortune was one of the chief disappointments of his life.

Combined with this personal ambition was a strong sense of social concern and responsibility. Stemming from his devout Protestant upbringing, nurtured by his childhood experiences in Toronto's slums and his early contacts with social reform movements, this sense of concern gradually dominated Kelso's life. Ideally, Kelso aspired to personal fame and fortune as well as to public service. But the role of wealthy philanthropist was not open to him, and he had to settle for the life of a public official. Although he frequently regretted his decision to become a public servant, it is doubtful that he would have made as lasting a contribution to social welfare as a private citizen. Social welfare services during the twentieth century came increasingly under governmental auspices, and, somewhat paradoxically, Kelso's main recognition stems from his role in the establishment of governmental child welfare services.

Notes

CHAPTER 1   Early Life

1 J.C. Beckett, *The Making of Modern Ireland, 1603–1923* (London 1966), 336–50
2 L.M. Cullen, *An Economic History of Ireland since 1660* (London 1972), 110–112, 131–9
3 Arnold Schrier, *Ireland and the American Emigration, 1850–1900* (Minneapolis 1958), 3–17
4 Protestant Irish emigration to North America is discussed in Donald Harman Akenson, *The United States and Ireland* (Cambridge, Mass. 1973), 34, 90–1.
5 Peter G. Goheen, 'Currents of Change in Toronto, 1850–1900,' in Gilbert A. Stelter and A.F.J. Artibise, eds., *The Canadian City* (Toronto 1977), 72–5
6 The following account of the social and economic development of Toronto in the second half of the nineteenth century is based on D.C. Masters, *The Rise of Toronto, 1850–1890* (Toronto 1947), and P.G. Goheen, *Victorian Toronto, 1850–1900: Pattern and Process of Growth* (Chicago 1970).
7 Richard B. Splane, *Social Welfare in Ontario, 1791–1893* (Toronto 1965), 256
8 J.M.S. Careless, *Brown of the Globe* (Toronto 1963), II, 289–98
9 Newspapers in late nineteenth-century Ontario are described in P.F.W. Rutherford, 'The People's Press: The Emergence of the New Journalism in Canada, 1869–99,' *Canadian Historical Review*, LV, 2, June 1975, 169–91; Masters, *Rise of Toronto*, 47–9, 163, and 167–8; and G.P. deT. Glazebrook, *The Story of Toronto* (Toronto 1971), 149–54.

CHAPTER 2   Young Reformer

1 Elisabeth Wallace, *Goldwin Smith: Victorian Liberal* (Toronto 1957), 104–7
2 Ibid.

3 G.P. deT. Glazebrook, *The Story of Toronto* (Toronto 1971), 146

4 Richard B. Splane, *Social Welfare in Ontario, 1791–1893* (Toronto 1965), 13–16

5 Wallace, *Goldwin Smith*, 104

6 Splane, *Social Welfare*, 16

7 Elisabeth Wallace, 'The Changing Canadian State: A Study of the Changing Conception of the State as Revealed in Canadian Social Legislation, 1867–1948,' (PH D thesis, Columbia University, 1950), 25–8

8 Splane, *Social Welfare*, 279

9 Wallace, 'The Changing Canadian State,' 53

10 Splane, *Social Welfare*, 280

11 Ibid., 46–51, and 280–4

12 Ibid., 53–4; Glazebrook, *Story of Toronto*, 143–4

13 Splane, *Social Welfare*, 40–1, and 56–64

14 Ibid., 18–19

15 See D.C. Masters, *The Rise of Toronto, 1850–1890* (Toronto 1947), 186–7.

16 Howland's election and term in office as mayor of Toronto are described in Desmond Morton, *Mayor Howland: The Citizen's Candidate* (Toronto 1973); the urban reform movement in the late nineteenth and early twentieth centuries is discussed in general terms in Paul Rutherford, ed., *Saving the Canadian City: The First Phase, 1880–1920* (Toronto 1974), ix–xxiii.

17 The evangelical movement is described in Masters, *Rise of Toronto*, 134, 158–60, and 186–7; the Prisoners' Aid Association is covered in Splane, *Social Welfare*, 176–8 and 185–6; the Industrial Schools Association is covered in ibid., 248–54.

18 Peter G. Goheen, 'Currents of Change in Toronto, 1850–1900,' in Gilbert A. Stelter and Alan F.J. Artibise, eds., *The Canadian City* (Toronto 1977), 66–70

19 The strike is discussed in Morton, *Mayor Howland*.

20 These notions are discussed in detail in Neil Sutherland, *Children in English-Canadian Society: Framing the Twentieth Century Consensus* (Toronto 1976), 13–28. See also T.R. Morrison, ' "Their Proper Sphere": Feminism, the Family, and Child-Centred Social Reform in Ontario, 1875–1900,' *Ontario History*, LXIX, March 1976, 45–64, and June 1976, 65–74.

21 Sutherland, *Children in English-Canadian Society*, 13–28

22 The history of child welfare policy in Ontario in the nineteenth century is detailed in Splane, *Social Welfare in Ontario*, 214–77.

23 Juvenile delinquency in nineteenth-century Ontario is covered in Sutherland, *Children in English-Canadian Society*, 91–107; J. Jerald Bellomo, 'Upper Canadian Attitudes towards Crime and Punishment (1832–1851),' *Ontario History*, LXIV, March 1972, 11–26; and Susan E. Houston, 'Victorian Origins of Juvenile Delinquency: A Canadian Experience,' *History of Education Quarterly*, XII, fall 1972, 254–80.

24 Splane, *Social Welfare in Ontario*, 265–6

25 Frank J. Bruno, *Trends in Social Work* (New York 1948), 61–2 and 67
26 P.F.W. Rutherford, 'The People's Press: The Emergence of the New Journalism in Canada, 1869–99,' *Canadian Historical Review*, LVI, 2, June 1975, 181
27 Splane, *Social Welfare in Ontario*, 259–60
28 Sutherland, *Children in English-Canadian Society*, 103

CHAPTER 3   Laying the Foundations

1 The appointment of the Royal Commission, its work and its findings are covered in R.B. Splane, *Social Welfare in Ontario, 1791–1893* (Toronto 1965), 54–5, 187–91, 268–71; and Neil Sutherland, *Children in English-Canadian Society: Framing the Twentieth Century Consensus* (Toronto 1976), 109–11.
2 Sutherland, *Children in English-Canadian Society*, 109
3 Kelso's evidence to the Royal Commission is found in *Report of the Commissioners Appointed to Enquire into the Prison and Reformatory System of Ontario, 1891*, Ontario, *Sessional Papers*, 1891, no 13, 723–9.
4 Details of the act are outlined in Splane, *Social Welfare in Ontario*, 273–7.

CHAPTER 4   The Superintendency

1 The immigration of British waifs to Canada is discussed in Neil Sutherland, *Children in English-Canadian Society: Framing the Twentieth Century Consensus* (Toronto 1976), 3–10 and 28–36; and Leonard Rutman, 'Importation of British Waifs into Canada: 1868 to 1916,' *Child Welfare*, 1973, 159–66.
2 The Canadian response to juvenile immigration in the 1870s is covered in Wesley B. Turner, 'Miss Rye's Children and the Ontario Press, 1875,' *Ontario History*, LXVIII, Sept. 1976, 169–200.

CHAPTER 5   Rescuing Juvenile Offenders

1 Industrial schools are described in Neil Sutherland, *Children in English-Canadian Society: Framing the Twentieth Century Consensus* (Toronto 1976), 106–7 and 136–40.
2 Ibid., 118–23

CHAPTER 6   Social Reform

1 Robert C. Brown and Ramsay Cook, *Canada, 1896–1921: A Nation Transformed* (Toronto 1974), 1–2 and 98–107. For the urban reform movement see also the Introduction to Paul Rutherford, ed., *Saving the Canadian City: The First Phase, 1880–1920* (Toronto 1974), and John C. Weaver, ' "Tomorrow's Metropolis" Revis-

ited: A Critical Assessment of Urban Reform in Canada, 1890–1920,' in Gilbert A. Stelter and Alan F.J. Artibise, *The Canadian City* (Toronto 1977).

2 Rutherford, ed., *Saving the Canadian City*, xiii
3 Ibid., xviii
4 Richard Allen, *The Social Passion: Religion and Social Reform in Canada 1914–1928* (Toronto 1971)
5 See Harriet Parsons, 'The Role of J.J. Kelso in the Canadian Settlement Movement' (unpublished paper, Toronto 1977).
6 'The Ward' is described in Robert Harney and Harold Troper, *Immigrants* (Toronto 1975), 23–32.
7 The findings of several such reports are recounted in Brown and Cook, *Canada, 1896–1921*, 100–1; Harney and Troper, *Immigrants*, 24–5; and G.P. deT. Glazebrook, *The Story of Toronto* (Toronto 1971), 200–5.
8 Rutherford, ed., *Saving the Canadian City*, xvi
9 See Benjamin McArthur, 'The Chicago Playground Movement: A Neglected Feature of Social Justice,' *Social Service Review*, XLIX, Sept. 1975, 376–95.
10 The following discussion relies heavily on 'Role of J.J. Kelso' by Harriet Parsons, who has generously given permission for this material to be used.
11 The settlement movement is discussed in Allen F. Davis, *Spearheads for Reform* (New York 1967), 3–14.
12 Allen, *Social Passion*, 21
13 Provisions for unemployment relief in Toronto in this period are discussed in Michael Piva, 'The Condition of the Working Class in Toronto' (PH D thesis, Concordia University, Montreal, 1975), 99–121.
14 J.A. Turnbull, 'What Does Associated Charities Mean and What Is Its Object?' in Rutherford, ed., *Saving the Canadian City*, 119–22
15 Frank J. Bruno, *Trends in Social Work* (New York 1948), 96–111

Note on Sources

The use of footnotes in this biography has been kept to the minimum. Most of the primary material has been drawn from one source, and detailed footnoting would have been repetitious. The major source is the John Joseph Kelso Manuscript Collection held by the Manuscript Division, Public Archives of Canada (Reference MG 30 C 97, Finding Aid 368). The Kelso Papers (as we shall refer to the collection) comprise twenty-nine volumes of materials collected by J.J. Kelso during his life, which were presented by the family to the Public Archives in 1974. The papers include autobiographical files, correspondence, diaries, daily journals, subject files, notes and drafts, notebooks, scrapbooks, newspaper clippings, broadsheets, and reports. In addition, a collection of photographs relating to Kelso's work has been deposited in the Picture Division, Public Archives of Canada.

Apart from the secondary sources, which are listed separately below, two other main sources must be mentioned. The Blakey Papers, held by the Archives of Ontario (Reference RG 8, II-22-B), are the records of the accountant in Kelso's office, and provide an interesting perspective on the later years of Kelso's career. Also, Martin M. Kelso, son of J.J. Kelso, consented to be interviewed for his recollections of his father's work. The interview was recorded and is available in the Sound Archives, Public Archives of Canada. Mr and Mrs M. Kelso also kindly permitted the authors to view some private correspondence of J.J. Kelso and photographs in their possession.

The background to Irish emigration to North America, described in Chapter 1, is based on Beckett, Cullen, Schrier, and Akenson. The account of Kelso's childhood in Ireland draws on the autobiographical files in Volume One of the Kelso Papers, and on the interview with Martin Kelso. The description of Kelso's youth in Toronto and his journalism career up to 1893 is also based on material in his autobiographical files, but relies most heavily on his diaries for the period 1885–91 which are also in Volume One of the papers. Bain contains an account of Kelso's early life and journalism career. Background to the social and economic conditions in Toronto in the late nineteenth century can be found in a number of sources. Those used most extensively for this work were Masters, Glazebrook, Goheen, and Chapter 1 of Morrison. Goheen's chapter in Stelter and Artibise is most valuable. Clark provides a fascinating contemporary account of social life in Toronto during this period, written in a muckraking style. Kealey's brief account of the conditions of the working class is also useful. Kelso's account of early child protection work contains his description of the conditions of the poor of the city. Rutherford, 'The People's Press,' describes the policies of newspapers such as *The World*, on which Kelso commenced his journalism career.

The account of the formation and early history of the Toronto Humane Society in Chapters 2 and 3 is based on several sources in the Kelso Papers, including autobiographical files (1), diaries (1), newspaper clippings (24), and annual reports of the Humane Society (27). [Bracket numbers refer to volumes of the Kelso Papers.] Kelso describes these events in *Protection of Children*, and the story is also told in Bain. Valuable accounts of the urban reform movement in Toronto in the mid-1880s are provided by Morton, the introduction to Rutherford, *Saving the Canadian City*, and Wallace's thesis and biography of Goldwin Smith. An analysis of the child welfare reform ideology in late nineteenth-century Ontario may be found in Morrison's thesis, Chapter 2. Splane also briefly examines the early history of the humane movement in Toronto. Sutherland is the leading source on changing conceptions of childhood in the late nineteenth century and resultant changes in child welfare, health, and educational policies.

Splane's book on the development of social welfare in Ontario to 1893 is the definitive work on this subject, and the authors relied on this source for background information on child welfare policies prior to Kelso's involvement. Chapter 6 of Splane's book, entitled 'The Welfare of Children,' is particularly relevant. Material describing Kelso's earliest campaigns in the field of child welfare including the Fresh Air Fund, the Santa Claus Fund, the licensing of newsboys, the 1888 Children's Protection Act, and Bands of Mercy can be found in several sections of the Kelso Papers: autobiographical files (1), diaries (1), subject files (5), notebooks (8), scrapbooks (18), newspaper clippings (24), and annual reports of the Fresh Air Fund (27). This early child welfare work is also described by Bain and Morrison. The descriptions in Chapter 3 of the events leading to the formation of the Toronto Children's Aid Society and Kelso's brief period as president are based on the Kelso Papers: diaries (1), subject files (4), scrapbooks (18), newspaper clippings (24), annual reports (26). There are several secondary sources dealing with these events of which the most useful are Bain, Jolliffe, and Kelso. The 1891 Prison Reform Commission, which played such an important role in the development of child welfare policy, has also been described in a number of sources including Fiser, Munro, Splane, a.1d Sutherland. The discussion of Kelso's appointment as superintendent and the passage of the 1893 Children's Protection Act is based on the Kelso Papers: autobiographical files (1), scrapbooks (18). The main secondary source is Bain. Evans gives a useful brief description of the general policies of the Mowat Liberal government which introduced the 1893 act. The provisions of the 1893 Children's Protection Act are discussed in a number of works, for instance Bain, Morrison, and Splane.

Chapter 4, which describes Kelso's early work as superintendent of neglected and dependent children, is based on the Kelso Papers: autobiographical files (1), correspondence (1), scrapbooks (18), newspaper clippings (24), and Kelso's annual reports on his work as superintendent (27–8). Kelso's annual reports between 1893 and the early 1920s were substantial documents, in which he discussed in detail his views on child welfare issues and the progress of his work, and they were used extensively in the preparation of this biography. A complete collection is available in the Kelso Papers, and they are also printed in the Ontario Sessional Papers. A number of secondary sources also discuss the early years of implementation of the Children's Protection Act. Ramsay and Morrison briefly describe the development of the child welfare system from 1893 to 1900. Baker provides considerable detail on the development of the Children's Aid Societies and the visiting committees between 1893 and 1921. Dawe focusses on the conflict between the supporters of foster care and those defending the use of institutions. Kelso's role as superintendent is described in detail by Bain. A lengthy report of the 1894 Ontario Child-Saving Conference is contained in Kelso's annual report for the year 1894. The account of his trip to Manitoba and British Columbia in 1898 has been compiled from the Kelso Papers: autobiographical files (1), scrapbooks (18), annual reports (27), and the annual report of the Winnipeg Children's Aid Society for 1898 (26). The trip is also briefly described in Bain. The emigration of British waifs to Canada has been described by Rutman, and by Sutherland. Both these accounts have been used in this work. See also Turner's account of the Canadian response to juvenile immigration. Kelso's role in this matter is also briefly described by Bain. Other material has been obtained from the Kelso Papers: subject file on juvenile immigration (5), and Kelso's annual reports (27). Kelso's report for 1897 contains a lengthy report on the whole juvenile immigration issue.

Kelso's campaign for the establishment of juvenile courts, which lasted from 1888 to 1910, is described in Chapters 4 and 5. The account is based primarily on materials in the Kelso Papers: autobiographical files (1), subject files on juvenile court legislation (5), scrapbooks (18), and his annual reports as superintendent (27). This material has been supplemented by secondary sources. Sutherland's account of the events surrounding the 1908 Juvenile Delinquents Act has been relied upon by the authors. Bain traces Kelso's struggle for juvenile courts from 1888 to 1908. Fiser describes the relevant legislative changes from 1888 to 1908. The discussion of Kelso's courtship and marriage which begins Chapter 5 is based primarily on correspondence in the possession of Martin Kelso of Toronto. The account of the industrial schools movement relied heavily on Kelso's annual reports, which contain his reports as inspector of industrial schools. Other sources in the Kelso Papers are the subject files on the industrial schools (5) and a Report on Victoria Industrial School (29, restricted). The early history of the industrial school movement is recounted by Splane. A detailed discussion of the whole history of industrial schools can be found in Fiser. Sutherland provides a brief but interesting description of the schools. The Kelso Papers are rich in materials describing the closure of the Penetanguishene Reformatory. Kelso considered this one of his greatest achievements and he wrote about the events extensively in his autobiographical files (1). His annual report on 1904 (27) contains a lengthy appendix describing the closure, including follow-up material on each boy released. Subsequent annual reports also discuss the experiment and the progress of the boys. Other materials in the Kelso Papers are: correspondence relating the closing of Penetanguishene Reformatory (1), subject files on reform of delinquent boys, reform and reformatories, reformatories and the nature of reform, reformatories and the closing of Penetanguishene Reformatory (5–6), scrapbooks (18), newspaper clippings (24), and Kelso's Registry of Boys from Penetanguishene Reformatory (29, restricted). Further material can be found in the annual reports of the inspector of prisons and reformatories for Ontario, which were printed in the Ontario Sessional Papers. Splane discusses the early history of the reformatory. Sutherland describes Kelso's illegal interception of children prior to their arrival at Penetanguishene. Nineteenth-century attitudes towards juvenile delinquency are discussed by Houston. The history of the Mercer Refuge for Girls can be traced through the annual reports of the superintendent which are recorded in the annual reports of the inspector of prisons and reformatories, Ontario Sessional Papers. Other accounts of this institution are by Splane and Fiser. Kelso discusses the closure in his annual report on 1905 (27). See also the Kelso Papers: Report on Refuge for Girls (29, restricted).

Urban reform in Canada in the early twentieth century, which provides the background to Chapter 6, is discussed in Rutherford's introduction to *Saving the Canadian City* and by Weaver in his article in Stelter and Artibise. Brown and Cook provide a general background to the period. The social gospel movement is described by Allen. Social conditions in Toronto are outlined in Glazebrook, and Harney and Troper. The development of Kelso's thinking can be traced through his annual reports. See especially his report for 1914 (27). Other sources on Kelso's life between 1908 and 1914 are the Kelso Papers: notebooks (8–9), and scrapbooks (17–18). The account of Kelso's role in the playgrounds movement is based on the Kelso Papers: autobiographical files (1), correspondence – playgrounds (1), subject file on playgrounds (5), scrapbook on play and playgrounds (15). See McArthur for the North American playground movement. The English and American background to the Charity Organization movement is described in Woodroofe. Piva is useful on unemployment policies in Toronto. Kelso's involvement in the establishment of the School of Social Work at the University of Toronto is described in the Kelso Papers: autobiographical files – university training courses (1), and subject file – School of Social Work (6). Bain also describes these events. The background to the settlement movement is described by Woodroofe and Davis. Parsons was the main source used for Kelso's role in settlements. See also the Kelso Papers: subject file on social settlements (6), and the annual reports for Central Neighbourhood House for 1912, 1913, 1915 (24). Kelso's views on other social issues in the pre-World War One years can be found in the Kelso Papers: autobiographical files (1), subject files on housing (5) and housing and slums (5), notebooks (8–9), and scrapbooks (17–18).

The work of the Children's Aid Societies in the early twentieth century, the subject of Chapter 7, is described by Ramsay. Insight into the workings of Kelso's office in the pre-World War One period, and Kelso's administrative style and problems, is provided by the Blakey Papers. Kelso's attitude to his work as superintendent in this period can be examined in the Kelso Papers: notebooks (8–9), scrapbooks (11, 12, 13, 15, 17, 18), annual reports as superintendent of neglected and dependent children (27). These sources also contain material on his visits to the Maritimes and Western Canada. These trips are also described by Bain. Material on Kelso's frequent visits to the United States can be found in the Kelso Papers: subject files – Conferences United States 1893–1924 (4). The account of Kelso's trip to the United Kingdom in 1914 is based on material in the autobiographical files (1) and on the interview with Martin Kelso, who accompanied his parents on the trip. Kelso's notebooks (8–9) and the Blakey Papers together provide the material for the section on Kelso's increasing administrative burden after returning from England. The account of the campaign in 1916 against the conditions in the Toronto Children's Shelter is based on the Kelso Papers: autobiographical files (1), scrapbooks (12, 15). A useful description of the decline of the Toronto Children's Aid Society between 1894 and 1920 is found in Jolliffe. A verbatim record of the 25th anniversary dinner held in Kelso's honour in 1918 is contained in the autobiographical files (1). Kelso's involvement in the campaign for mothers' allowances was compiled from materials in the Kelso Papers: autobiographical files (1), subject file – mothers' allowances (5), scrapbooks (12, 16, 17, 18, 19), newspaper clippings (24), annual reports of Superintendent of Neglected and Dependent Children (27–8). An account of the introduction of mothers' allowances is given in Munro. A number of secondary sources discuss the passage and implementation of the Children of Unmarried Parents Act: Ramsay and Baker provide the most useful accounts. The social goals of the Drury government are outlined in the memoirs of E.C. Drury. Oliver covers aspects of the provincial political setting. Kelso's concern for the children of unmarried parents can be traced through his annual reports (27–8). Other sources in the Kelso Papers are: autobiographical files (1), subject files – boarding homes (4), the illegitimate child (5), Unmarried Parents Act (6), scrapbooks (19, 20, 21, 22, 23). Material on the various amendments to this and other child welfare legislation during the 1920s can also be found in the Archives of Ontario (Records of the Provincial Secretary's Department, Office of the Clerk of the Legislative Assembly, Proposed Legislation and Precedents, RG 8 1–7-E). The Adoption Act of 1921 is discussed briefly in Baker and Ramsay. Material on Kelso's role in making adoption placements during the 1920s can be found in the Kelso Papers: subject files on adoptions (3), scrapbooks on babies and adoption (11), and on social work (19, 20, 21). Statistics on the administration of the act can be found in Kelso's annual reports (28). General developments in child welfare work in Ontario in the 1920s are covered in Ramsay. Mills' criticisms of Kelso are found in Baker, and in Archives of Ontario material (RG 8 1-7-E). Kelso's contribution to child welfare work in the 1920s and early 1930s can be compiled from the scrapbooks (18, 19, 20, 21, 22, 23) in the Kelso Papers. This is also the source for the account of Kelso's views on social issues during his later life. Jolliffe describes the development of the Toronto Children's Aid Society during the 1920s.

Kelso's private life during the 1920s and 1930s, the subject of Chapter 8, is based on the notebooks (8, 9, 10), scrapbooks (19, 20, 21, 22, 23), diaries (2), and daily journals (3) in the Kelso Papers. This material was supplemented by the interview with Martin Kelso. The formation of the Public Welfare Department and Kelso's subsequent retirement is discussed by Baker and Ramsay. Further material can be found in the Kelso Papers: autobiographical files (1), correspondence – retirement (1), diaries (2), daily journals (3), and scrapbooks (21, 22,

23). The description of Kelso's memoirs in Chapter 8 is based entirely on the autobiographical files (1) in the Kelso Papers. Details of his final illness and death were based on the interview with Martin Kelso. See also the Kelso Papers: correspondence – illness, death (1), scrapbook – obituaries (15).

Two attempts to assess the work of Kelso and the social reform movement with which he was associated are Bain and Morrison.

Finally, it should be noted that the Finding Aid to the Kelso Papers in the Public Archives of Canada, prepared by William Smith, will direct the reader to other valuable materials relating to Kelso's life and social reform movements of the late nineteenth and early twentieth centuries.

SECONDARY SOURCES

Akenson, Donald Harman, *The United States and Ireland.* Cambridge, Mass. 1973

Allen, Richard, *The Social Passion: Religion and Social Reform in Canada, 1914–1928.* Toronto 1965

Bain, Ian, 'The Role of J.J. Kelso in the Launching of the Child Welfare Movement in Ontario.' MSW thesis, University of Toronto, 1955

Baker, W., 'The Place of Private Agencies in the Administration of Government Policy, A Case Study. The Ontario Children's Aid System, 1892–1965.' PH D thesis, Queen's University, 1966

Beckett, J.C., *The Making of Modern Ireland, 1603–1923.* London 1966

Bellomo, J. Jerald, 'Upper Canadian Attitudes Towards Crime and Punishment (1832–1851).' *Ontario History*, LXIV, March 1972, 11–26

Brown, Robert Craig and Ramsay Cook, *Canada, 1896–1921: A Nation Transformed.* Toronto 1974

Bruno, Frank J., *Trends in Social Work.* New York 1948

Careless, J.M.S., *Brown of the Globe,* II. Toronto 1963

Clark, C.S., *Of Toronto the Good.* Montreal 1898

Cullen, L.M., *An Economic History of Ireland since 1660.* London 1972

Dawe, Jane-Louise K., 'The Transition From Institutional to Foster Care for Children in Ontario, 1891–1921.' MSW thesis, University of Toronto, 1966

Davis, Allen F., *Spearheads for Reform.* New York 1967

Drury, E.C., *Farmer Premier: Memoirs of the Honourable E.C. Drury.* Toronto 1966

Evans, Margaret A., 'The Mowat Era, 1872–1896: Stability and Progress,' in Firth, E.G., ed., *Profiles of a Province: Studies in the History of Ontario.* Toronto 1967, 97–106

Fiser, V., 'Development of Services for the Juvenile Delinquent in Ontario, 1891–1921.' MSW thesis, University of Toronto, 1966

Glazebrook, G.P. de T., *The Story of Toronto*. Toronto 1971

Goheen, Peter G., *Victorian Toronto, 1850–1900: Pattern and Process of Growth*. Chicago 1970

Harney, Robert and Harold Troper, *Immigrants*. Toronto 1975

Houston, Susan E., 'Victorian Origins of Juvenile Delinquency: A Canadian Experience.' *History of Education Quarterly*, XII, fall 1972, 254–80

Jolliffe, Russell, 'The History of the Children's Aid Society of Toronto, 1891–1947.' MSW thesis, University of Toronto, 1950

Kealey, Greg, *Working Class Toronto at the Turn of the Century*. Toronto 1972

Kelso, J.J., *Protection of Children: Early History of the Humane and Children's Aid Movement in Ontario 1886–1893*. Toronto 1911

McArthur, Benjamin, 'The Chicago Playground Movement: A Neglected Feature of Social Justice.' *Social Service Review*, XLIX, Sept. 1975, 376–95

Masters, D.C., *The Rise of Toronto, 1850–1890*. Toronto 1947

Morrison, Terrence, 'The Child and Urban Social Reform in Late Nineteenth Century Ontario.' PH D thesis, University of Toronto, 1971

– ' "Their Proper Sphere": Feminism, the Family, and Child-Centred Social Reform in Ontario, 1875–1900.' *Ontario History*, LXIX, March 1976, 45–64, and June 1976, 65–74

Morton, Desmond, *Mayor Howland: The Citizen's Candidate*. Toronto 1973

Munro, Don R., 'The Care of the Dependent Poor in Ontario, 1891–1921.' MSW thesis, University of Toronto, 1966

Oliver, Peter, *Public and Private Persons: The Ontario Political Culture, 1914–1934*. Toronto 1975

Parsons, Harriet, 'The Role of J.J. Kelso in the Canadian Settlement Movement.' Unpublished paper, 1977, deposited in the Baldwin Room, Metropolitan Toronto Library

Piva, Michael, 'The Condition of the Working Class in Toronto.' PH D thesis, Concordia University, 1975

Ramsay, Dean, 'The Development of Child Welfare Legislation in Ontario.' MSW thesis, University of Toronto, 1949

Rutherford, P.F.W., 'The People's Press: The Emergence of the New Journalism in Canada, 1869–99.' *Canadian Historical Review*, LV, June 1975, 169–91

– , ed., *Saving the Canadian City: The First Phase, 1880–1920*. Toronto 1974

Rutman, Leonard, 'Importation of British Waifs Into Canada: 1868 to 1916.' *Child Welfare*, 1973, 159–66

Schrier, Arnold, *Ireland and the American Emigration, 1850–1900*. Minneapolis 1958

Splane, Richard B., *Social Welfare in Ontario, 1791 to 1873: A Study of Public Welfare Administration*. Toronto 1965

Stelter, Gilbert A. and A.F.J. Artibise, eds., *The Canadian City*. Toronto 1977

Sutherland, Neil, *Children in English-Canadian Society: Framing the Twentieth Century Consensus*. Toronto 1976

Turner, Wesley B., 'Miss Rye's Children and the Ontario Press, 1875.' *Ontario History*, LXVIII, Sept. 1976, 169–200

Wallace, Elisabeth, 'The Changing Canadian State: A Study of the Changing Conception of the State as Revealed in Canadian Social Legislation, 1867–1948.' PH D thesis, Columbia University, 1950

– *Goldwin Smith: Victorian Liberal*. Toronto 1957

Woodroofe, Kathleen, *From Charity to Social Work*. Toronto 1962

Index